CITY LIMITS

CITY LIMITS

*Barriers to Change
in Urban Government*

by Diana R. Gordon

CHARTERHOUSE

New York

CITY LIMITS

LIBRARY OF CONGRESS CATALOG CARD NUMBER: 73–79959
MANUFACTURED IN THE UNITED STATES OF AMERICA
ISBN: 0–88327–021–8

To David

Foreword

Diana Gordon's studies combine in happy fashion the eye of a participant in New York City government, alert to nuances under Mayor Lindsay, and the ear of an observer recently in Cambridge, tuned to questions asked by academics. The result is illuminating, lively, argumentative, and individual. This book is neither memoir nor treatise but has some of the virtues of both.

Mrs. Gordon's book embodies many of the hopes with which at Harvard seven years ago we launched a set of visitorships for men and women from public life: Fellows of the Institute of Politics in the John F. Kennedy School, colloquially "Kennedy Fellows." Diana Gordon was in our fifth group of Fellows, and among the first named to a special category, with a special task, as a "Research Fellow." From all our Fellows we sought reasonable reciprocity between what we could learn through them and they through us. From Research Fellows we sought something more: attention in their own terms, out of *their* experiences, to inquiries on *our* research agenda. Mrs. Gordon did just that.

City Limits, while very much her own, owes its beginnings to her work with us. We brought her into a faculty seminar with a simple shorthand name, the May Group. This Group was pondering questions of implementation, questions rendered sharp by national experience: How account for the disparity so often seen between intentions and results in governmental programs? What part of the answer lies in organizational factors: bureaucratic procedures, personnel, internal politics? Pursuing these in the interests of the School's new Public Policy Program, we asked Mrs. Gordon to look not at Washington but at the City of New York in the Administration of John Lindsay, whence she had come straight from the Mayor's Budget Bureau. Several of the cases in this book were first researched on our behalf. Some not found here are featured in our courses. From the outset, we and our Research Fellow had different uses for her work—different but by no means incompatible. To us her cases, mingled with others, were raw materials for teaching and research, sparking arguments, suggesting hypotheses, posing further questions. On matters of interpretation we differed frequently among ourselves and with her. On matters of fact, we often hankered for more information and indeed still have one follow-up inquiry under way. To Mrs. Gordon, on the other hand, the cases done for us were a first step toward this book, incorporating her own further research, shaped by her own interpretations. With hearty agreement on our part, when she had done her stint for us, she went back to New York, taking our questions with her, and pursued them there to suit herself on her own terms and time. What better occupation for a former Fellow! As the then Director of the Institute of Politics, I hasten to claim not credit —that's all hers—but good sense in giving her a fellowship.

Now her work comes before a wider audience. I hope it

will be widely read. Sensibly, Mrs. Gordon rarely deals in general terms. Rather, she illuminates specific efforts of a lot of individuals at given times and places to pursue particular aims. Many fail completely; some succeed to a degree. Governments in actual operation are mosaics of such particulars. To grasp some of the problems of the would-be reformer in a city government, one cannot do better than read this book. It should be no less educative for those who deprecate than for those who espouse the aims of any given character in Mrs. Gordon's variegated cast. She has put on display a remarkable assembly of effortful men and women. I commend them to you.

Richard E. Neustadt

Cambridge, Massachusetts
June 14, 1973

Acknowledgments

Over the past two years I have interviewed hundreds of New York City employees, from commissioners to workers at the lowest level. Some of these people spent many hours with me, and some read and criticized drafts of individual chapters. Their good humor and patience in the face of my sometimes rude questioning was extraordinary. If I were to name all of those who gave me generous amounts of time and attention, the list would go on for pages. Since that is impossible, I must thank most of them anonymously and say that to them I owe the greatest debt. The workers of New York City are the essence of this book. A few whose contributions went far beyond professional courtesy should be singled out; they are Jack Birnbaum, Steve Disman, Vincent Guinee, Maurice Reichman, and Henry Rosner.

A number of friends and colleagues, some of them also former New York City employees, guided me in shaping both the whole of this book and its separate parts. They often influenced me as much by what they stood for as by what they said, as many of them have been actively working for change in urban government. I am particularly indebted to Kathryn Allott, Timothy Bates, Michel Crozier, Joan Dunlop, Susan Engel, Gregory Farrell, Joseph Featherstone, Lewis Feldstein, Peter Goldmark, Susan Harman, Marlys Harris, Frederick O'R. Hayes, William Josephson, Margaret Levi, S.M. Miller, Jack Newfield, Glenn Paulson, David Rogers, Geoffrey Stokes, and Jacob Ukeles.

This book grew out of a group of case studies prepared for graduate students in the public policy program of the Kennedy School of Government at Harvard University. Two case studies, which I later rewrote into chapters, were originally researched and written by Arnold Howitt and Steven J. Ross. Background papers for one study were written by Paul Orlofsky. Invaluable advice about the preparation and use of the studies came from faculty of the public policy program: Richard E. Neustadt, Graham T. Allison, John Steinbruner, Lance Liebman, and Mark Moore.

Many institutions supported this book along the way. I am grateful to the Institute of Politics of the Kennedy School of Government, and especially to its former director Richard E. Neustadt, for the fellowship that enabled me to begin, and to the Ford Foundation for the study and travel grant that enabled me to finish. The Fund for the City of New York and the New York City–RAND Corporation provided quiet, comfortable office space at various stages of the book's development.

Thanks must go to Carolyn Hicks, who typed the original case studies, and to Cassia Berman, who worked on the book manuscript. And finally my deepest gratitude goes to my father and my husband: Hallett Smith, who took upon himself the unenviable task of exorcizing jargon and flagging unreadable sentences; and David Gordon, whose insights and suggestions influenced almost every page. I hope they find the book worthy of their efforts.

D.R.G.

Contents

"Civilized" means, literally, "citified," and the state of the city is an accurate index of the condition of the culture as a whole. We behave toward our cities like an irascible farmer who never feeds his cow and then kicks her when she fails to give enough milk.

—Philip Slater

What is barely hinted in other American cities is condensed and enlarged in New York.

—Saul Bellow

1

Introduction

The United States of the 1960s was a restless place. Some of its citizens assaulted the barriers that kept them from realizing the American Dream. Others deplored the dream itself. Still others scorned those who railed, suggesting they were not true Americans. Even people who lived personally contented and successful lives felt uneasy with the general directions society was taking. A lucrative career did not stave off boredom and alienation. Physical safety did not conquer fear or anger.

Technological advance did not prevent the malaise. Although it eased the material problems of life for many people, it did not strengthen the social and spiritual core. In fact, the "progress" of our urban, industrial society often spoiled the simplest, most natural pleasures. The ordinary person now had the means to see his country, but trees were cut down for the highways on which he traveled and the air was darkened by the exhaust from his automobile.

Social progress lagged far behind the technological. The gap between rich and poor remained as wide as ever. Public schools—whether in slums or suburbs—did not teach students how to think. Job discrimination against women and minority groups kept equality of opportunity a classroom dream. Prisons did not prepare inmates for productive, noncriminal lives. Private and public shelters did not provide real homes for society's neglected children. And on and on.

Our cities often bore the brunt of our discontents. They were dirty and dangerous and decaying. People who could not easily contribute to their improvement were moving in, while those who *would* not contribute were moving out. We all spoke of the "urban crisis"—a catchall for the problems of society that most of us could not escape in daily life.

Part of the solution to the urban crisis seemed to rest inevitably with local government. After all, it is the bureaucracy of first resort. It hands out the welfare checks, it regulates the corner store, it sweeps the streets. Because its activities are most visible, people often turn to it first when a "new" problem arises that does not seem susceptible to private solution. And local government is often blamed when things go wrong. Is air pollution increasing? We must impose stricter local controls. Are the prisons overcrowded? Look to city administrators to correct the problem. Is there more garbage these days? The men who collect it must not be doing their job. No matter that pollution controls are more appropriately imposed by the state and federal governments; or that the actions of state courts and legislatures have been largely responsible for overcrowded prisons; or that the packaging industry and modern consumer habits create 6 percent more trash and garbage in New York City each year. It is commonplace for citizens to blame all retail sales tax increases on a city's mayor, even when they are proposed and legislated by state officials.

City governments are not well equipped to handle either the expectations or the abuse. For the urban crisis springs from conditions beyond local control, and its solution calls for resources unavailable to local administrations.

Many of the problems that create the urban crisis are national. Economic conditions are examples. In the last fifty years developing production and transportation technology has stimulated the spread of industry out from the central city, removing an important source of high-wage jobs. The influx of white-collar business into the downtown areas of big cities has distorted the traditional mix of commercial and residential land use, driving the price of land up beyond the point where it is profitable to build low- or even middle-income housing. As large corporations have grown into conglomerates, the discrepancy in wages and working conditions between big business and small, competitive enterprises has widened. This phenomenon is especially important in large northeastern cities where low-wage industries originally concentrated to take advantage of unskilled immigrant labor pools.

The great national demographic shifts followed from the economic conditions. Southern blacks migrated north by the millions. Country people continued the flow into the cities that had begun in the nineteenth century. As these developments brought poverty and increased density to urban areas, more and more middle-class families sought the space and greenery of the suburbs. During the 1960s alone, New York City lost a million white people, the large majority of them middle-class whites moving away from the increasing hazards of big-city life.

Finally, national budget priorities excluded the social programs that might have improved education, raised incomes, constructed low-income housing—and helped prevent the urban crisis. It was only in the 1960s that butter began to catch up with guns, and even then domestic programs rarely amounted to more than 20 percent of the federal budget.

The city governments never had the power to redress at

the local level the national injuries which led to urban blight. Cities are creatures of states, with their powers restricted to those specifically granted by the legislatures. They rarely have significant independent taxing power, and important new urban programs often require statutory authority from the state. Legislatures are often dominated by rural and suburban interests, and as a result cities get short-changed when it comes to state aid.

Even if city governments had more power, they might not know how to use it to solve the most pressing problems. Traditionally, local governments have acted only on problems that could be solved with the provision of a limited, tangible service. Fifty years ago New York City spent substantial portions of its budget on sanitation and highways, but nothing on public housing or welfare. These earlier functions were housekeeping services, not intended to affect or reflect people's basic values. In the 1960s, cities were confronted with demands for services which encompassed intangible aspects of life not previously considered the concern of government. No longer could a social service agency simply design and plan a community center; its potential users demanded participation in the planning process. The schools could not just teach designated subjects; they had to take affirmative steps to provide equal opportunity for all. It was no longer enough for correction systems merely to protect the rest of the society from its criminals; they were asked to "rehabilitate" prisoners. Adoption bureaus were now expected not only to find homes for children, but to ascertain and protect the rights of the natural parents.

During the mid-1960s these expectations challenged a number of vigorous, intelligent political leaders. Filled with reformist impulses and eager to apply sophisticated analytic and managerial techniques to local government, they vowed to halt the decline of our major cities. In Boston, Detroit, Atlanta, and New York, coalitions of concerned voters elected liberal mayors who hailed the coming of a progressive era at the local level. On taking his oath of office in January 1966, John V. Lindsay, one hundred and third Mayor of New York City, called on his fellow citizens to "enlist in the fight for a better New York":

The fight to revive the hopes of the downtrodden, the sick, the exploited.

The fight for new and better employment.

The fight against wretched slums, poisoned air, stifling traffic and congested subways.

The fight for excellence and equality in our education—and for the integrity of our historic system of independent free city colleges.

The fight for new parks and recreational facilities.

And fight he did. For neighborhood government centers, called Little City Halls; for a more streamlined city administration, with the sixty-odd agencies clustered under ten superagencies; for a civilian board to review complaints of police brutality; for decentralization of the operating authority for the city's schools. Each battle left him scarred, hardly closer to the "new city" his inaugural address had heralded. By the end of his first four-year mayoralty term, many of his earlier supporters thought he had failed. The streets were as grimy as ever, poverty as pervasive, drug abuse more prevalent. Strikes by municipal workers—including the worst teachers' strike in the city's history—had angered the public and led to serious drains on the city's already tight budget. The Mayor's critics called him an inept labor negotiator, a poor administrator, a leader only in championing the rights and interests of the city's downtrodden minority. He won a second term of office solely because his two opponents split the conservative vote. Many liberals who voted for him did so reluctantly, considering him the least of three evils.

John Lindsay was, to some extent, the victim of unrealistic expectations. New York City has what public administration professors call a strong-mayor form of local government, and people look to their mayor for aggressive leadership. The aura of glamor that surrounded Lindsay when he first took office—the clear-eyed Republican challenger in a jaundiced Democratic city—added to the usual expectations. Lindsay encouraged the unthinking faith by maintaining his own rather unthinking faith that goodwill and determination, nourished by a superior education, would right most urban wrongs in short order. He soon ran up against the reality of problems more deeply rooted than his executive power. Lacking the experience to make him cynical about his own potential for effectiveness, he called on rhetoric and reorganization to attack even the most fundamental problems. Not that other urban leaders were doing any better; but Lindsay's blunders made news both because he was swimming in a larger pond and because he had held out so much hope for change.

While Lindsay became the butt of national cartoonists, others of the men who had taken on the urban challenge simply conceded defeat. Resigning in midterm, the mayor of Denver said, in 1968, "With perhaps few if any exceptions, the financial and organizational structures of most large cities are hardly up to the needs of 1969 or '70." Commenting on his decision not to run for another mayoral term, Ivan Allen of Atlanta said, "At my age I question whether I would have been physically able to continue for another four years in the face of the constant pressure, the innumerable crises, and the confrontations that have occurred in the cities." Even though Lindsay won a second term, he was glum about the cities' future. "The cities of America are in a battle for survival," Lindsay said in 1971. "Frankly, even with help in Washington, I'm not sure we can pull out of the urban crisis in time."[1]

If the failures of the urban reformers seem obvious, most people think that the causes of those failures are equally obvious. Nearly everyone finds some simple explanation for the society's inability to solve the urban crisis. A sociologist has noted the American tendency, when we are faced with disturbing and contagious social disorder, to expect a "magic telegram," a single-ingredient medication for a complex and fundamental disease.[2] In much the same way, we usually attribute a set of complicated problems to some single cause—even though we ought to recognize that almost everything in a large and complex society is related to almost everything else. Both experts and laymen have favorite problems which they cite as singular, immutable obstacles to improving the urban condition. If we could only overcome these individual sources of crisis, they suggest, our problems surely would end. The panaceas abound.

Inept political leaders head the list. With better mayors, many argue, the cities would thrive. Blaming the mayors for the cities' continued decline is unfair but understandable. Political scientists and psychologists tell us that people vest their leaders with powers of rationality and control totally beyond the reach of any mortal being. If things do not go well, it is always easier to blame the failure on the leader's ineptitude than on something less tangible like systemic chaos or bureaucratic accident. The specific attribution of rationality and control, moreover, plays an important role. People most quickly scorn those leaders who do not appear to have identified, defined, and measured their adversaries. If the problems the leader encounters are diffuse, if they are not susceptible to simple strategies he can easily convey, the public is most likely to lose faith. Recessions are usually more damaging to national leaders than wars.[3] As long as our urban blight seems so undifferentiated, its causes so intangible, people may never have the confidence that their mayors can cope.

Exculpating their mayors, many blame the cities' decline on other people. The poor have been easy targets. They were moving into the cities in waves, taxing the already inadequate social services and swelling the public assistance rolls. The middle class also received abuse. Many affluent families, essential contributors to a healthy local tax base and a civic spirit, demonstrated their indifference to the fate of the cities by moving to the suburbs. Those who remained in the cities did their best to protect themselves from the dirt and crime; as they withdrew from city life, they left its direction to professionals whose judgments they scorned.

It seemed equally easy to ascribe the crisis to fiscal disaster. Money problems loomed large in the congeries of urban ills. Local tax structures were regressive and inadequate. Revenues could not grow rapidly enough to support the services demanded by the cities' low-income residents. Even at their present levels, taxes often seemed so high that taxpayers' rebellions broke out everywhere, with school and transportation bond issues sometimes going down to defeat. Frederick O'R. Hayes, former Director of the Budget for New York City, estimated in 1969 that City expenditures were rising about 15 percent annually—even without major program improvements—while revenues expanded by only 5 percent. Faced with such projections, urban officials turned urgently to the federal government, which had long since preempted the largest and most flexible revenue source, the progressive income tax. They urged their Congressional delegations to legislate the "Heller-Pechman plan," which would share a percentage of federal revenues with state and local governments. But this remedy, enacted in 1972 in a very modest form, has not substantially alleviated money problems for large cities. It is unlikely that other potential federal aid—like tax credits or large general grants for certain expenditure categories—will do so either.

In New York City, at least, many could also blame municipal employees. The growing strength of municipal unions has brought the salaries of City employees up to those of workers in the private sector—and, in some cases, above. Pensions now rival the generosity of private pensions anywhere in the country. With each new union victory, annual increases in employee salaries take larger chunks out of the City budget. In turn, these salary increases provide fuel for the charge that "capitulation" to union demands is seriously crippling City services.

To pick a final example, many also wonder whether the

cities' political structures permit their governance and management at all. Most cities have jurisdictional and managerial problems that seem to many to determine the cities' fates more surely than the competence or ideology of the mayor and his appointees. It is far from clear that general-purpose, central city government is the most efficient form of urban organization. Within the past few years both metropolitanism and decentralization have become popular panaceas. Each certainly has attractive features, but neither is the "magic telegram." Political scientist Norton Long expresses concern that support of metropolitanism is based on "the simple faith that big government will encompass big resources and challenge big men to do big things."[4] That faith does not itself guarantee solution to the most difficult problems. With metropolitan government, many city services would inevitably be standardized in the interests of greater efficiency. But as people demand more varied and more intangible services, the large cities' diverse neighborhoods will increasingly require special—rather than standardized—attention. The potential efficiencies of metropolitanism might be wasted as a result of neighborhood demands. The adoption of a more decentralized way of delivering local government services does not provide easy answers, either. Providing individual programs according to a neighborhood's special needs might well deepen the race and class divisions already threatening to polarize our heterogeneous society. It might also compromise the central governments' responsibilities for control over taxpayers' money. Those who have advocated governmental reorganization have not suggested clear resolutions of these contradictions. In urging reorganization, they have not pointed toward solutions any easier than have the proponents of better management, different tax structures, more "home rule," sterner labor strategies, or other panaceas.

I am troubled by many of the explanations for the cities' failures and the prescriptions for future success. My own experience with our cities has come neither as scholar nor as theorist. Instead, I began experiencing the problems of urban change as a worker within the large agencies that comprise the executive branch of the New York City government. As I tried to apply the abstractions to my own observations of how urban government works, I felt more and more dissatisfied.

The first problem with these explanations, of course, is that they are too simple. They are all partly right and partly wrong. They point up problems, but they do not help us determine the relative weight of the problems. (If cities had as much money as they needed, they could not spend it very well. The best managers in the world could not rebuild the slums or negotiate transit workers' contracts without conflict. A truly integrated city would not eliminate late-twentieth-century American anomie.) The experts' nostrums do not usually reflect the specific dynamics of individual cities and their problems—although our urban diversity ought to have taught us the dangers of overgeneralization. These prescriptions do not often enhance our understanding of the occasional signs of accomplishment. And they rarely take account of the people and the processes governing urban bureaucracies.

As an illustration of the problems of single-factor explanations, consider the fiscal dilemma. John Kenneth Galbraith once said, "I doubt that there is much wrong with John Lindsay that another billion dollars a year wouldn't cure." But is that really true? A large portion of that billion dollars would have to be spent not on social remedies but on what the City calls "mandated expenditures"—salary raises, pensions, medical benefits for 380,000 City employees. Another portion of it might not be spent at all because of bad management or inadequate program development. (That has happened more than once with federal funds intended to go for new social programs.) Furthermore, we assume that the improved service that additional money can buy will result in solutions to some of our problems; yet studies indicate over and over that there is little or no direct correlation between new programs in the schools and generally improved academic performance, or between additional police patrolmen and a drop in crime rates.

Many of these simple explanations of our urban failure seem deficient, in the light of my own experience, because they do not incorporate the lessons we can learn from the experiments of the past several years. Even though many of them have failed, serious efforts at urban change have been under way. Often motivated by abstract ideas about the urban crisis, these efforts serve as direct—though not very rigorous—tests of some of those ideas. If we are going to improve our understanding of the problems of urban change, we must be able to continue learning as we apply our provisional knowledge. All too often the people who have acquired this knowledge most intimately—those who have worked to bring about change—cannot contribute what they have learned to others, either because they do not recognize its importance or because they have retired from the urban fray in a state of exhaustion.

Some of my observations of New York City government have already indicated to me that we have neglected one of the most important forces constraining our ability to bring about change. I have been struck over and over by the importance of patterns of behavior within big-city government agencies, patterns that help determine how a policy imposed from above is interpreted and carried out. Perhaps that is not surprising. "In an age of large organizations," the political scientist Murray Edelman writes, "the decisions of officials about the allocation of tangible resources to groups of the population are controlled far more than in simple polities by the factual and value premises assembled through organization."[5] My own experience suggests that not only decisions but their impact and outcome are shaped by bureaucratic behavior. This behavior reflects not only the universal organizational tendencies to rationalize activities and develop hierarchy, but also the peculiarly American values and customs of the people who work in those organizations.

The experiments of the past several years provide other lessons as well. This book is intended to incorporate some of those lessons into our understanding of the problems of urban change. The six chapters that follow tell six stories of attempts to bring about change in the New York City government during the Lindsay years (1966–1973). Each change described was intended to be an innovation of some sort, not simply a marginal program improvement like increased police patrol or more numerous trash collections. Each was a sincere effort to provide service, though several were stimulated by unfavorable publicity that could not have been ignored by political leaders. Some of the problems on which the government took action have been partially solved, while some remain totally impervious.

In these narratives, I have sought to illustrate the ways in which all the simple, conventional explanations of the urban crisis become interwoven in the everyday activities of urban government. I also hope to underscore the internal institutional constraints on change. If I have a bias, I consider organizational politics as a particularly important variable in the problems of changing urban life through the activities of local government. Politics in its broadest sense is simply the control of human beings by one another. I am convinced that we must look at people within our urban bureaucracies in order to understand how they use politics to promote and defeat change.

My points are all simple. In preparing these stories, I have concentrated on four different phases of urban change —the processes of *stimulating, defining, implementing,* and *sustaining* change. I believe that stimulus for change comes about only rarely from rational perception by an experienced administrator within government. Instead, it is far more likely to come from glaring social dysfunctions or public uproar created by a small group of outsiders with special interests. I think that the processes of problem and program definition—where new and complex tasks are to be undertaken—are usually totally overlooked or undertaken in such haste that disaster results. I am also convinced that even the most carefully planned reforms often fail because they are initiated with very little understanding of the problems of implementation—and particularly of the people and institutions who must do the dirty work. Finally, I find that we do not often appreciate the problems of sustaining change. Once a problem seems solved, slippage takes place. Problems recur, over and over, but our memories are so short and our appreciation of the processes of change so limited that we do not often remember how we handled the problem before. While the lessons are there for the learning, we usually ignore them.

The first story looks at one familiar kind of stimulus for change—the pressure on government by a group of knowledgeable and powerful outsiders. In this case that group included scientists, doctors, and a muckraking journalist. They suspected that thousands of ghetto children in New York were being poisoned each year by lead-base paint, and they tried to force the City to treat the disease and prevent its occurrence. Their experience illustrates the difficulties of overcoming the sluggishness of a bureaucracy's business-as-usual approach and reveals some built-in limitations to even the most sophisticated attempts to prod government into action.

Although stimulus for a municipal drug program—the subject of the second case study—also came from outside the government, it grew from different kinds of external pressures. The lead-poisoning activists were professionals who knew a good deal about the disease; the disease itself was clearly both treatable and preventable. In contrast, the pressure to take action on drugs came from the general public, which was almost totally ignorant about the phenomenon of heroin addiction and was motivated largely by fear. Even the experts—medical, psychiatric, governmental—could not define the addiction problem. But political considerations—and the humane concern of liberal leadership—provoked Mayor Lindsay to reach for something, anything, that might make the problem go away. The story focuses, then, on the problems of change when a government is simultaneously beset by demands to *define* and to *solve* a serious and spreading blight.

Another sort of problem in definition frames the third story, which recounts the struggle over community control of a huge City-owned building on Manhattan's Lower East Side. City officials recognized the widespread citizen alienation that motivated the area's residents, but that recognition did not provide an equally adequate understanding of their responsibility in dealing with citizens' demands. Both community residents and government officials continually wrestled with the question of how to reconcile specific programmatic demands with more intangible appeals for community control.

The fourth story moves on to the problems of implementation. The problems of stimulus and definition were not at issue here. Officials of the City Budget Bureau and City Planning Commission understood the need for new, more rational analysis in the planning and construction of large capital projects. They knew what techniques they wanted to use. They knew what objectives more rational analysis might serve. They tried to introduce systems analysis in a specific problem—determining the type and size of a huge water distribution tunnel, the largest single capital project in the City's history. But the officials—reform-minded Lindsay appointees—may have placed too much faith in the validity of their cause. Their three-year tussle with the City Board of Water Supply illustrates some of the internal political problems that often plague the efforts of zealous reformers to alter the priorities and routines of bureaucratic institutions that, though nominally subject to the directives of high government officials, are actually quite autonomous.

The fifth story also examines the problems of implementation. It focuses more closely, however, on the needs and behavior of the workers within a large organization than on the life of the organization itself. It describes selected efforts to institute some prison reforms after the 1970 riots in New York City and the effects of those reforms on the

City's correction officers. Like the story of the tunnel, this chapter suggests the need for reformers to consider carefully the backgrounds, attitudes, and work routines of those who have to effect change.

The sixth story, finally, deals with the problems of sustaining change. Once a change, however superficial, is effected, how are its benefits maintained? In 1970, the City experienced a crisis over "welfare hotels." City-wide publicity revealed that more than a thousand welfare families were living "temporarily" in crowded, deteriorating, dangerous—and expensive—hotels. Twenty-five years before the same problem had existed on a smaller scale. The City's efforts to "solve" the modern crisis with emergency measures raise serious questions about our ability to learn from our previous failures.

Most of the problems presented in the following chapters are generated by the social and economic ills of the urban poor. To some extent, this is because those ills are the nub of what is driving the middle class away from the cities. An important source of crime is the drug abuse which particularly entraps New York's young black—and poor—males. The impact of the drug problem strikes poor and affluent alike. Similarly, the need for supportive services for the City's low-income people depletes the municipal budget and precludes the provision of amenities for the middle class. At every turn the problems of the poor affect the lives of more affluent citizens, often more directly than the government's policies for enhancing middle-class urban life. Even where a government program benefits the nonpoor at substantial cost to other services, that benefit seems often to have been won in reaction to problems of poverty. Salaries and pensions for municipal employees in New York are so high partly because the City has to pay dearly for the willingness of teachers and policemen to continue to deal daily with the saddest of urban ills.

But are these stories not peculiar to New York, aberrations that could not arise in smaller cities? Certainly New York is special—its bigness, the age of its housing, the size

of its ghettos, its importance as a port of entry for drugs as
well as people. But other cities have its problems, sometimes more oppressively if not so visibly. Many cities now
have one person in seven receiving welfare, as New York
does; a number have higher rates for the occurrence of
violent crime. Schools and libraries are closing for lack of
funds, even in small cities. Ghetto outbreaks have been
more damaging in most large cities than in New York, and
machine politics more wasteful.

But the relevant question is not whether New York is
better or worse off than other urban areas. It is rather what
New York's experience can tell us about the problems of
all of our cities. Perhaps simply to ask that question begins
the process of answering. Los Angeles is often described as
the place to go to see what's new in unconventional life-
styles—a sort of circus of exaggerated fashion. New York,
too, is a city of portents. But its drama has weightier substance. Its players articulate even the most sophisticated
demands, its plots raise the burning issues of the day, its
setting presents urban decay as almost an art form. The
New York scenario puts every kind of urban problem on
a superstage; by looking at that stage, perhaps we can know
something about what is on the way for other cities.

2

Getting the Lead Out

I

Large government agencies often fail to add new programs as quickly as their clients need them. Delays have many causes. The top policy-makers must decide that the new activity is a proper government function and comes within their jurisdiction. They must be sure that, as a practical matter, they can provide the service needed. In addition, budgets rarely include funds not already designated for an existing program. Shifting money around inevitably causes howls of outrage from the administrators on the losing end. Finding and hiring personnel competent to run the new program may take a lot of time, to say nothing of locating or leasing space. Tactically, the prospective clients' interests may seriously conflict with those of another, more politically powerful constituent group. Finally, starting something new creates a risk for the agency as an organization. Since the goal of maintaining the organization is almost always at least equal to the goal of service to the public, the possibility of failure in the new activity—leading perhaps to a weakening of the organization—dampens the interest of the agency personnel who sense the public need and would like to meet it.

This lag between client need and agency response is often overcome by pressure from beyond the agency. Dramatic events may trigger action: riots generate local recreation programs; outbreaks of crime in sleazy hotels speed up efforts to protect the downtrodden who live in them; rebellions lead to prison reform measures. A concerned political leader may give the agency an ultimatum that confers license to override the usual bureaucratic obstacles to rapid change. Or outsiders to government—journalists, special-interest groups, powerful individuals—may wield their own particular kind of power to push the agency into action. The latter kind of stimulus sometimes provides citizens with an opportunity to create a crisis of publicity which neither politicians nor agency administrators can ignore.

But that stimulus, too, can be constrained—by public apathy, by persistent institutional resistance, by the outsiders' other concerns. This chapter is about the efforts of knowledgeable professional people outside government to force New York City to eradicate lead poisoning in children. It explores the effects and limitations of gadfly activity on a large urban bureaucracy.

The story begins not in New York but in Missouri. In the fall of 1967, the Scientists' Institute for Public Information held a meeting in St. Louis on urban problems for its local committees. From all over the country came scientists and doctors, the most active participants in what its members call "the science information movement." The movement has grown because many scientists believe that they can and should communicate unbiased scientific information to the public about issues of critical general concern. Local committees conduct studies, testify before legislative bodies, publish pamphlets, and give school and university courses. The New York Scientists' Committee for Public Information (SCPI), for instance, has approximately one hundred members working on issues as diverse as biological warfare and noise pollution. SCPI declares that its purpose is "to give to citizens the scientific information needed for making sound judgments on public policy issues involving science."

SCPI originated in the late 1950s to provide a forum for scientists to express themselves publicly on the effects of radiation. When the Nuclear Test Ban Treaty was signed in 1963, the organization broadened its focus. It continued to attract the same kinds of members, however—professionals who felt a social obligation to use their scientific skills outside the lab. SCPI members tend to be young, usually with impeccable educational and professional credentials—medical doctors concentrating on research, physiologists with Ph.D.s, professors at the city's universities. While distinguished in their fields, they usually have little experience with politicians or government bureaucracies. Typical is Glenn Paulson, a short, friendly environmental scientist in his late twenties who became SCPI chairman while still a graduate student at The Rockefeller University.

A major agenda item at the St. Louis meeting was the problem of lead poisoning. This disease occurs when young children who have pica—an abnormal craving for nonfood substances—regularly eat or chew on chips of lead-based paint or plaster. Local committees from Rochester and Chicago reported studies showing a surprisingly high incidence of the disease among slum children in those cities. Excess absorption of lead may cause hyperactivity, mental retardation, kidney disorders, and occasionally death. It is estimated that from 250,000 to 400,000 American children, ages one to six, have absorbed damaging amounts of lead from paint.

Four New York SCPI members were attending the meeting—Glenn Paulson, Edmund Rothschild, Evelyn Mauss, and Joel Buxbaum. Although they had previously heard of lead poisoning, they were surprised at the high levels of incidence reported in other cities. They were also concerned to learn that other cities were testing and treating many more children threatened by lead poisoning than New York. The disparities could hardly be explained by the absence of lead in New York; although the use of paint with more than 1 percent lead had been illegal in the city for interior walls since 1959, hundreds of thousands of deteriorating apartments must still have lead-base paint peeling from their walls. It seemed to the four of them, as they talked about the reports on their way back from St. Louis, that the low number of reported cases in New York City must reflect, at least in part, ignorance and neglect of the problem. They discussed the need for studying the disease and disseminating basic information to New Yorkers who might be concerned. They constituted themselves a special subcommittee, delegated assignments, and held their first formal meeting in February 1968, when they reviewed what they had learned and planned their next steps.

Every urban dweller absorbs some lead into his system, principally from breathing gasoline exhaust, but also sometimes from swallowing water or food. But the ingestion of lead paint chips creates an abnormal burden far more dangerous than what most city dwellers sustain from usual sources. A lead level of 20 micrograms per 100 milliliters of whole blood would be quite normal in an adult city resident; a child who has symptomatic lead poisoning will usually have more than 60 micrograms per 100 milliliters. Recently, doctors working on lead poisoning have come to suspect that long-term damage may even occur in some children with lead levels as low as 40 micrograms. Since this measure represents exposure to lead, not damage done by it, it is difficult to say exactly what lead level will injure any given child.

Although lead poisoning is both preventable and treatable, it is often difficult to identify. A child may chew on paint chips every day for a few weeks without any noticeable effects. Initial symptoms—irritability, fatigue, nausea— can be attributed to many other causes. Misdiagnosis often occurs at this stage. If a child continues to accumulate lead in his system, he may go into convulsions or paralysis. At this stage, called lead encephalopathy, doctors speculate that the blood vessels of the brain swell. Permanent damage to the central nervous system occurs in 25 to 40 percent of cases that reach this stage, even if the child is treated. It is at this point that children may suffer severe, permanent mental retardation.

Treatment for lead poisoning has become quite effective in recent years. A poisoned child receives, intravenously, chemical agents that draw out the lead. This treatment is usually given in a hospital. The chances for complete recovery are very good if the disease is discovered early. Those chances decrease markedly each time a child is successively repoisoned. In severe cases, treatment serves only to reduce the damage, not to eliminate it. Death from discovered cases is now rare, though deaths attributed to other medical causes may, in fact, be lead deaths.

Though the principal causes and effects of lead poisoning are known, many questions of physiology and epidemiology remain. What causes the craving for nonfood substances (called "pica," from the Latin word for "magpie," a bird with an indiscriminate appetite) that leads children to nibble on paint chips? Why does the same absorption of lead in the blood cause some children to have severe symptoms of the disease and others none at all? What activates the conversion of lead from an insoluble phosphate stored in the bones to a soluble form that circulates in the bloodstream? Why do three-fourths of acute episodes of lead poisoning occur in the late summer?

Estimating the incidence of the disease, in the absence of "hard" numbers, is a subtle problem of inference. Studies show that as many as 25 percent of urban slum children in the East and Midwest may have a dangerous lead burden, and that up to 5 percent have actual, clinical symptoms of the disease.¹ The children at risk are, of course, all those whose homes contain leaded surfaces or who regularly spend time outside the home at another place with lead-base paint on the walls. An estimate based on the Housing and Vacancy Survey of 1968 finds 1,350,000 people living in deteriorated or dilapidated housing, old enough to have lead-base paint still on the walls. Nine percent of the city's population is between the ages of one and six. Applying that percentage to the number of people in substandard housing, the number of children at risk is 121,500. Another estimate projects 352,000 children in the susceptible age range who live in the city's sixteen officially designated health districts, poverty areas where dilapidated housing is the rule. No one knows how many of them have pica. Dr. Julian Chisholm, a Johns Hopkins Medical School expert who has studied lead poisoning for over fifteen years, guesses that this craving affects up to 50 percent of all children between one and six.

At the time the SCPI members were learning about lead poisoning, no one had bothered to make a careful count of the number of poisoned children in New York. Once the problem surfaced, the estimates varied. Health Department officials have guessed at various times that from 6,000 to 30,000 New York children have lead levels of at least 60 micrograms. Others who have studied the problem believe the number to be much higher; they also maintain that damage is done to some children with lead levels lower than 60 micrograms. If the exposure level were measured at 40 micrograms, the numbers of affected children might triple.

A study of lead poisoning prepared by the New York City–RAND Institute in late 1969 interprets the present impact of lead poisoning on the 150,000 children born in New York City each year as follows:

1. Approximately 16.9% or 25,000 of these children will be born to an environment containing large quantities

of lead and will be a part of the population of risk approximately one year after birth;

2. Approximately 3,750 of the 25,000 children will ingest extensive quantities of lead during their first six years of life;

3. As much as five per cent of these children could subsequently die from lead poisoning;

4. As much [sic] as 1000 could suffer irreparable brain damage;

5. An unknown number could develop disorders such as kidney malfunction and cardiovascular and renal damage.

The costs of lead poisoning to its victims are obvious. The costs to society are also staggering. Dr. Chisholm has estimated that a severely brain-damaged child will accumulate $220,000 in institutional costs over his lifetime. Special education for a mildly retarded child could come to $17,000. Treatment for a child whose case is diagnosed early runs between $1,000 and $2,000; patching or repairing the walls of his home is about the same. The greatest social cost may be the tragedy of undiagnosed brain-damaged children in ghetto classrooms.

SCPI members soon discovered that they were not the first New Yorkers to recognize the problem. Each year the Health Department recorded several hundred cases, and the City's hospitals provided chemical treatment for diagnosed cases. In the 1950s, Dr. Mary McLaughlin, then a City public health officer and later Commissioner of Health, supervised a Health Department study that identified significant numbers of lead-poisoned children living in dilapidated housing in Jamaica, Queens. As a result of this study, the City's hospitals and child health stations developed procedures to report discovered cases of lead poisoning to the Health Department. But children were not routinely tested for absorption of lead, and many doctors knew little about the disease. Incalculable numbers of cases were undoubtedly overlooked. The department was also in charge (until 1965) of directing landlords to repair apartments so the disease would not recur. But enforcement was lax, and the fines were too low to force adequate repair. The lead-poisoning recurrence rate remained high in New York City hospitals.

Why was the City doing so little about a major health menace to a large portion of its children? The Health Department has a long history of concern for the city's youthful poor. In the early twentieth century, its new child health stations provided comprehensive pediatric care for thousands of malnourished and tubercular immigrant children. From free milk to universal inoculations, New York has pioneered in public health for the young. Lead poisoning had been found to affect more than 5 percent of slum children in other cities—an incidence higher than other diseases to which the department had given high priority. It affected innocent victims with devastating permanence. Yet in the late 1960s neither the Health Department nor the municipal hospitals had taken aggressive measures to prevent or control it.

Paulson and his colleagues quickly discovered some of the reasons for the Health Department's lethargy. Testing hundreds of thousands of "lead belt" children would tax the already overburdened public health personnel and laboratories. Funds for a full-scale effort would have to come from a budget stretched so tight that other programs would suffer. General ignorance about the disease would necessitate educating medical people as well as the public before its victims could be identified. The technology of testing children was not well advanced. The most reliable test—measuring lead levels in the blood—was expensive to administer, time-consuming to interpret, and traumatic for the child. Finally, those who know anything at all about lead poisoning knew that the key to its elimination lay in prevention, which could be effective only if small children were simply not exposed to leaded surfaces. With the city's housing vacancy rate close to zero for the poor, relocation of tenement families with small children was impossible.

To order repair or renewal of all areas painted with lead would place an unbearable financial burden on the city's landlords. It would also probably be unenforceable.

These reasons comprised a rational basis for inaction— or for a level of activity that did not reflect the high incidence of exposure to lead which existed among the city's poor children. But for government—perhaps particularly for local government, which is so exposed to its constituents—rational calculations as to what is the best course of action always include the extent and kind of the demand for a service under consideration. In this case, a need existed but not an actual demand. The potential clients of a lead-poisoning program were virtually voiceless—helpless toddlers and their parents, usually poor, uneducated people to whom it would not have occurred to fight City Hall or even to approach it. That fact alone probably explains the Health Department's bureaucratic stasis as forcefully as all the substantive obstacles combined.

II

During the spring of 1968 the SCPI subcommittee began to collect and disseminate information on lead poisoning. Paulson estimates that he spent more than twenty hours a week for several months working on the issue—phoning health centers for statistics on the number of poisoned children they had seen, speaking with representatives of community groups about the need for public information on the disease, talking with social workers about their observations of the prevalence of lead-poisoning symptoms in ghetto children. Each member of the committee tried to find sympathetic individuals who would give time and expertise to aid the effort. They went from friends to friends of friends. They became more and more convinced, as they enlarged their group of loyal workers and collected more information, that New York's lead-poisoning problem was serious and as yet largely undiscovered.

Perhaps because of their scientific backgrounds, SCPI

members began to plan an experiment—a summer program to test for lead poisoning all children in a given neighborhood. They hoped their findings would dramatize the
problem and prove its prevalence. They intended to analyze urine samples—a test which, though less reliable than
blood tests, was easier to administer—in an area of the city
with a high rate of substandard housing. Hoping to find a
community group to sponsor the study and provide volunteers to collect urine specimens, SCPI invited more than
two hundred organizations to a meeting at The Rockefeller
University in late spring. Although the thirty-five groups
who sent representatives expressed polite interest in the
problem, it was a new and unfamiliar issue to most of them,
and they were not ready to commit scarce resources to it.
An Albert Einstein Medical School student was present,
however, and he thought he could interest some classmates
in running the project and doing the lab analysis. While he
persuaded the medical school to loan lab space for the summer, SCPI raised money and borrowed equipment.

In June, Paulson met Paul DuBrul, an intense, red-
headed housing specialist in his early thirties, with a long
history of involvement in liberal and radical causes. Du-
Brul had been a labor journalist and organizer, a teacher
(urban planning at Pratt Institute), and housing director
for a large community service organization on the Lower
East Side. Although DuBrul had never heard of lead poisoning before Paulson looked him up, he responded immediately to the issue. "I had always thought there was
literal truth in the adage 'Slums kill,' " he says. "Now I had
concrete evidence." He began to call upon his vast network
of acquaintances to help SCPI members gain access to
media people, local politicians, and community organizations. He also helped Paulson, Buxbaum, and other SCPI
people focus on strategies for getting City government
more involved in the problem.

After a couple of unsuccessful attempts to arrange appointments with the Commissioner of Health and the
Housing and Development Administrator, DuBrul, Bux-

baum, and Paulson finally met with Dr. Donald Conwell, Assistant Commissioner of Health for Preventable and Chronic Diseases. Dr. Conwell, a pleasant, articulate man, was on leave from the United States Public Health Service to spend two years in New York. Although the Health Department reported only about 700 cases of lead poisoning a year, Dr. Conwell freely admitted that thousands more went undiscovered. He even suggested that his visitors' estimate of 9,000 to 18,000 affected children was probably too low. He cited budget problems and medical ignorance as significant deterrents to effective Health Department action on the problem. But he also implied that outside pressure on the agency would put him in a better position, internally, to get funds for tests and treatment. As for the preventive remedy of more effective Health and Housing Code enforcement, Dr. Conwell clearly thought that was impossible. He said that burning off lead-base paint was illegal, sanding it off only sprayed lead dust around the apartment, and covering it with plaster board did not constitute "removing" it within the meaning of the law.

Paulson and DuBrul had similar experiences at City Hall. DuBrul had reasoned that the Mayor's assistants were more likely than health and housing officials to respond to the menace of lead poisoning with aggressive action. They were young, vigorous, and liberal, too new at the bureaucratic game to be cynical or tired. And the 1969 mayoralty election was only a year away. But the Mayor's men were cautious. They recognized lead poisoning as a serious child health problem, and they were sympathetic with the outsiders' interests in doing something about it. They feared, however, that the City could not mount an effort that would effectively combat it. John McGarrahan, the housing assistant, talked generally with housing officials about the problem and asked the administrators of the federally funded Model Cities program about including among their projects an effort to de-lead apartments. But the task just seemed too immense. As McGarrahan reported ruefully,

"All the housing people say you just can't solve the problem in the context of so many old buildings." Discouraged,
he referred the problem to the health officials in what he
admits "looks like pretty bad buck-passing."

The Mayor's assistant for health matters, Werner Kramarsky, had somewhat more influence around City Hall
than McGarrahan. Yet he met with little more success at
getting priority for lead poisoning. He told the people who
visited him that he had read the 1967 Chicago study and that
he wanted to get the Health Department to set up a small
pilot program of testing children and repairing apartments; he hoped to develop some procedures that could
eventually be applied to all of the affected population. But
the program never materialized. Kramarsky either lacked
sufficient clout with the Health Department officials or he
failed to push hard enough. He did lobby for the allocation
of new funds for lead poisoning, but those efforts also
failed.

By the middle of the summer DuBrul and the SCPI
group decided that they needed to pursue a specific and
conscious strategy for getting the City government to act.
Past performance seemed to suggest that no significant investment would be made in eliminating lead poisoning
until the City was faced with what Paul DuBrul calls "a
counterbalancing cost of *not* making such an investment."
One such counterbalancing cost, which might provoke the
administration, was bad publicity. A convincing story of
the City's failing to meet its responsibilities by tacitly allowing irreparable damage and even death to thousands of
innocent children might produce action where persuasion
could not. So the lead-poisoning "activists," as they came
to be called by Health Department officials, set out to demonstrate that the prevalence of the disease, combined with
the City's handling of it, had produced a lead-poisoning
crisis. An "Action Program," written by DuBrul a month
or two later, sets forth the group's aims:

> No progress will be gained in the battle against lead
> poisoning without massive mobilization of the ghetto

community. We have already been told by the Health Department that no money can be found for a testing program until the black community begins yelling "Murder." Previous experience has shown that existing agencies only respond in the face of crisis; the crisis exists; we have to draw attention to it.

Medical identification of lead-poisoning victims was chosen as the most profitable immediate goal. The root cause of the disease, to be sure, was dilapidated housing, and ultimate solution of the problem rested on extensive repair of old tenements. But noting the numbers of leaded apartments was not likely to have much impact on public policy; the public had already been saturated with complaints about the City's inadequate housing supply. Emphasizing the medical issue would be much more specific, and probably more dramatic.

As the group worked out its strategy—which centered on political action, community education, and awakening the press to the problem—its members realized that they needed a new organizational form. The SCPI subcommittee had not been created to act as a pressure group or to deal directly and continuously with community organizations. Its members, chosen from the academic scientific community, had no experience with directing or participating in action programs. It contained no families of lead-poisoning victims, the natural group to demand action. What was needed was a frankly activist organization, with a leader who could pursue whatever forms of advocacy seemed appropriate.

Paul DuBrul was an obvious choice for leader of the new group. And the formation of the activist organization came just as he was deciding to make a much more substantial personal investment of time and effort in the lead-poisoning cause. DuBrul had previously visited City officials and talked to community groups. He had also tried to persuade the city's Community Development Agency, for which he worked as an occasional consultant, to train poverty workers to refer slum children for lead-poisoning tests. But he dates his real commitment from August 19, 1968. That evening he spoke—along with Joel Buxbaum of SCPI and the mother of a poisoned child—at an open meeting of the Central Brooklyn Coordinating Council. The atmosphere was charged with worry and anger. At one point an intern from Kings County Hospital rose to display samples of lead-base paint he had collected from the walls of the same pediatrics ward where poisoned children were sent to be treated. After the meeting a group of those on hand, including DuBrul, sat down and formed Citizens to End Lead Posioning (CELP). The new organization included residents of Brooklyn slums, representatives of health groups in other parts of the City, and a few SCPI members. Over the next few weeks they developed a program which called for three kinds of activities: case detection, to be conducted by residents of the affected areas through anti-poverty programs, neighborhood health councils, etc.; aggressive code enforcement, to be accomplished by community pressure against the responsible agencies; and community organization, to bring the danger home to those people whose children were threatened by it.

It is worthwhile to pause a moment and consider the motives of the people moving most aggressively to make lead poisoning a major public issue. DuBrul and Paulson had no personal acquaintance with lead-poisoned children, except as they encountered them through their growing involvement with the issue. Their concern stemmed primarily from a general social idealism. It also bore some relation to their professional goals. One of his friends has said of Paulson, "Glenn has wanted for a long time to be Mr. Environment of New York." And DuBrul's career as activist and organizer depended on his uncovering issues of significance and bringing them to public attention. Finally, the role of gadfly fit each man's self-image, though in different ways. Paulson sees himself as a helpful expediter, eager to spread his knowledge widely to activists in other cities who will repeat the New York experience. DuBrul relishes the position of challenger to established practices and institutions which he finds harmful or inert. A 1971 comment reveals his attraction to the role of David with his slingshot: "We stole mimeo paper in the first days, and we are still stealing mimeo paper, which I think is a measure of our credibility."

III

Some time in the spring or early summer of 1968, Commissioner Edward O'Rourke of the Health Department formed a task force to study the City's lead-poisoning problem and assess the Health Department's efforts to solve it. Several department bureau directors took part in the task force; a senior public health physician, Dr. Felicia Oliver-Smith, was assigned to work under Dr. Conwell as staff for the task force and coordinator of lead-poisoning activities for the department.

The origins of the task force are not clear. Disagreement persists as to whether it was appointed before or after SCPI and CELP began to apply pressure on the City, so one cannot assess the presence of defensive motives. One Health Department official has said that an increase in reported cases of lead poisoning (from about 200 in 1960 to almost 700 in 1968) combined with evidence of concern among community groups to push the Commissioner to determine what the Health Department's responsibilities in this area were supposed to be. The task force was not announced as a prelude to action, but as a fact-finding device.

Dr. Oliver-Smith had two handicaps. She was not particularly well organized or responsive, and her new job was an almost impossible one. The position had no precedent; she had no staff; the scope of her duties was only loosely defined. She was responsible for checking on individual cases to see whether the department had ensured repair of leaded apartments. She was also supposed to develop a register of lead-poisoning cases and to certify them to the

Housing Authority so that families with a lead-poisoned
child would receive priority for public housing units. But
she lacked strong department support, and she apparently
did not have the strength to press for it on her own. She
was never able to work out an effective means of referring
cases to the Housing Authority; she was unresponsive to
the "lead activists" when they asked for information; and
she could not seem to formulate research objectives that
bore on the immediate problem.

But the City's failure at this time to launch either a new
program or a systematic survey of the problem went much
deeper than Dr. Oliver-Smith's ineptitude. For one thing,
cost had to be considered. As Dr. Conwell put it, how could
you justify cutting funds from the critical venereal disease
program to start an uncertain attempt to control lead poisoning? The lead problem caused fiscal headaches as well
as technical and educational ones. But even more fundamental bureaucratic problems help explain why the Health
Department did not act quickly—pre-existing departmen-
tal conditions and daily operational problems which present a classic picture of institutional torpor.

The late sixties were lean years for the department. Pervasive personnel problems had lowered the formerly high
morale. During the Depression doctors of great ability had
come into public health because it promised security. By
and large they had either left those careers altogether or
moved out of the New York City Health Department. The
likelihood of getting superior doctors into middle-level positions where they could run a lead-poisoning program was
slight in 1968. A new Bureau Director in that year received
only $14,000, hardly competitive with the rewards of urban
private practice for even a mediocre doctor. Other health
worker positions simply went unfilled. Job slots for
sanitarians—the inspectors who went into a poisoned
child's apartment to find the leaded surfaces—remained
vacant because, although they paid extremely low salaries,
they required a college degree.

If the right kind of doctor could have been found to run
a lead-poisoning program, he would have faced a massive

job of coordination. The Health Department's organizational units sometimes focused on the patient group to be served, sometimes on the service provided or type of problem attacked. What services there were for detecting and treating lead poisoning were allocated among several different bureaucratic units: the Bureau of Public Health Education supplied information about the disease to community residents; the Bureau of Public Health Nursing provided the public health nurses who went to see a poisoned child's family; the Bureau of Child Health supervised the child health stations, where many children were tested; Environmental Health Services sent out inspectors to find the source of the poisonings; and the chronic disease section of the department retained some residual responsibilities.

Out in the District Health Facilities, fragmentation was overshadowed by alienation. Health officers there were overworked and underpaid. They often felt cut off from the problems and policies of the central Health Department offices. They resented new procedures and programs, which they felt were imposed on them by administrators too far removed from the "firing line." As a result, they sometimes overreacted to pressure for change. They portrayed the annoyances of adjustment to the policy-maker as insurmountable obstacles. When pressure for a large testing program mounted, lead-poisoning tests became one such obstacle. Excited senior health officers protested loudly in department meetings that their doctors could not all be expected to learn to take blood from the jugular vein of a one-year-old.

The budget problem that Dr. Conwell had cited transcended questions of adequacy of funds and weighing of priorities. The Bureau of the Budget, which had to approve every program change in the department, even when it meant no new expenditure of money, had begun to emphasize comprehensive child health care. The use of scarce funds to attack what the Bureau of the Budget saw as an isolated problem did not seem efficient or appropriate.

Although Health Department officials told SCPI and

CELP members in the autumn of 1968 that they intended to move on lead poisoning as aggressively as possible, the next year did not produce much change. To the impatient outsiders measures often seemed to move the program one step forward and two steps back. A pilot study of a screening device to be conducted at Brooklyn Jewish Hospital was planned, but a year later had not begun. From August 1968 to the fall of 1969 the Housing Authority requested opinions from the Health Department on 200 applications from families alleging that the hazard of lead poisoning in their apartments should give them priority for placement in public housing. No one acted on the requests for more than a year. Despite Dr. Conwell's hope for vastly increasing public awareness of the dangers of lead, the Commissioner's approval of a warning poster took nine months to obtain. It took fifteen months to get approval of notices to be sent in envelopes containing welfare checks. When a pamphlet about lead poisoning finally appeared, it was full of complicated information presented in technical medical language. An official sent to community newspapers an editorial on lead poisoning, but he failed to follow up on it, and only one or two papers ran it. A sanitarian was assigned to develop better procedures for testing apartments for lead, but he was given no authority over his colleagues, and his improved testing plan coud not be effected with so many vacant sanitarian positions.

Consider the bureaucratic problems that beset Health Department efforts to increase lab capacity for analyzing blood samples and to find an easier method of testing children's absorption of lead. Most laboratories are equipped with metal fume hoods to prevent noxious odors from circulating in the air. When the Health Department's new lab was built in the mid-sixties, it was discovered that it had not been properly designed to accommodate the old fume hoods. Additional construction work made it possible to install some of the fume hoods, but the City's lab capacity for blood tests was reduced by more than half. And this was just as doctors in hospitals and child health stations were becoming more aware that tests for lead should be run even on children without clear symptoms of poisoning.

The problem with the fume hoods predated the lead-poisoning concern and provided an unintended, if useful, means of resisting the pressures from people outside the Health Department. When thousands of urine tests were donated, the Department handled the pressure much more purposively. Delta-amino-levulinic acid (ALA) in the urine accumulates in amounts greater than ten times the normal level when the body has absorbed dangerously high amounts of lead. In 1968 a new technique for extracting the ALA seemed to offer a means of measuring the burden of lead in a child's system that would be easier, cheaper, and faster than the usual blood test. A Chicago doctor, using the urine ALA to test almost 70,000 children over a two-year period, found a 91 percent correlation between elevated ALA levels and dangerous absorption of lead. But another study doubted the usefulness of ALA as a screening method. The Bio-Rad Laboratory, a commercial outfit marketing test kits, wished to prove the reliability of ALA measurement and offered 40,000 free tests to the City. It hoped to get valuable information from the mass screening the Health Department could undertake and to receive favorable publicity.

The offer put City officials in a rather uncomfortable position. If they refused the offer, and their refusal became known, they would appear callous. But they doubted the validity of the device, and they did not really want to expend the time and money necessary to administer something that might prove inaccurate. They also probably worried that the tests would correctly identify so many poisoned children that the department would then be unable to cope with the treatment and prevention problems.

Resistance to the ALA testing proposal took different forms at different stages. At first the Health Department refused the Bio-Rad offer outright, saying it believed the test to be unreliable. But when SCPI and CELP brought public and political pressure to bear, the department reversed itself. It agreed to accept 2,000 of the test kits immediately—a number that could be used right away. Once the commitment had been made, actual use of the test was further delayed. Some debate ensued over whether the Mayor or the Health Commissioner should be the one to accept the gift formally. Once the tests were actually in hand, Health Department officials seemed reluctant to distribute them, and no procedures were promulgated for their use. At one point Metropolitan Hospital was prepared to go out and purchase the tests, even though they had been given free to the Health Department.

The bureaucratic stasis illustrated by these incidents was caused, in part, by individual personal and professional conflicts within the Health Department. The period when public awareness of lead poisoning developed—stimulated by SCPI and CELP and by the publication of studies documenting the problem in other American cities—was also a time when intense uncertainty about status and responsibility permeated the administrative levels of the City's health bureaucracies. From late 1968 well into 1969, the turmoil of competition among the department's top staff, some of whom were career City officials and some federal Public Health Service doctors brought in by Commissioner O'Rourke, sapped energies and deflected attention from programs. Personal animosity flourished, perhaps primarily because several areas of functional responsibility had to be divided up among Assistant Commissioners.

Dr. Conwell, who was in charge of improving the Health Department's lead-poisoning efforts, was one of those caught in the power struggle; his fight to retain responsibility for some federal program areas necessarily detracted from his focus on other programs. His jurisdictional problems did not end there, either. He had no power to go directly to the Budget Bureau to request funds, and he could not alter lines of authority to pull together all program functions under one administrative mantle. Within a framework of bureaucratic constraints, he did what he could. During 1969 he met regularly with the "lead activists" and helped to get several community programs started.

Above the Health Department and its supervising agency, the Health Services Administration, sits the Mayor, John Lindsay. During 1968 he had become increasingly dissatisfied with his Health Commissioner, Edward O'Rourke. February 1969 brought the *coup de grace*. The fuel workers had struck two months earlier, and the year's heaviest snowstorm had paralyzed the city for days. The Mayor, it was reported, was ready to leave New York for a vacation in the Bahamas, when the Board of Health—acting under O'Rourke's guidance—declared the City to be in a state of imminent peril. Lindsay fired O'Rourke immediately. Bernard Bucove, the Health Services Administrator, was also said to be in the Mayor's disfavor.

In late 1969 the bureaucratic wheels began to turn a bit faster. In July Dr. Mary McLaughlin became Commissioner. Her early concern for lead poisoning, combining with her recognition that lead was becoming an important public issue, prompted her to request a budget modification that would give lead some priority. After considerable pulling and tugging between the department and the Bureau of the Budget, the Commissioner was allowed to shift $150,-000 from a $500,000 fund for some low-priority programs. On October 5 the new Commissioner announced "a stepped-up attack on lead poisoning," which would include (1) an attempt to get the Health Code revised to require landlords to cover lead-painted surfaces with wallboard; (2) the development of a small staff to work solely on lead poisoning; (3) an extensive study of the ALA tests; and (4) the purchase of new lab equipment for lead tests. This increased activity was intended to expand the department's lab capacity, enabling it to perform, each week, 500 blood-lead tests (a 400 percent increase), 250 ALA tests, and 100 paint analyses. It was estimated that these increases would permit the Health Department to identify an additional 2,500 cases of lead poisoning during the coming year.

A number of other developments also spurred the pro-

gram. Under considerable pressure, Dr. Oliver-Smith pro-
cessed some certifications of lead poisoning for the Housing Authority, and a few units of public housing were
found for families with one or more lead-poisoned children. (Partly as a result of the Housing Authority problem,
Dr. Oliver-Smith was relieved of her responsibilities and
left the department.) In response to a Health Department
sit-in, Dr. Conwell helped a group of Young Lords, a militant Puerto Rican group, start a community project in
which volunteers took the ALA tests door-to-door in East
Harlem to reach children who might not come into clinics
or hospitals. Finally, conversations between the Health Department and the Bureau of the Budget made clear that a
sum much larger than the $150,000 already committed
would be necessary to make a real impact in the future. The
department was asked, for further budget action, to document the need for a new program and the dimensions of the
existing one. The Health Department, in turn, contracted
with the New York City–RAND Institute to do this study.
It became available for discussion within the City government by December 1969.

It is easy to conclude from the Health Department's
behavior in 1968 and 1969 that the bureaucrats there were
simply not interested in finding and curing sick black children. But that explanation ignores the costs to them of
turning a perfunctory, sporadic service into a major program. DuBrul and Paulson were motivated to action partly
by professional considerations; the same considerations led
City officials to resist change. Many Health Department
doctors and administrators held powerful images of professionalism that were threatened by the proposed program.
They did not wish to accept less than reliable testing methods or involve themselves with physicians generally unsophisticated in public health matters. They did not want to
undermine the plans being made for a "comprehensive
child health care system" which would presumably include
lead-poisoning tests and treatment within its scope. Their
jobs were best done by keeping the existing public health

services running smoothly, maintaining rather than innovating. What the lead activists wanted would disrupt both the organization as a whole and the work of individuals within it.

IV

For the lead activists, 1968 had been a year of marshaling forces. By the end of the year the troops had clearly broken through on several fronts.

Beginning in late August, when the *Daily News* ran a story about lead poisoning in Brooklyn—triggered by the case of a two-year-old boy in a coma at King's County Hospital—the New York press took grudging notice both of the existence of the medical problem and of the outsiders' attack on it. In September the *News* and the *New York Post* covered Glenn Paulson's testimony at a City Hall hearing to consider the poor maintenance of painted walls as a Housing Code violation for which tenants could withhold rent. In October the *Post* ran a story focusing on Health Department figures that showed that the disease was increasing at an "alarming" rate, its victims more than tripling in the first eight years of the 1960s. The first *New York Times* story, in mid-December, presented the problem and referred to SCPI and CELP as the principal sources of information of the disease.

The lead activists had also begun to capture the interest and concern of some of those most affected by the disease —the poor residents of the City's worst housing. Lorie Fargo, a graduate student in social work, had organized groups of mothers, many of them welfare recipients, to present community demands to the Health Department. Adolescents from the South Bronx had collected urine samples for testing in the Einstein project during the summer of 1968. That project revealed that of the 409 samples from children under six living in dilapidated housing, 89, or 22 percent, might be poisoned, even though they had no discernible symptoms. Two representatives of poor, black neighborhoods appeared with SCPI members in one of a series of radio discussions of lead poisoning.

But these efforts still reached only a very limited number of people. The publication of those few newspaper and medical journal articles did not immediately arouse widespread general interest in lead poisoning, nor did they create a special audience, attentive to the problem of the disease. Community groups in affected areas of the city had so many other concerns and so little information about lead poisoning that they often responded slowly to its dangers. The data from the Einstein summer project was never made public. (SCPI members say the results were so striking that a high hospital official withheld them in hopes of using them to get a fat federal grant to study the problem.) And the radio programs were broadcast only over WBAI-FM, a listener-sponsored station with a very limited audience.

In 1969 the organizing efforts of the preceding year began to pay off. The public—including both the affected groups and those who, though in no danger of the disease themselves, were outraged at the toll it was taking in the slums —became aware of the menace of lead. Politicians took up the cause, and research increased. The activists' campaign quickly gathered momentum. The issue generated sympathetic concern for many reasons. No one could dispute the innocence and helplessness of the victims of lead poisoning. The disease clearly caused extensive waste of human resources. Perhaps most important, it illustrated vividly the dangers that modern industrial society can create for those who have not been able to keep up with its "improvements." As people became more and more aware of lead poisoning, many could not help agreeing with Dr. René Dubos, a highly influential microbiologist and environmental scientist, who said of the problem: "If we, with a complete knowledge of the problem and adequate technological means to deal with it, are not willing to make the limited effort that would get rid of this disease, then our society deserves all the disasters forecast for it."

The occasion for Dr. Dubos's words was also the realization of a six-month effort by Glenn Paulson to convene a group of medical and scientific experts and community representatives to consider the lead-poisoning problem. SCPI, the Health Department, the Public Health Association, the Health Research Council, and the Scientists' Institute for Public Information jointly sponsored a two-day conference at The Rockefeller University in March 1969. Although the meeting did not produce major new findings, it was useful for other reasons. The conferees emphasized that deteriorated housing was the root of the problem. They noted that without correcting poor housing conditions, no ultimate solution to the problem could be expected. The conference helped to legitimize the lead activists in the eyes of the city's medical establishment. Perhaps most important, a continuing committee on lead was formed at the close of the conference. It included some of the scientists and doctors who had previously agitated for change. More significantly, it also included some public health specialists, like Dr. Bernard Davidow, head of the Health Department's labs and an important ally in the effort to get more testing.

During 1969 local politicians, including Congressman William F. Ryan, Jonathan A. Bingham, and Edward Koch, began to take up the lead-poisoning cause. The first to raise the issue were two candidates for New York City offices: Carter Burden, running for City Council; and Robert Abrams, a Democratic State Assemblyman from the Bronx running for Bronx Borough President. On April 22 Janet Scurry, age two, died of lead poisoning at Morrisania Hospital in the Bronx. Her death seemed especially tragic because, although her mother had taken her to the hospital on April 15 with mild convulsions, the Health Department had sent her home and did not process her lead-poisoning test until the day she died. Paul DuBrul went to Abrams with the story. On June 2, Abrams, with the dead child's mother at his side, charged publicly that the Health Department had been "scandalously slow" in responding to the evidence of New York's lead problem. He called for routine testing equipment for slum hospitals and the use of Neighborhood Youth Corps and anti-poverty programs to provide community education and conduct a mass testing program of all children living in deteriorated housing.

Carter Burden, a reform Democrat running for the City Council from the Upper East Side and East Harlem, explored the lead-poisoning problem in greater depth. Unlike most young and inexperienced politicians, Burden, who comes from a very wealthy family, had the resources to pursue new issues, even as a first-time candidate. When DuBrul told him about lead poisoning, he assigned a staff member to gather information and soon became convinced that it was a serious problem for his area. He wrote to Mayor Lindsay, expressing his concern, but got no response. Staff calls to Dr. Oliver-Smith elicited only an explanation of why the Health Department could not do more. Finally he and his staff decided to demonstrate the need for action with their own testing project. But even there they met resistance. The East Harlem Health Council refused to help Burden's staff conduct a block survey of apartments, and the Neighborhood Youth Corps decided that testing children to help a political candidate was not a proper use of enrollees' time.

Although Burden referred occasionally to lead poisoning in campaign speeches during the summer of 1969, it was not until September that he found a way to hammer home his concern. A doctor at Metropolitan Hospital called him about a two-year-old boy, Gregory Franklin, who had been so badly damaged by his absorption of lead that he could no longer see, hear, or recognize people. Gregory's family lived in an East Harlem tenement which, at the time of the child's admission to the hospital, had ninety-six outstanding housing code violations. Tests of wall surfaces in the Franklin apartment showed that every room in the apartment was a lead menace. Burden's press conference on the case got television coverage, but not attention in the daily press.

As Burden's idealistic young staff workers pursued the

Franklin case, they got some depressing glimpses of the bureaucratic sluggishness they would have to confront continually if their candidate was elected. Once they had seen the conditions in which Gregory's family lived—and in which his younger sister Liza was daily exposed to the hazards of lead—they were determined to find public housing for them. They wrote to many City officials who could have helped—among them Maurice Reichman, Commissioner of Rent and Housing Maintenance; Dr. Oliver-Smith of the Health Department; Miss Dorothy Spencer, District Supervisor of the Central Harlem District Health Office; and Ira Robbins, vice-chairman of the New York City Housing Authority. Only Mr. Robbins indicated any willingness to take action. After an exchange of three or four letters, in which Mr. Robbins detailed the many bureaucratic obstacles to getting the Franklins into an apartment quickly, he finally found one.

Political action took other forms, too. SCPI and CELP members had protested for some time to the Health Department that the 1959 provision in the Health Code prohibiting the use of lead-base paint for interior walls had never been enforced. Health Department officials had alleged that paint-removal methods were all either illegal or dangerous to tenants and workmen. Dr. Oliver-Smith had also once said that the Health Department works by persuasion, not coercion. But persuasion had been strikingly ineffective in getting the lead out of painted slum walls, and the new Commissioner recognized this. Dr. McLaughlin announced in October that she would press for a new Health Code provision allowing the department to cover lead-painted walls with wallboard or other sheathing material. CELP members thought this did not go far enough. With the aid of lawyers from the Martin Luther King Health Center in the Bronx they developed an alternative proposal that made the responsibility of the Health Department mandatory instead of permissive. The Health Department would be required to issue an order to cover or remove the paint to any landlord whose building had interior walls covered with paint containing more than 1 percent lead. If the landlord did not comply within five days, the Health Department would be required to call in the Emergency Repair Program of the Housing and Development Administration to do the work and bill the landlord.

To the surprise of CELP members, the department accepted substantial portions of their proposal. The Board of Health ultimately sponsored a successful resolution which made the department's responsibility mandatory and required the Health Department to "request" the Emergency Repair Program to cover the leaded walls. (The Board of Health found impractical CELP's provision for covering leaded surfaces to a minimum height of five feet, nor did it endorse the requirement that public notices in English and Spanish be posted in the hallways of buildings found to have leaded surfaces.)

SCPI also tried to stimulate federal legislation. With the help of Upper West Side Congressman William Ryan, who had sponsored a bill to provide support for local lead-poisoning programs, the organization held a breakfast meeting in Washington to which it invited all members of Congress. Senator Edward Kennedy spoke to the group—most of whom represented urban areas—and announced that the following day he too would introduce a lead-poisoning bill. (It was eventually passed, but the President has never approved spending the money authorized.)

Nonetheless, the most important development of 1969, from the lead activists' point of view, was neither the growing sophistication of experts, nor the embryonic interest among politicians, nor the shreds of evidence that the Health Department was slowly developing resources to test and treat more children. These events showed progress, but they did not generate a general enough concern to bring about the level of change being sought. The most important catalyst of public pressure and bureaucratic response was the writing and advocacy of Jack Newfield, a widely read political writer and an editor of *The Village*

Voice. On September 18, Newfield told the story of Janet Scurry on the front page of the *Voice.* From that case he elaborated on the dangers of the disease, the institutional indifference of many City hospitals to its victims, and the inertia of City government. He called the efforts of SCPI and CELP "a lonely crusade, bereft of money, manpower, and organizational support, to pressure the City and the health establishment, and to alert parents." He credited Carter Burden with being "the only politician in the city who seems genuinely involved in the issue." Perhaps most important, he lambasted the news media for not seizing upon lead as a major public health issue. Expressing his frustration with journalists who didn't find lead poisoning "newsworthy," he noted that

> lead was a story hard to make visible or dramatic for the television networks. It didn't involve famous leaders or exotic militants, or public violence. How do you show a *process,* how do you show indifference, how do you show invisible, institutionalized injustice in two minutes on Huntley-Brinkley? How do you induce the news department of a television network to get outraged about nameless black babies eating tenement paint, when the public health profession, schoolteachers, housing experts, scientists, the NAACP, and the politicians haven't given a damn?

Newfield followed the initial article with a piece about Gregory Franklin, the poisoned child whose family Carter Burden and his staff had helped. In two succeeding articles he attacked "the anonymous individuals responsible for this tragic situation: City officials, landlords, newspaper editors" for their tendency to "act irresponsibly because they feel protected by their anonymity." Each of the five articles he wrote elicited letters and phone calls from outraged readers, most of whom would never feel the threat of lead poisoning in their own homes, but whose liberal and altruistic tendencies were roused by Newfield's passion. Later Newfield went beyond his commitment to the issue as a professional journalist. He appeared on television, interested other writers who might reach the readers of the popular press, and pushed Albany and Washington legislators to get involved.

It is easy to underestimate the political importance of Newfield's articles. They aroused only a few thousand people—a consistently upper middle-class liberal, rather intellectual group, a tiny fraction of potential Lindsay voters. But these readers had friends among the Mayor's men; they were New Yorkers of influence in many realms. Half a dozen highly placed City officials, when asked a year later why it became necessary to do something serious about lead poisoning in 1970, responded in some surprise that such a question should be asked. "Political pressure," they said. "Jack Newfield's pieces—you know," trailing off vaguely.

But the Newfield catalyst worked only because the groundwork had been laid. Hundreds of community meetings, dozens of confrontations between CELP and the Health Department, and scores of negotiations with the hospitals had prepared the growing number of lead activists for the time when the public at large—and particularly those with political power—would take notice. By the time Newfield's articles attracted attention community programs—most of them small projects run by anti-poverty and health groups—were springing up all over the city. The East Harlem Health Council was surveying the lead-poisoning problem in that area, a group of Upper West Side agencies had banded together to force slum landlords to repair leaded walls, and some of the hospitals were responding to CELP pressure for routine testing. Kings County Hospital had initiated a special test for all children between one and six years of age who came into its clinic. The Brooklyn Jewish Hospital and Brookdale Hospital, both in central Brooklyn, were setting up large community education programs. Brookdale also conducted a study of 100 children living in Brownsville slums, and in October the District Health Supervisor reported that fifty of those children had absorbed dangerous amounts of lead, fifteen to the point of requiring hospitalization. By the end of 1969, several dozen organizations had become involved with the issue—through code enforcement, case detection, community education, or grass-roots pressure on the Health Department or City Hall. In many cramped offices of community organizations, xeroxed copies of Newfield's articles hung by strips of tape on dirty walls, reminding workers of the new danger they had committed themselves to fight.

Although there is disagreement about when and how he first saw them, it appears clear that Mayor Lindsay was also influenced by Newfield's articles. Both his health and housing assistants had tried to bring the issue to the Mayor's attention during 1968 and 1969, but they apparently had not been insistent enough. McGarrahan sent out a memo in 1968 to a number of City officials, urging attention to the problem, but he did not direct it specifically to the Mayor, nor did he ask for a response. Kramarsky remembers bringing up the issue in conversation with the Mayor some time that year, but he never drew his attention by scheduling a briefing on it or asking in writing for directives on how to proceed on the issue. By 1969 both assistants seem to have accorded the issue little significance in comparison with problems that might have serious impact on the upcoming mayoralty election. A third assistant, Peter Goldmark, feels sure that Lindsay was not really aware of the lead-poisoning problem until after the election.

Perhaps Lindsay failed to see the drama of the wasted minds and bodies of a few thousand ghetto children when it was presented as a statistically uncertain part of a larger set of health or housing problems. Perhaps he was subject to some of the blindness that Newfield found unforgivable in the medical people whom he excoriated in his articles. Perhaps he needed evidence that lead poisoning was an issue that stirred the reform Democrats whom he was wooing for 1969 election support. Even when that evidence did surface, it did not have much force. He already had the allegiance of most of the two constituencies who cared about the issue—the liberal, middle-class *Village Voice* readers, and poor black families. He was not likely to lose that support over lead poisoning.

Lindsay took note of lead poisoning in only one way before the 1969 mayoralty election. In a major speech delivered to the Educational Alliance, he called for a "new coalition for justice" between discontented middle-class Americans and poor people. He blamed the costs of the Vietnam war for the general disaffection of Americans, charging that the City of New York got a very poor return on the tax monies it sent to Washington. He said, "I want this money kept here, in our homes and schools, in our neighborhoods, in our lives . . . I want it to complete Gouverneur Hospital here, I want it fighting the menace of lead poisoning in our neighborhoods. . . ."

Many of the accomplishments of the lead activists came about because they could rely, to an extraordinary degree, on the resources and positions of personal acquaintances. Lindsay's September speech, delivered before the Mayor had taken any action on lead poisoning, was written by Jeff Greenfield, an old friend of Newfield (with whom he was later to collaborate on a successful book about "the new populism"). Dr. Dubos, whose presence as chairman of the lead-poisoning conference gave it prestige and importance, originally became interested in lead poisoning through Glenn Paulson, a former student of his at The Rockefeller University. The 1968 radio broadcasts of information were possible only because Paulson had his own regular WBAI show, "Scientists Speak Out." And DuBrul's wide acquaintance with local radical-liberal politicians gave him the opportunity to enlist support for his cause at every turn.

V

The day after Lindsay's re-election as Mayor of New York City, he called a meeting to discuss the appointment of a new Health Services Administrator. Gordon Chase, the chief fiscal officer of the City's Human Resources Administration, was chosen to succeed Bernard Bucove, whom Lindsay was letting go. In his new job, Chase would have responsibility for overall planning and research for the City's health services and for supervision of the Departments of Health and Hospitals, the Community Mental Health Board, and the Office of the Chief Medical Examiner.

It was a rather daring appointment. Chase was a management whiz who had worked for the federal government—in the State Department, as a White House aide, with the Equal Employment Opportunity Commission—but he had not had administrative responsibilities of this size and complexity. More significant for the City's tightly knit medical Establishment, he was not a doctor and knew nothing about health issues. The outcry was immediate. In answer to the protests of doctors and medical administrators all over the City, Lindsay maintained that the problems of the gigantic and unwieldy health bureaucracy could best be handled by a first-rate manager.

With that advertisement, Chase needed to demonstrate his managerial abilities promptly. The opportunity arose through Peter Goldmark, an executive assistant to Mayor Lindsay. Goldmark had first seen the Newfield articles in a friend's home right after the election and had sent them to Lindsay with a cover note requesting permission to push hard on the issue. With Lindsay's endorsement of lead as a top priority for City Hall, Goldmark alerted the health planner in the Budget Bureau, the Mayor's new assistant for health matters, the Human Resources Administrator, and the head of the Project Management Staff, a group that rode herd on projects with which the Mayor had some special concern. And Goldmark introduced the issue to Gordon Chase, who had heard of it only vaguely and had not read the Newfield articles.

For many reasons, lead poisoning seemed suitable to Chase for an immediate attack. The population most vulnerable to the disease was easy to identify. A reasonably reliable testing method existed. Treatment was usually effective if the disease was caught early. Furthermore, Chase was a father and a compassionate, liberal man. He was, he says, "emotionally affected" by the evidence that, in such an affluent and technologically sophisticated nation, such large numbers of children were victims of a preventable disease. He also knew that the issue was generating a good deal of public heat, though it appears that was not the principal influence in his determination to focus on it.

Chase first needed to inform himself. He read the newly completed RAND report. He also called together as many people as possible who had been working on lead—CELP and SCPI members, Carter Burden's staff people, District Health Officers who had become involved, and health and housing officials. He began to survey the Health Department's resources for fighting the disease. The Mayor's Project Management Staff prepared a project plan for him, setting forth alternative goals for a new program. All of this happened within the first month of Chase's tenure.

Chase discovered right away that both the Health Department's central staff and the personnel in its operating facilities felt very defensive about what they could do about lead poisoning. To overcome their resistance to a new mass program, Chase apparently reasoned that he should proceed a little bit at a time. He met weekly with Health Department officials, doling out specific assignments and taking careful notes. Discussion of progress on the previous week's agenda always formed the basis for the next week's meeting, and after each meeting a memo summarizing assignments went around to all the participants. The meetings continued for about three months until Chase had found new leadership for the program.

Chase tried hard to build permanence into the program changes he was making. Although he assigned new employees to handle aspects of the program—"we had to get a few tigers in there," he says—he also selected leadership from within the department. He worked to make the staff incorporate new procedures into their usual routines. He knew that eventually the pressure from above and beyond the Health Department would slacken, and he wanted to minimize the tendency, when that happened, for those actually operating the program to slip back into the old ways of doing things. With the help of the Project Management Staff, he developed quantifiable standards by which he could measure progress at regular intervals and ensure himself of a somewhat consistent reporting system.

Chase's strategies were very conscious. Good management seemed to him the key to stimulating change and maintaining higher levels of effort. He says:

> A good manager will know when something starts going wrong because he will have a reporting system which enables him to tell at a glance when slippage begins. He has to stay on top of the new program until that system is established. Once that happens, the actual monitoring of the program can be left to those below the top administrative level.

He feels the interaction between the manager and the program operators is key:

> You only get things done by deciding what you need and setting quotas for the operators of the program. The main thing is to count, and let everybody know you're counting. . . . That approach is good for the people working under it—they know when they've succeeded and they know that you know. . . . Our job is to provide for the operating units the resources they need to meet their quotas.

Chase attributed the new program's success in its first year to a technique he had used in previous jobs: putting a manager and a specialist together. By early spring he had established in the Health Department a new Bureau of Lead Poisoning Control with Dr. Vincent Guinee as its head and James Kagen as his deputy. An epidemiologist in his late thirties, Guinee had been a public health specialist for most of his medical career. Kagen is ten years younger, a casual, confident Harvard Business School graduate—what Chase calls "a damn good manager." Chase impressed upon the two men, as well as upon other health officials who advised on the problem, that they should think of their task as both medical and managerial.

Guinee had demonstrated an earlier interest in dealing with medical problems in a larger context. Before his assignment to lead poisoning he had run a successful program which both administered and disseminated information on the new rubella vaccine. He had also developed a reminder program for new mothers to help them take advantage of immunizations and other preventive measures that the public health system provides for them and their babies. So Guinee was particularly sophisticated about the importance of educating mothers to the need for lead tests for children. Quite early in his new job, he arranged for WPIX, the television station with the largest children's audience in the City, to broadcast frequent public-interest announcements which included brief descriptions of pica and lead poisoning and provided information about where to get children tested. Within a few months of the start of the new program, informal surveys showed that both small children and mothers were at least familiar with the images and general message of the commercials.

Guinee was in a good position to be able to develop the new program quickly. As a bureau director, he would normally have had to report to an Assistant Commissioner, through whom his requests and progress reports would have gone first to the Deputy Commissioner and then to the Commissioner and Administrator. But because both Chase and McLaughlin wanted priority for the program, Guinee reported directly to the Commissioner. In addition, he was given a Health Services Administration title—HSA Coordinator for Lead Poisoning—and in this capacity reported to Chase. This special double status undoubtedly helped him in the early days of the program to gain access to hospital officials and staff of the Housing and Development Administration.

But developing the new program quickly was not easy, even though both the Mayor and Chase had determined that it should receive immediate attention. At first Chase tried to reorganize Health Services Administration resources, hoping that new funds would not be necessary. When he discovered that to be impossible, he requested $2.4 million from the Budget Bureau for the fiscal year 1970–71. The Budget Bureau, also pressed for money, first proposed that the Model Cities program include a major lead-testing project. But the Model Cities administrators turned down the proposal, perhaps because inadequate staff work failed to interest the local policy boards, perhaps because the area directors thought lead was not competitive with other demands on their scarce resources. Further delays arose because of disagreements over matters like the numbers of clerks needed to code lead-poisoning tests and allocations of space for the central unit in the Health Department. Finally the Budget Bureau agreed to the $2.4 million sum, and a supplementary amount of $100,000 a month enabled the program to begin before the fiscal year started in July 1970.

Chase now had support from all sides. Commissioner McLaughlin and Dr. Guinee were pushing within the Health Department, the Budget Bureau had finally complied, and City Hall seemed to be trying to make up for its former neglect of the problem. (Mayor Lindsay once said candidly to a reporter, "Our staff work on this issue was just bad. That's all there was to it.") The Mayor's press secretary, Tom Morgan, was genuinely concerned about lead and kept track of what Chase was doing. Although Peter Goldmark, who had brought City officials together immediately after the election, stepped out of the picture, his place was taken by a new Mayoral assistant, Mrs. Ronnie Eldridge. An influential Democratic reform leader from the Upper West Side, Mrs. Eldridge had campaigned hard for the Mayor in 1969 and was chosen by him to work as his liaison with many different political groups. A warm, concerned liberal, she picked up immediately on the lead-poisoning issue. In a memo to Deputy Mayor Richard Aurelio, she expressed her shock over the "enormity" of the lead menace, and said simply, "Couldn't we be naïve and try to do something?" Her experience at political organizing suggested methods of providing the necessary community education. She pointed out:

> For the Health Department to say that they will within four months distribute 20,000 pieces of literature is absurd. We are able to distribute more than that and make a lot of noise during a political campaign in weeks. Why can't we employ similar techniques now?

Chase and Mrs. Eldridge were equally committed to action on lead poisoning. They were also both unusually relaxed bureaucrats, perhaps partly because they were both new to their jobs. Far from evading the lead activists, they encouraged their criticisms and program suggestions. They set up regular meetings with DuBrul, Paulson, Carter Burden, and others. For a time the group discussed with Chase and Mrs. Eldridge the possibility of an official advisory council to the Mayor on lead poisoning. Although that did not materialize, the activists continued to act as officially sanctioned gadflies during the early days of the new effort to eliminate lead poisoning.

Once the program began, Chase and McLaughlin kept careful track of its progress. In addition to Chase's strict supervision of the early staff meetings, the Project Management Staff set out program milestones that helped the administrators to check progress. And each District Health Officer provided a weekly report on his area's lead project. These memos were summarized by an Assistant Commissioner so that problem areas could be isolated at a glance.

It was easier to find money for medical tests than to do anything effective about lead paint on walls. For one thing, it appeared that the costs of repairing the apartments of damaged children would run close to $10 million in the first year. In addition, the repairs were to be done by the Housing and Development's Emergency Repair Program, which was principally accustomed to fixing defective boilers in the winter when landlords did not respond promptly. To add the job of repairing leaded apartments would require expanding the training workshops for the low-income ERP workers and finding large numbers of new people. The Emergency Repair Program was not efficiently administered, to begin with; its new responsibilities would surely worsen an already inadequate service. (It has since come to light that ERP was riddled with graft, which probably did not help, either.)

Housing officials who were involved in planning and helping administer the City's lead-poisoning effort generally regarded their task as hopeless. They knew that fixing up the apartments of diseased children would not eliminate all possible exposure to lead. Suppose a child's mother worked during the day, and the child stayed with a friend or relative who lived in a leaded apartment? Suppose the child's family moved? And what about the child who had not begun to eat lead when tested but would start within another few months? The only immediate housing solution to the lead problem was to de-lead every apartment in a dilapidated building where a child of susceptible age lives, at a cost of perhaps $150 million. And of course that would not solve the other, less superficial problems of those tenements. The leaking pipes and decaying timbers would simply be hidden behind new wallboard. Housing officials could not give much attention to the problem while it seemed so inherently unsolvable. They dragged their heels at almost every step of the way. A demonstration project conducted to determine the most effective method of making repairs was supposed to be completed some three weeks after its inception. It took three months. The Housing and Development Administrator never gave the lead problem the same priority it received from Chase.

Despite the obstacles, a much-improved medical testing program went into operation in the spring of 1970. Two years after its beginning, its annual budget was $2.4 million for the health aspects and $1 million for housing repair. About half of the medical funds were spent for finding and testing children, and the rest for testing surfaces, research, and program administration. Some 5,000 tests were performed in 1968, 115,000 in 1971. In 1970 and 1971 the program identified 4,574 children with lead levels at or above 60 micrograms per 100 milliliters of whole blood, the City's definition of a "case" of lead poisoning. Blood tests are given in or near almost every poverty neighborhood of the City, at 130 locations. The number of cases discovered decreased from 2,649 in 1970 to 1,925 in 1971, although the number of tests increased. This may mean, in part, that the educational and housing repair aspects of the program had had an effect.

But the program had problems, too. Its goals included not only the identification and treatment of poisoned children but also the prevention of poisoning and repoisoning. And in this area, it proved less than successful. In 1970, the Surgeon General of the United States Public Health Service issued a policy statement on lead poisoning that emphasized the importance of remedial action for children with borderline lead levels, "before the state of overt poisoning is reached." Effective programs, the statement said, should have medical follow-up on these children as well as "adequate and speedy removal of lead hazards from their homes." Neither of these guidelines was followed in the New York program. Public health officers of the department alleged that screening of large numbers of children takes place "without sufficient attention given to the medical and environmental follow-up of children discovered to have high blood levels." No regular, periodic attempts were being made to retest a child who is treated and released or one whose blood lead is abnormally high but not high enough to be considered "poisoned." Once a poisoned child's home has either been repaired or determined not to have leaded surfaces, no reinspection is made, despite the fact that a dangerous lead environment can develop as soon as a wall begins to peel or crumble.

Much of the follow-up problem rested with the Housing and Development's Emergency Repair Program. Although Dr. Guinee reported in 1972 that the average cost for ERP to de-lead an apartment was $450, an HSA staff report says, "According to random checkups of work performed by ERP, only 60 percent of the apartments repaired by them met the qualifications set forth in the New York City Health Code." This means that the effective cost of apartment repair is over $800 per apartment, and that many apartments may be almost as dangerous after the City has stepped in as before. Even repaired apartments that meet Health Code standards may be dangerous, since ERP will not go into intact walls, and only those walls that test positive for lead content are repaired. Retesting of some walls has indicated that inadequate samples are often taken. And ERP always has a large backlog of apartments that it has not repaired but to which children return after receiving hospital treatment. For January and February of 1972, the average time between Health Department order and certification of ERP repair was 58.56 calendar days.

Because apartments are often not fixed or have fallen immediately into disrepair again, doctors sometimes refuse to release a treated child from the hospital. The lead activists say some children have remained in hospitals for as long as four months after their treatment was completed. This adds to the hospitals' bed shortages and may affect a hospital's willingness to accept poisoned children for treatment. Despite the program's stipulation that children with lead levels of 60 micrograms should be treated, some hospitals have refused to treat children under 80 micrograms. And Chase's hope that children would be routinely tested for lead when they came into hospitals and clinics for other reasons has failed to materialize in some facilities.

Many observers of the program are distressed because it has not expanded its aims or activities. It does not include research or the experimental use of new tests for children or painted surfaces. Although many doctors feel that long-term damage may be done to a child whose lead burden is between 40 and 60 micrograms, the New York program is neither studying this possibility nor acting on it. In 1969 SCPI developed a paper on techniques for repairing housing, but none of them has ever been tried or evaluated by the City.

Of course there are answers to these criticisms. Close to 20,000 children were found to have lead levels at 40 micrograms or higher during 1971; if it were determined that these children needed treatment, the costs of the program would increase drastically. And the use of even the most sophisticated methods for covering over or removing the lead in walls would not improve substandard ghetto housing in any other way. On the other hand, the program's defects often subvert its accomplishments; Kings County Hospital reports that one-third of its lead-poisoning cases are repoisonings—a situation which presumably would not exist if the City exercised the proper attention in seeing that lead was really removed from the environment of a poisoned child.

For the first year of the new program's existence, the lead activists met regularly with Chase, Health Department officials, and Mrs. Eldridge. They pressed for relocation of families with poisoned children into lead-free apartments, tax abatements for landlords who voluntarily remove or cover leaded surfaces, and more thorough apartment inspection by Health Department sanitarians. But as the public pressure diminished, so did both the bureaucrats' tolerance for these outside kibbitzers and the outsiders' vigilance. When Chase no longer came to every meeting, indicating that lead had become for him something less of an immediate concern, Dr. Guinee's natural reaction was to wish to shoulder more of the responsibility for the program's operation himself, and the "lead group" often seemed to get in his way. He complained that they focused too narrowly on a few people in trouble; "they can't possibly understand my horizon of eight million people," he said. The activists, too, were shifting focus. Newfield began to write about other urban tragedies, Ed Rothschild became concerned about more general health issues as the youngest member of the City's new Health and Hospitals Corporation, and Glenn Paulson was appointed to the Mayor's Council on the Environment. As Dr. Rothschild said in early 1971, "Part of the problem that you get into is that you get diluted out. Paul is now with the Borough President, I'm now with the Corporation, Glenn is with the whole world's environmental problems, Jack's with the prisons and everywhere else."

VI

In May 1970 Richard Aurelio, Deputy Mayor of New York City at the time, met with twenty college students working as interns in City agencies. He answered questions about political processes and goals and spoke about the art of government. Students questioned him closely about the extent to which City Hall responds to problems in political, rather than programmatic, ways. "I don't think you can separate the two," *The New York Times* quoted him as saying. "I don't think the political is necessarily at odds with the programmatic. Lead poisoning came to the attention of the Administration because of the emotional issue that was generated. That doesn't mean that the City isn't responding in a way that it would respond if it had learned of it from the administrator in charge."

The latter part of Aurelio's statement was clearly wrong. Without "the emotional issue that was generated," the administrators in the Health Department would have developed a less ambitious lead-poisoning program at a much slower pace. Stimulus for change is merely the event (or group of events) that alters the balance between the costs of action and inaction as those who must effect the change see them. In this case, no one within the Health Department, acting in the normal course of things, could have shifted that balance to motivate speedy program development. It took an entrepreneurial assault from outside the bureaucracy to create a sense of crisis which made the costs of inaction seem to health officials greater than the risks of change.

The sense of crisis developed by the lead activists had several important effects. It cast the City's responsibility in terms of the capacity to respond with speed and efficiency. It created a secondary constituency for the program—not the poor people who would be the program's clients, but the liberal upper-middle class who would be its public monitors. Finally, it shoved the issue onto the desks of the top policy-makers, bypassing agency bureaucrats who had insufficient power or energy to act on their own. Once there, the problem could not be ignored, even by those who believed it was relatively insignificant. Late in 1970, after Chase's program had been operating for over six months, Frederick O'R. Hayes, Director of the Budget from 1966 to 1970, still thought lead poisoning was "a phoney issue." One of the most powerful men in City government, not even he could withstand the forces demanding response from the City.

For the Mayor, action on lead poisoning became worthwhile when it was evident that it was not solely the concern of a special-interest group. That the issue aroused people of different stations and for different reasons promised political support, to be sure. Equally important, the emergence of lead poisoning as a matter of interest to diverse groups must have appealed to the reformer's interest in coalition.

Chase needed very little prodding to respond to the stimulus that the lead activists had set in motion. For him the cost of acting was minimal. As new blood in the Lindsay administration, he was supposed to "get a few tigers in there," as he put it, to bring about change. If he passed up this issue, he risked not finding a better one on which to build his reputation in the Health Services Administration. (The timing of Chase's involvement was crucial. If he had assumed his duties even a year earlier, he would probably have encountered much resistance to a new lead-poisoning program from the Health Department, the Bureau of the Budget, and City Hall.)

If stimulus from outside the government was so effective in activating medical solutions for the lead-poisoning problem, why did it have so little impact on the more fundamental environmental aspects? The housing administrators were less concerned with the problem than Chase and McLaughlin. In addition, the costs of repairing all the leaded apartments in ghetto areas was so high as to be almost incalculable. Housing officials knew they were not doing the job. As Bruce Gould, then Deputy Commissioner of Rent and Housing Maintenance, said in 1970, "Paul Du-Brul says what we're doing is just a knee-jerk reaction. He's right, of course. What we can do is totally inadequate." And John McGarrahan asks, "Is it really better to spend your money to de-lead 100,000 apartments than to build 10,000 new ones? It *is* a zero-sum game."

Finally, the lead activists did not bring the same kind of pressure to bear on the housing officials as they did on the health people. Their energies dwindled because the task was so enormous and the challenge no longer novel. Preventive remedies excited people less than the treatment of dramatic symptoms—and were much more difficult to effect. The outsiders could not transfer their talent for effective stimulus to the more fundamental level of change.

This, then, is a crucial limitation on the value of the gadfly. Too often, like the bee, he can sting only one opponent. Other kinds or sources of stimulus must take over if change is to continue and spread. Perhaps a powerful political leader who follows certain issues very closely can maintain the movement begun by outsiders. Or perhaps one gadfly can take over from another. Evidence is mounting that as many children may be poisoned by the lead emissions from car exhaust as by lead paint. Successors of the New York City lead activists (a Washington group, called the Public Interest Campaign, is already working on the emissions problem) may force national medical programs or legislation prohibiting the sale of gasoline containing lead.

A final point illustrated by the lead-poisoning episode is that prevention is usually more difficult to stimulate than treatment. Altering bureaucratic routines in order to bring about the visible, immediate change of de-leading a child is hard enough. Changing them for the long-range, immeasurable objective of de-leading apartments requires greater dislocations for less certain benefits. The lead activists were able to cope with bureaucratic sluggishness to the extent that they could show damage that was clearly the City's immediate duty to correct. The fundamental environmental problems were less clearly the City's responsibility, and forcing the government to act on causes rather than symptoms was a task of another order. Faced with that challenge, the outsiders faltered, lost steam, and settled for half a loaf.

3

The Junkie Dealers

I

New York City is not only the financial and cultural center of the country; it is also the narcotics center. Drugs of many kinds are smuggled through its airports and distributed to local dealers by its underworld. Though estimates of the number of heroin addicts vary widely, no one doubts that New York has a larger proportion of "junkies" than any other large city. Federal government officials and *The New York Times* assert regularly that at least half of all the addicts in the United States live in New York City.

In the early 1960s drug abuse emerged in New York as a pressing political issue. Urban crime appeared to be increasing, and most people believed that addicts were responsible, stealing in order to buy heroin. Drug-related deaths were on the rise, as were arrests for selling and possessing illegal drugs. The press and the public cried out to the City's political leaders for help.

John Lindsay, running for Mayor in 1965, could not ignore the pressure to "do something" about drug abuse. He promised solemnly, "If elected Mayor I will carry out an intensive, progressive, four-year program for wiping out this city's cancerous narcotics problem." He proposed treatment programs, new legislation, and a campaign against "pushers" of illegal drugs. He asserted that he would treat addicts as sick people rather than as criminals and noted that their ultimate cure could come only from improving the environment that bred them.

Lindsay's declarations ensnared him in a dilemma. He had promised to solve a problem he could not yet define. Neither he nor anyone else could adequately explain how the phenomenon of addiction worked. Even the experts could only speculate about what caused occasional or regular drug abuse. Its long-term implications for American society were still obscure. Although conventional wisdom held that the impulse to alter one's state of consciousness with drugs was a product of social and economic deprivation, LSD and other hallucinogenic drugs had appeared on Ivy League college campuses. The public's usual association of drug-taking with deviant behavior seemed open to question as evidence mounted that many law-abiding Americans depended on barbiturates, "pep pills," and tranquilizers.

For the first two hundred years of this country's existence, local government provided services clearly understood by the citizens. These generally included the "housekeeping services" of garbage collection and highways repair as well as police protection and public education. But times have changed, and Lindsay's dilemma had become a common one in the mid-twentieth century. As the most exposed flank of American government, municipalities have increasingly faced political pressure to provide services in areas that touch the most intimate aspects of people's lives and that are not yet completely understood by either the public or the experts. This task of simultaneously defining and solving problems is awesomely complex. On the one hand, the public pressures politicians to come up with immediate answers. This pressure, exacerbated by confusion about the nature of the problems, may be extreme. On the other hand, government administrators need time and freedom for research and experimentation in these "new" and thorny areas. Responding to both these imperatives taxes even the most competent and well-meaning leaders. Choosing the perfect balance between immediate action and considered study requires the wisdom of Solomon.

Defining these kinds of problems produces further complications. Government must deal not only with issues themselves but also with the public's perception of them. Pressure for solutions arises from expectations as well as from reality. Many of the problems new to city governments have existed for many years but have generated public demand for governmental action only recently—air pollution, for example. Still others are problems that may have existed in other generations but are now distributed among the population in more visible or troublesome ways—drug addiction and unemployment. Finally there are the most intangible problems, problems that touch on all the other problems, dilemmas made manifest in vaguely expressed but intensely held values. The anomie or alienation of many contemporary Americans comes under this heading. In each of these categories need for solutions arises from a different mixture of worsening reality and escalating public demand. Progress in reaching a governmental goal may be almost invisible to the general public if the goal becomes gradually more ambitious.

The nation's largest city, guided by a reform-minded Mayor, was bound to have to deal with many of the "new" problems. In some areas the continual tension between defining and solving problems was certain to produce a period of haphazard policy and wasteful programs. It is hardly surprising that drug abuse—particularly the use of heroin—was one such area. The following story illustrates the inescapable confusions and inevitable failures that accompany governmental exploration of completely uncharted territory, guided by neither map nor compass.

II

To most mid-twentieth-century Americans, heroin addiction appears to be a relatively recent social problem. Before the 1960s it seemed an exotic phenomenon, found among occasional athletes and jazz musicians—like the drummer in the film *The Man with the Golden Arm*. This is partly because it was concentrated in black ghettos, usually unpublicized and untreated. Malcolm X writes in his extraordinary autobiography of taking opiates in Harlem during World War II, and a younger Harlem black has written that "the hippest thing was horse"[1] among his friends in the late 1940s. One New York City hospital recorded 251 Harlem teenagers admitted as heroin addicts in 1951.[2] Harlem was, not surprisingly, the focus of most illegal drug activity in the city in those days. A prominent black psychologist points out that the use of narcotics was almost ten times as prevalent in Harlem between 1955 and 1962 as in New York City as a whole.[3]

Because heroin addiction principally afflicted and affected slum residents, it did not become a matter for widespread public attention for many years. During the 1950s the City provided detoxification beds in several municipal hospitals and a treatment program at Riverside Hospital, but the experience was disheartening. Most of the treated addicts became readdicted as soon as they returned home. Medical authorities, including Dr. Ray Trussel, Commissioner of Hospitals under Mayor Robert F. Wagner, Jr., were skeptical that addicts could ever be cured.

Drug abuse became an issue of urgent public concern because one of its external effects was increased urban crime. As the city's Narcotics Register, a list of known narcotics users compiled by the Department of Health, recorded increasing numbers of heroin addicts, reported property crimes—burglary, robbery, auto theft—rose in both poor and wealthy neighborhoods. The police and press hypothesized that much of this increase could be attributed to addicts who stole to support their habit.

In the early 1960s the public fear of crime caused by drug abuse was supplemented by an inchoate uneasiness among middle-class parents about the effects drugs might have on their own children. Reports of adult "pushers" seen lurking in schoolyards spread quickly. The press made much of the small number of college students who were experimenting with the "consciousness-expanding" drugs. As evidence mounted that smoking marijuana, a commonplace recreation in the slums for many decades, was becoming popular among middle-class young people, a public debate raged. Although there was little indication that "grass," smoked in moderate amounts, held greater dangers than alcohol, many people believed that it was addictive, or that it produced psychotic behavior, or that smoking it would lead to heroin use.

The general ignorance about marijuana is not surprising. Confusion and misinformation characterized public views of all kinds of drugs through the 1960s and into the 1970s. Fear and stupidity undoubtedly contributed to this state of affairs. But equally important was the inadequacy of the information that was provided to a frightened, angry public. Sometimes the official statistics were incomplete, sometimes one could not really tell what they measured, and often one had to rely on totally informal and inaccurate sources.

Take the problem of estimating how many addicts there were in New York. Doctors are supposed to report addicts whom they see to the Narcotics Register, but many do not, and many addicts are never seen by doctors. In 1965, the Register listed 23,000, but City officials generally maintained that there were probably twice that number. A few years earlier Harry J. Anslinger, head of the federal Bureau of Narcotics from 1930 to 1962, had estimated the number of New York City addicts to be about 30,000. Many experts would have agreed, however, with the addict who said, in response to that figure, "I don't think Mr. Anslinger knows what he's talking about. He took that census while he was asleep. Certain areas of six square blocks on the Lower East Side or in Harlem could fill his estimate up. There are probably 50,000 addicts in colored Harlem alone. He's way off."[4] During the early 1960s *The New York Times* variously estimated between 40,000 and 60,000 addicts in the City. In the 1965 mayoralty campaign all the major candidates used different numbers. Abraham Beame (the Democratic candidate) claimed 40,000; Lindsay (Republican-Liberal), 60,000; and William F. Buckley Jr. (Conservative), 40,000 to 80,000.

There simply is no reliable way to count addicts. An addict who can support his habit without resorting to crime, and who can continue an otherwise normal life, will not become visible through his addiction alone. Additionally, no one has developed a good definition of addiction, and such a definition would probably be useless even if it existed. Doctors say that addiction "takes place when profound changes occur in the chemistry and physiology, or the workings, of the body—profound, but reversible, changes."[5] But the public concerned about drug abuse wants to know not only who is addicted, but who behaves as though he were addicted. Included in that category is the person who is dependent—that is, who is thrown into a state of disorientation if he cannot get a drug he takes regularly. At present, many experts maintain that heroin purchased on a ghetto street corner is so diluted that, for most users, it cannot produce the profound physiological changes in body chemistry that characterize real addiction. Yet the dependence is enough to cause "junkies" to steal in order to buy the drug that is available.

The fear caused by all the information and misinformation about drugs led, inevitably, to the emergence of drugs as a political issue. In the 1965 mayoralty campaign in New York City, it was important principally because the public believed that addiction drove its victims to rob and molest innocent people. It did not matter that the federal Bureau of Narcotics claimed that most addicts had criminal records before using drugs. Anecdote outweighed statistical argument; people who had been robbed by those they thought were addicts spread the bad news.

Politicians responded to the public's fear. Abraham Beame asserted in August that "Almost half of all violent crimes committed in the City are attributable either directly or indirectly to addicts." Lindsay also focused on the connection between drugs and crime. In his October 24 white paper, he estimated that New York's addicts annually stole money and personal property worth half a billion dollars, committed almost half the "serious misdemeanors," and were responsible for at least 20 percent of the felonies against property. The paper also pointed out that a large number of the City's prisoners voluntarily admitted to being addicts, and that 80 percent of the convicted prostitutes in the Women's House of Detention were drug users.

Law enforcement in the drug area appeared to be ineffective or worthless. If the drug supply could be curbed, people would presumably take smaller amounts of drugs, or perhaps people would be deterred from starting down the road to addiction. On the other hand, a smaller drug supply might simply drive the price up, forcing addicts to steal larger amounts of personal property to feed their habits. In any event, the supply of drugs seemed to be beyond the control of local law enforcement. Organized crime probably regulated the flow of most hard drugs, customs inspections were too haphazard to be effective, and prohibitions against search and seizure limited the techniques of federal narcotics investigators. Furthermore, crackdowns on drug traffic, if they worked at all, had strange and annoying side effects; after one such federal effort, in May and June of 1965, the Bureau of Narcotics reported that during those months the amount of narcotics stolen from New York

State drugstores had doubled. Finally, the shadow of police corruption and involvement in the narcotics traffic hung over police attempts to round up pushers and users. The enforcement effort in New York seemed to be part of both the solution and the problem.

Perhaps because of the professional cynicism about curing heroin addicts, the City of New York had very few drug programs of any kind in 1965. A small Health Department narcotics office had opened only one treatment center and three referral offices in the six years of its existence. The treatment center provided no job training or placement and very little therapy; its primary activity seems to have been the regular testing of addicts to see if they were "clean." Other departments did not do much more; the Police Department Speakers' Bureau sent out men to speak to school audiences and community groups about the dangers of drugs, and the health education course given in junior high schools mentioned drugs briefly. City funds also supported a number of private agencies providing social services like counseling and meals for addicts. Though these programs rarely kept anyone off drugs, City officials were loath to withdraw support, since their boards of directors generally included many prominent business and professional leaders.

During the months before John Lindsay took office as New York City's one hundred and third Mayor, a number of events pointed up the public's concern about drugs and the need for a political response to it. In February 1965 Mayor Robert Wagner chaired a three-day Conference on Narcotics Addiction which, although it produced no consensus on what to do about the problem, resulted in the formation of a commission to examine it further and report to the public. Headed by Paul Screvane, President of the City Council, the commission included many distinguished New Yorkers and added to the pressure on mayoralty candidates to take a firm stand on addiction. Its program, finally released in December, looked much like the recommendations of Lindsay's white paper: it called for treatment programs with many approaches, experimentation with drug-maintenance programs, tighter federal law to cut the narcotics supply, and narcotics coordinators who would be responsible to the Mayor and the Governor. It also recommended establishing a program of civil commitment and involuntary treatment for addicts.

Governor Nelson A. Rockefeller also stepped up state concern about drug abuse during 1965. Responding to charges that the State Department of Mental Hygiene had failed to produce a plan to prevent or control addiction, he asked the legislature for new funds for rehabilitation programs, and toward the end of the year two state committees produced reports commending the establishment of a state drug agency and stressing the need for public education about the drug problem.

A third event also provided political force on the drug issue—the emergence of methadone as a treatment method for heroin addicts. In 1964 Drs. Vincent Dole and Marie Nyswander had received a federal grant for an experimental program using methadone as a substitute for heroin. Methadone is a synthetic opiate that prevents both the euphoric effect of heroin and the "drug hunger" that addicts usually feel when they are deprived of heroin.[6] Drs. Dole and Nyswander set out to prove that an addict maintained on methadone could live an otherwise normal life. On the strength of their first successes with a small group of addicts, they had received money from both the state and the City for an expanded program. By late 1965 about one hundred patients were involved, none of whom had returned to heroin.

But public interest in the methadone program was tempered with doubts. To many people the substitution of one drug for another did not seem to be a "cure" for addiction. The essential characteristic of the addict—his dependence —went unchanged. Furthermore, if methadone maintenance was acceptable, why not heroin maintenance? Blacks especially resisted these solutions, suggesting that white leaders wanted to keep ghetto blacks drugged in order to keep them quiet. Chemical treatments also flew in the face of the development of American law and public policy since the twenties. Public debate broke out over the question of adopting the British system, which provides for legal dispensation of heroin to registered addicts. *The New York Times* and the New York County Medical Society both came out in favor of adopting the British system on a limited basis. Mayor Wagner stated his basic opposition to that solution, and a U.S. Senate subcommittee turned down a heroin-maintenance proposal. Senator Robert F. Kennedy supported experimentation with methadone; Senator Jacob Javits went further and urged adoption of the British system. The growing excitement about treating drug addiction with drugs was tempered somewhat in October when two state health officials returned from a trip to Great Britain and reported that the drug problem there had worsened, that since 1958 the number of addicts had increased ten times. Whether the allegation was correct or not may have been less important to policy-makers in New York City than the fact that it helped keep alive the continuing public controversy about drugs and addicts, a controversy that marched insistently across the pages of the City's newspapers all during the months of the mayoralty campaign.

III

John Lindsay knew he didn't know much about drug addiction. He asked Dr. Donald Louria, author of *The Drug Scene* and *Nightmare Drugs,* to draft his white paper, and he stuck to the views expressed in it when he spoke about addiction during the campaign. Though he proposed a hospital specializing in different forms of drug treatment and neighborhood addiction treatment centers, he could not say what programs they would contain nor what assumptions about drug abuse they would be guided by. He supported continued experiments with methadone maintenance, but he was not convinced enough of its superiority as a treatment method to recommend that it be adopted as City policy.

Though he lacked information, he had strong feelings about the drug-abuse problem. He was genuinely sympathetic with its victims and concerned that its ravages were the responsibility of all members of society. He said in his white paper, "Drug addiction is symptomatic not only of a sick individual, but a sick society. . . . The ultimate answer to drug abuse will be found in our ability to cure not only the individual but the environment that contributed so much to the individual's use of drugs." But his concern was diffuse and uninformed; he was uncertain about the kinds of values that ought to dominate his future activities in the drug area. Although the white paper stated that "the punitive emphasis is largely misplaced" and that addicts should be viewed as "sick," it also noted that pushers, who are generally addicts also, "shall be treated severely."

As a new political executive takes office, he must decide which of his pet issues to watch over himself and which to delegate. Understandably, he often tries to get rid of those he does not understand, particularly if he thinks there is someone around him who does. As Lindsay looked at the murky problem of drug abuse in New York, he could think only that he needed to do something, and do it fast and visibly. In a sea of ambivalent experts, one person stood out who might be able to shoulder the burdens and provide some answers: Efren Ramirez.

Ramirez thinks of himself as an architect, a philosopher, an existentialist. The people who worked for him in New York City from 1966 to 1968 came to think of him as a superb salesman, a charismatic leader, and, occasionally, as "an authoritarian psychiatrist." The ex-addicts who came out of his programs to find constructive new lives saw him as a kind of savior. His critics in the medical profession and on the New York City Council sometimes called him a fraud. And Mayor Lindsay once referred to him, with a mixture of admiration and despair, as "my witch doctor."

Ramirez was a plump, friendly psychiatrist who, in 1965,

had had four years of experience in running a 1,500-patient addiction treatment program in Rio Pedras, Puerto Rico. He had noted, during his residency in psychiatry, that addicts grew up in fundamentally alienating environments, developing character disorders that prevented them from facing reality and coping with it in responsible ways. Dissatisfied with traditional therapeutic techniques, which did not seem to change addicts' behavior, he set out to create a total environment where addicts could live and undergo a complete process of personality reorientation. Much later, in a 1967 television appearance, Ramirez stated that the addict needed "a complete barrage of therapeutic activity," and went on to describe the activities of his ideal therapeutic community:

> It doesn't mean that [the addict] is with a psychiatrist twenty-four hours a day—that's impossible. But it means that new extensions of therapeutic exchange and transactions are developed and are built into a therapeutic community—day-by-day functions, the management of the community, the cleaning details, the community government, occupational therapy, education, discussions, encounters, sessions, seminars, you name it. Sometimes you even try things as esoteric as Haiku writing . . . even yoga exercises . . . religious orientation, every kind of human activity that would help the individual reorient his character in a more productive way.

The reorientation should take place in stages, at each of which the challenge to change intensifies. Treatment is complete only when, as the 1964 annual report of Ramirez' Puerto Rican program stated, the patient has "undergone fundamental changes in his personality which make possible his reintegration (after trial period) into the community as a productive citizen."

Ramirez' views of addiction are intimately connected to his views of life. He called his form of treatment in Puerto

Rico "existential psychiatry," and he believes firmly that "it is necessary for any human being . . . to make a decision, to take a stand, to take a position in front of himself and his circumstances." He saw the therapeutic community, with its continual confrontations among peers and staff, as the best way to help the addict take that stand—to force him, as the report says, to face "the requirements and challenges of reality." Perhaps Ramirez' own background as a poor boy who accepted discipline and self-sacrifice to put himself through medical school and psychiatric training contributed to his view of the individual's responsibility for his own existence. For whatever reason, that view was crucial to both his Puerto Rican successes and the building of his New York City program.

Ramirez' appointment as Narcotics Coordinator of New York City was not the culmination of a systematic selection process. No comprehensive recruitment was undertaken and no evaluation of program alternatives preceded the search. Local professionals in the field were not consulted. Lindsay had heard of Ramirez' Puerto Rican program and asked an aide to bring Ramirez around to talk when he was in New York. Lindsay interviewed Ramirez once before the election, and immediately afterwards he asked Nancy Hoving, a personal friend and wife of the new Parks Commissioner, to look in on Ramirez' program while she was vacationing in Puerto Rico. When her report was very positive—she wrote the Mayor that "Dr. Ramirez is an excellent combination of expert who knows addicts first-hand and yet sees the broadest implications of the problem"—Lindsay was convinced that Ramirez was his man. He called him in to talk again and was impressed with Ramirez' remarks about breaking down the giant cities into "villages," "human communities" that would not engender the kind of alienation from which addiction springs. Perhaps this sounded to Lindsay much like his own interest in making municipal government more responsive to people at the most local level. In any event, the two men did not —and could not—get down to the hard, cold specifics of

how addiction could be stopped at this particular time in
this particular city.

It is perhaps instructive to look at what the two men
thought they were agreeing to. The Mayor wanted someone who could locate and pull together the existing small,
disparate programs and provide evidence that the new administration was concerned about the City's burgeoning
drug problem. In talking with Ramirez, and in the press
conference announcing his appointment, Lindsay used
words like "flexible" and "comprehensive" to describe the
kind of municipal program he envisioned. For Ramirez,
those words were encouragement enough. He assumed that
the Mayor meant, he said later, a "full sequence of services," serving many geographical areas and many types of
drug users. He also says he thought the Mayor wanted to
try many forms of treatment, though it is hard to imagine
that Ramirez' dedication to drug-free rehabilitation would
have allowed him to acquiesce easily in the newly popular
experiments with chemotherapy, or drug-maintenance,
programs. In any event, it seems quite probable that
Ramirez interpreted the Lindsay language as a mandate for
action beyond what the Mayor had intended to convey.
The Mayor thought he was asking Ramirez to orchestrate;
Ramirez thought he was being asked to compose.

IV

Even though he knew where he wanted to go, Ramirez saw
immediately that he would have a difficult time getting
there. He had no budget and no staff; the agencies he was
supposed to coordinate did not want to be coordinated;
much of New York's powerful medical establishment was
suspicious of his views; and City Hall was not nearly so
committed to setting up a major new drug program as he
was. He did not know the ins and outs of the City's
bureaucracy at all, and he was not a naturally skillful administrator. Nancy Hoving, who volunteered to help

Ramirez get the office set up, says of the first few months, "It was total chaos. Nobody knew how to find his way out of a paper bag."

But over the next year and a half, Ramirez turned the Office of the Coordinator of Addiction Programs (OCAP) into a thriving little bureaucracy, operating a number of new programs and monitoring some of those that had existed before. The innovator and philosopher in Ramirez shaped the City's new anti-drug effort to an extraordinary degree, and the pervasiveness of his personality determined both OCAP's successes and its failures.

First, he had to find out what all the drug programs run by private social services agencies were doing and how they could fit in to the treatment system he envisioned. As he visited them, he became more and more appalled. He felt they usually had no concrete goals, and in most cases were only providing services to addicts, not trying to cure them. Ramirez says he asked these programs only "to adhere to the minimal clinical criteria of my own program," such as regular urine tests and staff evaluations of addicts' progress. But the "voluntaries," as these agencies are often called, had usually operated with relative freedom from the City agencies that funded them; they were annoyed at Ramirez' questions and at the notion that their programs would now be more carefully scrutinized.

The voluntaries had a powerful trump card. The New York Council on Narcotic Addiction, made up of members of the board of directors of each of the larger agencies, was dominated by well-heeled WASPs, members of Manhattan's elite, with strong connections in the Mayor's office. They disliked Ramirez' unorthodox views on addiction and his somewhat abrasive approach to their agencies. When Ramirez began to tell some of the voluntaries bluntly that he could not justify extensive City refunding of their programs, the Council complained to the Mayor and various members of the New York medical establishment. Lindsay, anxious to placate his powerful friends and also to keep them from tearing Ramirez apart in public, appointed a

City Hall assistant, Michael J. Dontzin, to mediate between Ramirez and the voluntaries. The conciliation effort met with only partial success.

Ramirez was not disheartened to find that he could not use most of the pre-existing programs as part of his total rehabilitation system. He was prepared to build his own program units, starting with store-front Community Orientation Centers (COCs), where addicts came to get used to the idea of going into treatment. A major activity during 1966 and 1967 was finding funds and staff to support his ideas for providing different kinds of surroundings for program participants at different stages of their commitment to change. Ramirez' considerable powers of persuasion turned out to be very effective; he used City funds from the Community Mental Health Board and negotiated state contracts and federal grants. By the fall of 1967, two COCs had opened; an induction center at Manhattan General Hospital was providing extensive therapy; and the state's new Narcotics Addiction Control Commission had asked the City-run OCAP to conduct a voluntary therapeutic community for up to 2,000 addicts who were prisoners at Hart Island. Small community projects using Ramirez' therapeutic techniques and emphasizing his "existentialist psychiatry" were beginning to reach juveniles, relatives of addicts, and citizens interested in the drug problem all over the City. More than one hundred new OCAP employees, including seventeen ex-addicts, worked under the three Deputy Coordinators, Larry Bear (Administrator), Mitchell Rosenthal (Rehabilitation), and Martin Kotler (Prevention). In fiscal 1967–68 OCAP spent almost $3 million.

Ramirez conceived his rehabilitation program in three phases, each including several steps. Phase one, the induction period, begins with contact between an ex-addict and an addict considering making a serious effort to give up drugs. It ends with detoxification. Phase two, the treatment period, takes place in a therapeutic community which surrounds, protects, and challenges the addict twenty-four hours a day. There the addict participates in many different types of therapy, usually led by ex-addicts, but supplemented by psychiatric social workers and other professionals. He learns responsibility by performing tasks necessary to maintain the community, starting with the most menial chores and gradually proceeding to the supervision of other, more recent residents of the house. The third phase begins when the addict seems in command of all aspects of life in the therapeutic community. He moves to a re-entry house, where routines are much less rigid and from which he can venture forth into a job or further education. He works as a clinical aide in the detoxification ward, then in a staff role at a therapeutic community, and finally as an interviewer and counselor in a COC. When he is certified as totally rehabilitated, the ex-addict may get a job in the outside world or he may apply for employment with the program.

The process of personality change that defined Ramirez' rehabilitation system necessarily took a long time and required the undivided attention of many people for even a small group of addicts. The intensity of the experience emerges in the ways its adherents speak of it. The total process is called "the concept," and the conversation of staff and patients in a therapeutic community is liberally sprinkled with words like "confront," "concern," and "engagement." Ramirez has described the treatment steps, in order, as "contact" ("not just meeting, but meeting in a watchful way"); "developing commitment" ("to stop existential destructive behavior"); "engagement" ("a contract . . . to behave as if I were a healthy, well-functioning human being"); "behavioral conditioning" ("achieving the status of being a patient"); and "attitudinal reorientation" ("takes the person into the positive zone of society"). Nancy Hoving expresses less abstractly the totality of the process: "You might say treatment is the job of helping the dope-fiend baby come to the point of being able to make the choice of being a man. It could be called a concentrated course in growing up."

Reliance on what Ramirez' former Deputy for Rehabili-

tation, Dr. Mitchell Rosenthal, has called "emotional sur-
gery" has led to many criticisms of "the concept." Some
psychiatrists have opposed such a behavioristic approach,
arguing that the confrontation therapy does not improve
its subjects' understanding of why they act as they do.
Other critics have felt that since the therapeutic community is so protected from the outside world, it cannot possibly train the addict for reality. The use of ex-addicts as
therapists often disturbs health professionals, who fear that
they do not know how to handle complex psychological
problems and may even exacerbate them.

Another frequent criticism of "the concept" is that it
seems to adjust people to hierarchical, conventional middle-class society as it presently exists, without recognition
of the defects in that society that have directly or indirectly
contributed to the spread of addiction. OCAP staff argued
that once an addict has been rehabilitated through "the
concept," he is his own man in such a way that he can
evaluate freely the standards of society and reject those that
do not further his own goals. Nonetheless, a recent conflict
at Daytop, a private New York therapeutic community
program, failed to resolve the issue of what social roles
ex-addicts should be trained to play. The Daytop struggle
may be symptomatic of an irreconcilable schism between
being resocialized into responsible middle-class behavior
and being taught to work for social change.

OCAP's single most important early program was born
almost by accident. In mid-1967 six patients were discharged from the narcotic detoxification center at Beth
Israel Hospital, determined to stick together to help each
other stay off drugs. Ramirez assigned Peter Falcon, an
ex-addict and new employee, to help this group realize its
ambition. Pooling their welfare checks to cover rent and
buy provisions, they moved into one large room of a roach-
infested rooming house on Manhattan's Upper West Side.
Neighbors and families of the group brought food and
clothing and funds to keep it going, and Falcon persuaded
the Welfare Department to provide extra rent money.

Gradually, with most of the labor done by the addicts, they took over and rehabilitated the entire fifth floor of their building. Ramirez' deputy, Mitchell Rosenthal, transferred another group of patients to the little therapeutic community and gave it a tremendous amount of time and encouragement. The addicts called their new home Phoenix House. As the program developed and became for a time the principal institution of the second phase of Ramirez' rehabilitation system, its participants wrote out "The Phoenix House Philosophy":

Our philosophy is that every man has an inborn dignity and self-pride. But pride is like a young sapling that must be trained, channeled and nurtured until it is able to become deeply-rooted and stand alone, self-supported and unshakable in the conviction that its firm foundation can withstand the test of any ill wind that may attempt to uproot it. An ill wind has stunted the growth of our pride, but with each other's help, we will, *we must* dig our roots deeper, make our foundation stronger and learn to combat and defeat all obstacles that stand between us and our goal of maturity, dignity and self respect.

Our symbol, the Phoenix, derives from the Egyptian myth of the great bird which is said to have destroyed itself by fire and rose again from its own ashes. It is what we, who have destroyed our lives by drug addiction, are striving to do; rise from the ashes of our defeat to once again take our rightful place in society. Society will accept us, for once we have regained our dignity *we* will be society.

The nucleus of treatment at Phoenix House is the "encounter." This may mean a two-hour session with twelve to fifteen participants, or a three-day "marathon" with a larger number of people. In these groups, each addict must face the character defects evident in his "acting out" behavior, and the group leaders, as well as his fellow addicts, do not spare him even the most fundamental challenges to his self-image. Frank Natale, program director of Phoenix House, has said of encounters, "Basically, in a program like this we smash the superego . . . what the church taught us, or the synagogue, or mommy and daddy, or the whole society."

After five years of operation, the Phoenix House program houses about eleven hundred residents in thirteen different locations. It runs a training institute for Phoenix House workers, a number of whom are ex-addicts from the program. It has broken away from the City and is now almost totally supported with private funds. Approximately three hundred graduates had completed the full two-and-a-half-year program by mid-1972. Virtually none of them had reverted to drugs, though no truly systematic evaluation has been done. No good data exist on the program participants who left before the final "re-entry phase" of the program. Of the first six addicts who went with Pete Falcon on 85th Street, only one has gone back to drugs. One other now owns his own business, and the rest work as addiction specialists with various addiction treatment programs.

By mid-1967, Ramirez' program had become a source of considerable controversy both inside and outside City government. Many doctors thought it "unprofessional" and unwise to use ex-addicts as therapists; Ray Trussel, former Commissioner of Hospitals and an influential spokesman for New York's medical community, criticized the program publicly for inadequate research. Observers of other therapeutic community programs—notably Synanon, a private, California-based organization—worried that the "mystical orientation" of OCAP's program would keep it from being widely replicable. Beyond the medical and ideological questions, Ramirez' system seemed bound to have serious political problems. Ramirez was trying to reintegrate distorted personalities—a long, costly process not suitable for mass production; Lindsay and other political figures wanted to reduce crime as rapidly as possible, which meant quick, cheap treatment of large numbers of addicts. The two goals were incompatible.

City Hall was faced with a dilemma. On the one hand, Ramirez had antagonized many of the groups he had been hired to coordinate, his program had been labeled as a "hoax" on the floor of the City Council, and he was said to be unable to follow even the simplest administrative procedures mandated by the City's personnel and budget agencies. Perhaps he should be fired. On the other hand, he had developed a plan for addiction services in the City and was putting that plan into effect. Furthermore, he was raising non-City funds to support it; the federal Office of Economic Opportunity had committed the largest health-related grant of its existence—$4.8 million—to support OCAP's community prevention and induction projects. Ramirez' departure might mean the loss of grant monies that his ideas and persuasive powers were attracting to the City. OCAP now looked more like a small City agency than like a branch of the Mayor's office intended to provide only a public spokesman and an expediter. It was easier for the Mayor to recognize its nature by elevating its bureaucratic status than it would have been to replace Ramirez as Coordinator or eliminate the office entirely. In November, Lindsay announced the formation of "the first municipal agency dealing solely with drug abuse," the Addiction Services Agency (ASA), with Efren Ramirez as its Commissioner.

It may seem ironic that City Hall would advance the status of an office which it felt had not been very successful and which, as yet, had no formal bureaucratic existence to make it difficult to destroy. The irony is only superficial. The key to explaining this behavior lay in the Mayor's lack of a sense of the nature of the addiction problem and its solutions, and in Ramirez' correspondingly clear assertion of those matters. Though Lindsay might not have liked Ramirez' approach to the problem, he could not easily get rid of him because, without his own definitions, he could

not point to ways in which Ramirez had not measured up
to standards dictated by them. He could not justify firing
him for such puny peccadilloes as OCAP's administrative
problems or the occasional public criticisms; the former
could be too easily attributed to the inevitable growing
pains of a new bureaucracy, and the latter were to be expected in moving the City into a controversial new program area. The only other powerful standards by which to
measure Ramirez' achievement were the increase of funds
and functions that he had attracted to his role, and on those
grounds he could hardly be faulted.

The bureaucratic transformation of Ramirez' office did
not, of course, solve any of its problems. As treatment
centers proliferated and the program expanded its focus—
still supporting character reorganization in drug-free programs—even more public doubt surfaced. Attacking ASA
made good press. In late 1968, when Julius Moskowotz, a
City Councilman from Brooklyn, called its program a
"fraud" and "a total failure," the City papers carried the
charges and denials for days.

Part of the difficulty lay in Ramirez' unwillingness to
play "the numbers game." When the Councilman pointed
to hundreds of addicts maintained on methadone now living normal lives, ASA could say after almost two years of
treatment that only 69 of its patients were now in the
re-entry phase, 552 in full-time treatment, and 560 at the
induction level. The numbers did not look good, and that
was the criterion by which the press and the public were
bound to judge the program. Ramirez might have appointed a strong evaluation team to develop statistics that
showed that once an addict made a commitment to the
ASA program, he was unlikely to drop out and go back to
drugs. Or he might have demonstrated that, though program costs per addict were very high for therapeutic communities during their first year or two, they dropped off
substantially once re-entry began. But Ramirez cared very
little about adhering to traditional standards of program
measurement if they did not coincide with his own. It was

not until mid-1968 that the Bureau of Applied Social Research at Columbia University was hired to evaluate the Phoenix House program, and that research has not been considered by most experts to be sufficiently objective or empirical.

Added to the public criticisms of the ASA approach were some perplexing administrative problems. Over and over the ideological focus of the ASA programs interfered with establishing and maintaining regular bureaucratic procedures. Particularly difficult were clashes of ASA staff with employees of the City's overhead agencies which provided necessary services to the new agency—the Department of Personnel, the Bureau of the Budget, the Department of Real Estate. These offices are in charge of the acquisition of facilities, the hiring and promotion of employees, and other administrative matters. They are generally staffed with career civil service men whose jobs are most easily performed when the procedures they must handle are regular, uniform, and impersonal. In setting up ASA, almost every negotiation involved making bureaucratic exceptions, defining new program standards, or solving individual problems. ASA officials did not do anything to minimize the dislocation either. Initially Ramirez was impatient with the bureaucratic rigamarole necessary to get the agency started, and he passed that feeling along to his aides. A member of his staff who regularly dealt with budget matters and watched Ramirez' relationship with budget and personnel examiners said recently, "In those days, everyone who was not part of 'the concept' was against us." Another, on hearing that Ramirez had described himself as an "architect," commented ruefully, "Perhaps, but one who never supervised the building."

City bureaucrats found puzzling the fusion of roles and responsibilities between the providers of the service and its beneficiaries. An addict who had proven himself, during several months of treatment in a Phoenix House, to be a responsible person, might go on the ASA payroll and rise, over a two-year period, from addiction aide ($4,650) to senior addiction specialist ($10,300). To a budget examiner, accustomed to approving $600 raises for only a small proportion of an agency's employees each year, the perpetual ASA requests for "merit increases" covering half the staff —sometimes for employees with only their previous addiction to qualify them for their work—seemed to indicate that the whole program was out of kilter.

Some of ASA's administrative problems stemmed from the agency's unique character as the bureaucratic embodiment of a set of ideas, the organizational manifestation of a philosophy of life going far beyond the mere provision of a service. A budget examiner once estimated in some dismay that office-hours "encounters" for ASA top executives cost $28,000 a year. Another instance of what seemed unreasonable expenditure was the payment of overtime to personnel who were spending those hours playing basketball with addicted kids. To budget and personnel people working with ASA, there seemed to be an air of laxity and indulgence about both the program and its leaders which jarred their sensibilities, clashing with experience and backgrounds which had taught them to honor sacrifice and discipline. Jack Pevny, the budget examiner for ASA during its first three years, describes his initial reactions to the program:

> First of all, it was voluntary. An addict could come in to the storefront and sit around all day and then decide he didn't want to do it. I don't know, I guess I found that hard to understand at first. My father died when I was six; I always worked for everything; I went to college at night. My wife is the sociologist in our family, and she is always saying that it's the problems of society that made these kids the way they are.

Unsurprisingly, the suspicion was mutual. The field personnel who spent fourteen hours a day coaxing junkies into ASA Community Orientation Centers could not believe that those old men who did not answer their phones after five in the afternoon and who were holding up requests for additional staff understood as they did the values and pains of hard work. Differences of style, emphasis, and background completely obscured a great irony: that in the dominant value structures of their lives, the bureaucrats and the addiction workers had a strong common bond. As the older men had grown up with Emersonian self-reliance, the younger ones were articulating it as a core idea of the City's newest social service.

Other bureaucratic problems resulted from simple ineptitude. After the Department of Personnel had finally approved the establishment of a new series of civil service titles, with job specifications tailored to fit ex-addicts and community workers who would not normally have qualified for professional positions, ASA continually proposed candidates for the new slots who could not qualify for them, or asked for promotions without adequate justification. Maddened by the sloppiness and apparent ingratitude of the agency, the budget personnel would process the requests at a snail's pace, which in turn infuriated ASA staff.

Ramirez and his staff often acted on impulse, creating problems for the overhead agencies. They tended to disregard the provision of the City Charter that mandated that contracts of more than $2,500 had to be approved by the Board of Estimate, and after they had made an expensive commitment to rent and equip a store-front treatment or prevention center, they would call upon the Department of Real Estate to honor it without delay. Ramirez once promised a job to a newly arrived Puerto Rican friend, telling her merely to show up at the agency and get put on an addiction specialist line. When she arrived, she supplied such scanty information about herself that she could not be paid at the promised level. Jack Pevny cites another instance of maddening disregard for bureaucratic norms: a new employee was put on the payroll as director of a new Community Orientation Center to be established in Far Rockaway, Queens. Although community resistance to a drug program in the neighborhood necessitated abandoning plans for the center, its director remained on the payroll until the Budget Bureau caught it. When confronted with this error (which seemed particularly important because it occurred during the mayoralty campaign), ASA staff replied, "But what should we have done? The guy had no money. His wife was sick. We had to do something."

That spirit was one of the great attractions of ASA and was never communicable in terms that impressed the bureaucrats, the politicians, or the press. Larry Bear, Ramirez' first deputy and successor as Commissioner, describes ASA as "an agency where people relate as human beings, not civil servants or government workers." To support that contention, he points to a federal Department of Labor study of eight government agencies that employed and trained disadvantaged workers. The study concluded that, while each agency had hired workers without hesitation, ASA was the only one that had advanced them regularly. The report was very enthusiastic about the job the agency had done in building the employees' pride in their work.

If the agency had been able to present a united front to its critics, both inside and outside City government, perhaps the strains would have lessened as time passed. After all, though the number of program graduates was still small, some impressive human beings were emerging from this crazy system. But the agency was honeycombed with dissension, with staff loyalties split between Rosenthal, the Deputy Commissioner for Rehabilitation, and the rest of top management. These divisions came to dominate many internal agency relationships and perhaps to retard the development of the program.

It is difficult to trace the beginnings of the discord. One thing appears quite certain: Ramirez and Rosenthal shared some important character traits, and their similarities clashed. One staff member has called them both "authoritarian psychiatrists"; another, "men of monumental ego." But while both men wanted control of the agency, Ramirez

wanted it only for the time it took to breathe organizational
life into his ideas; Rosenthal wanted it only insofar as he
could get the agency to devote its resources to the Phoenix
House program. For each of them, indifference to one aspect of the program was as important as the struggle for
power over the rest. Finally, Ramirez' inability to track the
implementation of his ideas gave way before Rosenthal's
domination of the agency's one good-sized visible program.
Though Ramirez had never been very enthusiastic about
the Phoenix House program, preferring the idea of hospi-
tal-based therapeutic communities and many different
treatment levels rather than one dominant kind of institution, he could not stop the growth of Phoenix once Rosenthal had put it together.

As soon as the split between Ramirez and Rosenthal
became pronounced, Rosenthal let it be known that he was
running Phoenix House as he saw fit and that any attempt
to wrest control from him would fail. By the time Ramirez
wanted to fire him for insubordination it was too late.
Rosenthal threatened to take all the trained ex-addicts in
the program with him and set up an independent Phoenix
House elsewhere. It was a real enough threat; alliances to
Rosenthal were strong, and Phoenix House funds were
already independent enough of ASA so that if most employees had walked out, those monies would have followed
them.

City Hall could not avoid involvement with the internal
ASA disputes, but it proffered no easy solutions. If the
Mayor's office supported Ramirez in his wish to remove
Rosenthal, and Phoenix House split off from ASA, what
would justify the agency's existence? And yet how could
Lindsay undercut his Commissioner when it seemed that
Rosenthal had created his own fiefdom and in doing so had
neglected the general welfare of the agency? Lindsay and
his advisors decided to stall. Mike Dontzin, the Mayor's
assistant for narcotics, advised Ramirez not to remove Rosenthal, and no one faced head-on the question of firing
Ramirez.

Personal differences between Lindsay and Ramirez may have complicated their political and administrative relationship. The ease and security of Lindsay's New York WASP background contrasted markedly with Ramirez' difficult climb from poor Puerto Rican boy to husband of the Governor's daughter and noted psychiatrist. The mutual distrust engendered by this difference of background was heightened by the passionate, ideological intensity of Ramirez' approach to his job. His single-mindedness prevented him from being particularly concerned with protecting the Mayor from excessive adverse criticism. This is a qualification for high office in the City that was understandably important to Lindsay, but it may be important to his administrators only in proportion to their own political concerns. Ramirez' lack of political ambition definitely worked against Lindsay's interests.

Lindsay's indecisiveness may have been caused in part by the realization at City Hall that Ramirez would shortly resign, even if not pushed to do so. As he had less and less control over the agency's principal program, and as the Commissioner's job increasingly involved the daily drudgery of running the agency rather than spinning schemes or winning converts, Ramirez' interest in his job waned. He seemed preoccupied and distant to many of his staff, almost from the time OCAP became ASA and he became Commissioner. By the summer of 1968, he spent little time at the agency, preferring to travel around advising other cities and states on drug programs, missing agency meetings because he had scheduled simultaneous meetings elsewhere in the City, rarely looking in on the programs that the agency had started.

In an organization where every employee participated in regular group therapy, this behavior could not go unremarked for long. A meeting of some top staff members to discuss "the Rosenthal problem" turned into an encounter session, as the participants began to tell Ramirez that he was acting as though he didn't want to be Commissioner. They pointed to his inability to control Rosenthal, his lack of direction in developing the prevention side of the program, and his failure to perform the lobbying and negotiating necessary to nail down a large program grant from the National Insitutes of Mental Health. He greeted their criticisms with relief, admitted that the details of running the agency were proving to be an administrative burden he could not bear, and promised then and there to resign. By November he had left to open a private psychiatric practice. Larry Bear, his First Deputy, succeeded him.

V

Many of the acute social problems of the 1960s posed a new kind of challenge to government. They were issues that aroused massive public concern—crime, drugs, welfare—and this concern demanded as careful attention as the problems themselves. While evidence mounted that violent crimes were increasing, and people became more fearful, the public relations function of law enforcement became more crucial. Making people feel safer seemed as important as the prevention of crimes and the apprehension of criminals.

The task was a complicated one. It meant assessing the sources of people's fears and determining what kinds of programs seemed to the public to reach the evils they most feared. In some cases it also meant devoting resources to programs that might not have the greatest impact on the substantive problem but might most effectively reassure the citizens. Neither bureaucrats nor professional experts were very sophisticated about how to handle the problems of public confidence, partly because they were outside the range of the traditional tasks of local government and partly because the problems shifted rapidly. Often, public anxiety about relief chiselers and rapists seemed to bear little relation to the statistical pictures of welfare families and criminals. It became difficult for even sophisticated observers to distinguish between mythology and reality.

By early 1969 a major determinant of City policy on drug abuse was the interaction between the reality of the problem and the public's fear of drugs. It was true that drug use outside the urban ghettos was on the increase; a Gallup poll showed that a large percentage of university students had tried heroin at some time, and the slick magazines were full of stories about youthful experimentation with LSD and mescaline. On the other hand, little hard evidence existed to show that significant numbers of young Americans were regularly taking anything more dangerous than marijuana. Nonetheless, middle-class parents were beginning to mix and sometimes confuse their fears of drug related crime with their intense concerns for the possible effects of the "drug culture" on their children's lives. Understandably, parents reacted with panic to journalistic accounts of heroin sales in high schools—in February, a former addict was reported to have stated at an NAACP conference that "there are more drug users in the schools than there are on the streets"—and to the New York *Post*'s weekly tally of heroin deaths. The panic became nearly as serious a problem for government as drug abuse itself.

In combating public fear, the policy-makers had to face the fact that their efforts to stem the drug-abuse problem had met with little success. ASA had not yet produced a significant number of "cured" addicts, estimates of the number of addicts in the City continued to rise, and the average age of arrested drug abusers was lower every year. The money spent by federal, state, and local governments had not made much of a dent in the problem. Neither had the 50 percent increase (over three years) in the Police Department's Narcotics Squad, nor the state's distribution to the public schools, in 1968, of four million pieces of literature on the dangers of drugs. The involuntary commitment program of the State Narcotic Addiction Control Commission—announced in 1967 as the way to achieve a "significant reduction in crime in the city and state"—had fallen on its face.

The only effort that appeared to be getting results was

the Dole-Nyswander methadone program. Some 1,500 patients now participated, most of whom held jobs or went to school. They were able to maintain stable family units. Most important from a political standpoint, they did not seem to be committing crimes.

Many of the problems at first associated with methadone subsided before its proven successes. The concern of some of those who felt that maintaining an addict on methadone was just substituting one addiction for another gave way as methadone patients showed no signs of dazed or irresponsible behavior. Per capita costs of the program diminished as some addicts no longer needed to report to the treatment centers every day. Even federal restrictions on the use of methadone were easing, so that larger-scale programs could be developed without having to be justified solely as research.

Although methadone successes were tentative and short-range, they took on special importance because they were visible and comparatively easy to achieve. They did not depend on elaborate physical facilities or costly therapy. They could be easily quantified and reported to the public. Their very essence lay in jobs held and families reunited. Little wonder that methadone should seem to politicians the answer to one of their most acute problems—the public's fear of drugs.

During the latter half of 1968 City Hall began to feel some pressure to get a City methadone program started. ASA programs were still reaching only a tiny proportion of the City's addicts, and it did not appear that number could increase very rapidly if the programs were to retain their highly personal character. The next mayoral election was only a year away, and Lindsay would have few concrete achievements to point to in the drug area unless he could develop something that would treat large numbers of addicts right away. If the Mayor was to take the initiative, he had no time to lose. Rumor had it that the City Council would soon approve legislation calling for methadone treatment of all the heroin addicts in the jails. It was certainly better for a Mayor with an activist image to lead the bandwagon rather than be pushed aboard.

In August, Mike Dontzin, Lindsay's assistant for drug problems, called together ASA and Health Services Administration officials to discuss how the City might use methadone treatment. The initial responses were negative. Bernard Bucove, the Health Services Administrator, pointed out that Dr. Vincent Dole had recently said methadone had proven itself so that private doctors ought to be able to administer it. If that was the wave of the future, the Health Services Administration (HSA) ought not to assume responsibility for a major new program, Bucove felt. ASA officials asserted that their agency's funds could currently be used only for their existing treatment programs and the new prevention efforts they had been making in response to the burgeoning drug problem.

To no one's surprise, Ramirez did not come to Dontzin's meeting; he sent his deputy, Larry Bear. Ramirez' opposition to methadone was well known, though he had never tried to subvert existing programs. He felt that the use of methadone simply delayed the day when an addict would have to come to terms with his basic personality problems and that it was to be condoned only in cases where an addict had unsuccessfully tried drug-free treatment. He made clear that he would not approve the diversion of funds currently being used for drug-free treatment into chemotherapy. Most of the ASA staff shared his hostility to methadone, especially those ex-addicts who felt that everyone should have to undergo the psychic agonies that had shaped their own cure.

While Dontzin explored the methadone route with health and drug officials, another City Hall assistant mined its potential as an antidote to crime. In 1967 Lindsay had responded to the crescendo of public outcry against urban crime by forming the Criminal Justice Coordinating Council, an advisory group of private citizens and City officials whose mandate included recommending new program directions in various crime-related areas. Jay Kriegel served as staff for the Council. A bright young man with bound-less energy and a good eye for politically profitable pro-jects, he suggested to Lindsay that the Council's subcom-mittee on crime and heroin addiction ought to sponsor a feasibility study of City involvement with methadone. An indication of interest was all he needed to be off and run-ning; as Dontzin's initiative faltered, Kriegel's flourished. By October he had nudged Lindsay into negotiations with the Vera Institute of Justice to mount a one-man study of methadone programs in other cities around the country.

Under other circumstances, Kriegel might have had sub-stantial internal political problems in developing his initia-tive in this way. He was bypassing the medical and social service bureaucracies of the City, virtually ignoring the Mayor's appointed drug experts, and relying on a private source to develop administrative mechanisms for which the City would take credit. But the situation made such a course appear relatively costless. Lindsay had little confi-dence in either Bucove or Ramirez, and ASA's record of distrust for drug maintenance programs provided an easy justification for failing to consult with its staff. Further-more, by mid-autumn Ramirez had resigned to go into private psychiatric practice, and ASA's new Commis-sioner, the former Deputy Commissioner Larry Bear, was fully occupied with building staff loyalty and strengthen-ing existing programs.

The Vera Institute of Justice, hired to consider whether and how the City should sponsor and conduct methadone programs, had pioneered a number of experiments in such areas as bail reform, treatment of alcoholics, and the release of criminal defendants on their own recognizance. In real-izing its aim to "improve the techniques and concepts and institutions which, in combination, represent New York's response to the problems of crime and anti-social behav-ior," Herbert Sturz, Vera's director since its founding in 1961, has mastered the art of conducting small controlled tests of simple, but often bold, ideas. In recent years he has worked closely with the City on many matters and has developed close personal relationships with both Lindsay and Jay Kriegel. When the Mayor asked him to turn his attention to methadone, Sturz was ready. He had already thought about the association of crime and addiction and was eager to apply to heroin addicts some of the notions he had tested with alcoholics. He had followed the Dole-Nyswander program with interest and thought its successes warranted experimentation with higher-risk patients, a shorter in-patient period, and younger participants. Thinking of his aims for a City-sponsored program, he said later, "I was willing to sacrifice some success in the interest of getting more addicts cured. I would rather have a success rate of forty percent with a thousand addicts than eighty percent with only a hundred."

It was almost inevitable that the Vera study, conducted by a young Legal Aid lawyer during the late fall and winter, would recommend City sponsorship of a methadone program. Equally unsurprising was the planned emphasis on treating large numbers of addicts and using a private corporation instead of a City agency to administer the program. The mayoralty election was only ten months away when Kriegel, the Vera people, and other Mayor's office representatives sat down to plan the implementation of the report. They all recognized that crime and drugs were crucial, interlocked issues on which Lindsay had to take affirmative and visible action immediately. Since neither ASA nor HSA had responded to Dontzin's first feelers, the group felt justified in accepting Sturz' view, derived from experience with Vera projects, that small private corporations are more effective administrators of innovative projects than government agencies motivated as much by bureaucratic imperatives as by the substantive rationale of the project.

City Hall drug policy at this point was determined not only by political exigencies and bureaucratic conflicts. The Mayor trusted his inner circle of advisors, and their attitudes and interests influenced him strongly. In this case, those attitudes were unequivocal. Kriegel's group felt that

ASA had failed. Its program was one-sided, it had not produced many "cured" addicts, it seemed perpetually riven by internal staff conflicts, and the people who ran it were a bit crazy. ("They spend a lot of time over there hugging one another," Kriegel once remarked acerbically.) By contrast, of course, the Kriegel team was rational, analytic, and realistic.

This half-conscious self-assessment was fairly accurate. Sturz had practice in framing clear, limited objectives and planning the most efficient ways of realizing them. Kriegel and Carol Ryan, the Vera staff lawyer, combined natural political and intellectual aptitudes with the training in rational analysis that good legal education often provides. And Joan Leiman, who was to help find funds for the new program, represented the best of a talented group of young analysts from the Budget Bureau. But none of them had an expert understanding of the roots or consequences of addiction, any more than had any of the City officials who had wrestled with the drug problem before them. And with all their combined abilities, they were no more skillful at avoiding the temptation to grab at one solution to a problem they did not understand.

During early 1969 plans for the new program—called the Addiction Research and Treatment Corporation (ARTC) —developed rapidly. Decisions about funding, administration, location, and participant standards were made. By March, a $2.4 million proposal to submit to the National Institutes of Mental Health (NIMH) had been drafted. At this point ASA and HSA were asked for comments. The proposal contained provisions for minor program elements to be supplied by the two agencies—a strategy intended to placate them for not being otherwise involved. Agency officials reacted so negatively to the proposal, however, that it was sent off solely as a creature of the Criminal Justice Coordinating Council. HSA objected generally to a City investment in such an experimental program. ASA staff had more specific complaints: they were skeptical of the feasibility of gradual withdrawal from methadone, they doubted that adequate social services would be provided to the participants, and they feared that the residents of Bedford-Stuyvesant, where the program was to be located, would be hostile to it.

Others also resisted the City's new initiative. Dr. Dole, who had originally supported Vera's interest in planning a program for addicts picked right off the street rather than carefully chosen for their potential success, became very opposed. He argued that the inevitable lower success rate of the new program would cast doubt on the inherent value of the treatment method itself. Adherents of drug-free programs predicted that ARTC would be closed down forcibly by people who saw methadone as the substitution of one addiction for another. And a number of important New Yorkers, including a prominent politician's wife, tried to pressure the Mayor into abandoning the project.

But Lindsay was not deterred. He had decided that methadone was the wave of the future, and he was determined to show that his administration supported it. By late spring Nicholas deB. Katzenbach, former Attorney General of the United States, had agreed to serve as chairman of the ARTC board. City Hall pressure brought about the granting of NIMH funds in time for the program's first Bedford-Stuyvesant center to open in October, one month before the mayoralty election.

Three years after opening, ARTC was treating 1,400 patients. In addition to methadone maintenance, it provided counseling, social services, and job placement to its participants. Although the program met with some community resistance in the first two years, it was not fatal to the organization, perhaps because such care had been taken to employ minority people from the area in most staff positions. Because it refused to make public its per patient costs and dropout rate, the success of the program was difficult to evaluate.

Shortly after the beginning of Lindsay's new term, Governor Rockefeller—probably moved in part by his own need to be re-elected in 1970—announced that the state would provide generous funding for locally administered methadone projects. Gordon Chase, the new HSA Administrator who had done such an impressive job setting up the new lead-poisoning detection and treatment program, was eager to work on the drug problem, so City Hall looked to him for a proposal to submit to the state. His staff quickly developed a plan for a large, decentralized methadone program, using existing HSA facilities as clinics. Once again—this time over the strong objection of the Commissioner—ASA was given only a very minor role in the planning and operation of the program. It seemed clear by mid-1970 that the City was shifting its emphasis from drug-free treatment to chemotherapy; the program grew quickly, and Lindsay began to emphasize its achievements over those of ASA. Within the first year, 17 HSA clinics were treating 1,200 patients, with very few dropouts.

Although the Mayor's men would not concede that ASA had really changed, the agency had broadened its focus considerably by the time the state methadone money became available. Larry Bear, the new Commissioner, had recognized for a long time that, while the Phoenix program had many strengths, ASA's reputation should not stand or fall on it. Furthermore, he believed rehabilitation programs reached drug abusers much too late, and he began to try to strike a balance in the agency's repertoire of programs between prevention and treatment efforts. So, although 1969 began with a major political defeat for ASA, it turned into the agency's busiest year to date. By mid-1970, fifty-four ASA facilities contained a wide range of programs.

It seems clear that nothing ASA could have done, however, would have improved its image at City Hall. The reasons for this seem to be beyond the inevitable lag between the changes at ASA and City Hall's perception of them. The Mayor's men were interested in the "numbers game," and ASA wasn't. Even after Bear took over—he had been the only possible successor to Ramirez whose appointment would not have caused massive resignations—the ten-

sions of the Ramirez-Rosenthal conflict were apparent,
down to the $7,000-a-year field employees. No concrete
evidence existed to show that the agency's new prevention
programs conducted in the schools really deterred kids
from drug taking. And, although Bear seemed to be vastly
easier to deal with than Ramirez, he still lacked the tightly
analytical bent of the City Hall planning group and the
new HSA bureaucrats.

The deliberate fragmentation of the City's drug program
had both positive and negative consequences. Perhaps it
muted the public criticisms of the City's efforts, since it
became more difficult to find a single target. With the resources of the huge HSA bureaucracy, and a bright young
planning and management staff, Chase was probably better
able to handle a large new methadone program than ASA,
with its relatively small staff and informal methods of operating. On the negative side, the inevitable interagency conflicts and lack of coordination made it difficult for HSA or
ARTC to profit from the "street experience" of ASA in its
early days. Without even the pretense of viewing ASA as a
"comprehensive" agency, much of the intense staff loyalty
to the program sagged. Perhaps most damaging, the deflec-
tion of authority from ASA meant that there was no place
except City Hall where overall policy questions on drugs
were handled. Inevitably, political judgments dominated
programmatic ones. The growing youth drug problem
might have been met with a strong program focus on prevention; but with City Hall at the policy helm, emphasis
was bound to remain on the more dramatic evidence of adult
addicts returned to responsible middle-class society. ASA's
capacities for evaluation, innovation, and research remained undeveloped for some time, though that agency
would have been a likely place from which to monitor the
HSA and ARTC programs.

VI

The story does not end here. The early 1970s have proved to be a time of great expansion for drug programs all over the country. Even at a time of budget cuts for many domestic programs, all levels of government have continued to give priority to efforts to curb drug abuse. Sources for both drug-free and drug-maintenance programs have continued to expand, and the City's interest in taking advantage of all monies available seem, for a time, to have subsumed the earlier tendency to promote one treatment form over another. Officials at both ASA and HSA now speak proudly of a "balanced policy" and of their "multi-modality" treatment program. In mid-1972 $33.9 million of public money was being spent in New York City on 12,357 people in drug-free programs (an average of $2,740 per person); $36.6 million was being spent on 17,629 methadone patients ($2,076 per person). Programs experimenting with variations of each of the treatment forms exist all over the city—methadone programs with heavy doses of encounter therapy, programs that gradually decrease the dose of methadone until the patient is totally abstinent, ambulatory therapeutic communities, and so on. At Downstate Medical Center in Brooklyn four different kinds of treatment—drug-free, methadone, cyclazocine, and a methadone program where the doses are decreased to abstinence—are providing opportunities for informal comparative evaluation. The City's policy-makers are now in agreement that no one solution is likely to work for every addict, at least for the time being.

The difficulties of bureaucratic negotiation over drug programs have eased significantly in the 1970s. ASA's most recent Commissioner, Graham Finney, a city planner and former Deputy Superintendent for Planning of the Philadelphia school system, proved to be skillful at working with the City's "overhead" agencies. He also turned the agency in important new directions. While continuing to broaden its program base with added prevention units, ambulatory drug-free and detoxification programs, and school activities, he reorganized the bureaucracy to minimize competition between programs and strengthen middle management. He placed great emphasis on fitting the treatment program to the individual needs of the client; as a result the agency developed a central diagnosis and referral system so that an addict could be sent immediately to the program deemed most appropriate. Finney has also implemented fully what Bear hoped to begin—the transformation of ASA from an administrator of programs into a coordinating body that contracts out most of its activities. Gradually ASA has become primarily a grant-making institution, providing evaluation for its delegate agencies and training addiction workers. Lindsay's original intention for Ramirez is thus being realized on a much larger scale. The "coordinator" is an agency instead of a mayoral aide, and this time there are real programs to coordinate.

ASA's new role is most evident in the state program that it now oversees. Governor Rockefeller, under pressure to take action on drugs in an election year, announced in mid-1970 a $200 million program for which $65 million was being immediately authorized. And $40 million of that money has come to ASA. The emphasis of this program is on youth, and drug-maintenance efforts are proscribed. Both treatment and prevention projects can be financed. ASA acts as a grant-giver, contracting with dozens of groups to run projects that range from a $2 million program at Kings County Hospital to a preventive Outward Bound unit at the United Nations International School. ASA provides its grantees with help in fiscal planning and management and evaluates their efforts. Many of these groups have little or no previous experience with the drug problem; the challenge to ASA of making this program work is probably as great as the agency's initial mission.

A new body has stepped into the policy vacuum created by the events of the drug program's early years. One of Lindsay's 1969 campaign promises was for a mayoral council made up of City officials—from the Police Department, the Department of Correction, ASA, HSA, the Board of Education, and others—whose programs touched in any way upon the drug problem. The Mayor intended the council to be directed by the new Deputy Mayor, former U.S. Attorney Robert Morgenthau. When Morgenthau resigned to seek the 1970 Democratic nomination for Governor the Mayor himself took over the chairmanship of the Narcotics Control Council, and it has become the central policy body in the drug area. Although the Mayor takes an active personal interest in the Council, chairing meetings and often providing direction, it is the group as a whole, registering its diverse vantage points on the problem, that resolves key policy and program questions. A City official who has watched the politics of the drug-abuse problem for several years said in 1971 of the council:

> It is a way of keeping Corrections and Police on their toes, embarrassing the Board of Education, and making officials generally justify their actions in the drug field. It legitimizes individual projects, and considers all major proposals which might represent a change or development of policy for the agency involved. And the Mayor listens. At the next meeting Herb Sturz will propose a heroin maintenance project that is bound to provoke strong reactions; the grunts and groans will have an impact on the Mayor.

The council is, however, a predominantly political influence. Unlike some other areas, Lindsay does not have much solid professional advice in the drug area to guide him. For, although progress has been made since 1965 in understanding drug issues, those efforts have not kept pace with public demand that the drug problem be solved. We now know more about the epidemiology of heroin addiction, but we do not know whether "heroin hunger" is a permanent metabolic effect, whether addicts are victims of a basic psychopathology, and what biochemical reactions occur from the effects of drugs on the central nervous system. No one yet has a sound, operational definition of the evil our society says it wishes to combat.

Policy-making can always become the handmaiden of party politics, personal interests, or unregulated market forces. Without the security of a good problem definition to work with, it is more susceptible to those influences. Addiction treatment policy in the City of New York has repeatedly been determined by substitutes for a real understanding of the drug-abuse problem. At first the endorsement of drug-free programs sprang from the Mayor's eagerness to do something—anything—about the problem, and his discovery of a man who thought he had the answer. Then when City Hall discovered that "the concept" could not cure enough addicts quickly enough to be politically acceptable, the upcoming election—and personal relationships within the Lindsay administration—largely determined the choice and development of an alternative.

Although the City seems now to have achieved a balance among the best known treatment methods, nothing guarantees that a judicious exploration of all the alternatives will be maintained. In fact, some evidence would point in the contrary direction. In the fall of 1972 City Hall announced that ASA would henceforth operate under the aegis of HSA, a move widely interpreted to mean that methadone would subsume other treatment possibilities within the next year or two. Certainly Graham Finney saw it that way: he resigned immediately as ASA Commissioner. He says of the rapid development of New York's methadone programs, "All the other efforts were overwhelmed by the political necessity of this solution."

All of this is not to say that methadone is not a very effective solution for many people. But it surely is not the political panacea hoped for. Increasingly, methadone-maintained addicts are found to be using other drugs—cocaine, barbiturates, and so on—the effects of which are not blocked by methadone. In addition, many addicts appear not to want to give up their lives as heroin addicts. The waiting lists for methadone treatment have dwindled, and it seems that future programs cannot rely on voluntarism.

If both methadone and therapy have reached the limits of their appeal (there are now vacancies in therapeutic communities), what route will public treatment programs take? One possibility is the direction that rumor gives to future federal programs—involuntary segregation of addicts from the rest of society. Such a policy sounds like a desperate response to our ignorance about the drug problem. It suggests that if we, as a society, do not have solutions, it is best to put the problem out of sight where we will not be reminded of our failures. This may receive immediate political sanction from those not overly concerned with civil liberties, but it does not bring us nearer to any long-range solutions.

But is there really any solution to this dilemma of definition? On the one hand, with hindsight we can see that our ignorance about drug abuse should have argued against adopting policies that promoted only one way of doing things. Varied needs should beget varied programs; in a blind world, the one-eyed man is too likely to be not a king but merely a cyclops. Initial program choices in such a fuzzy area are too likely to foreclose later ones that seem appealing as values shift and knowledge increases. As ASA Commissioner, Ramirez was a cyclops, reducing the agency's capacity to move toward total sight. The ideal bureaucrat, faced with this fuzzy issue, should perhaps have placed great stress on the value of experimentation; attempted to communicate to the public a spirit of inquiry, trial, and the inevitability of error; contracted out with organizations that could mount a number of small, controlled experiments; and developed the agency's capacities for sophisticated evaluation and research.

But could that hypothetical bureaucrat have survived? Political and bureaucratic pressures of the kind ASA officials encountered would surely have had equal force against an empiricist. The citizenry wants to think its government has the answers, and an equivocal stance would probably have created among City Hall-watchers an almost immediate opposition to the administrator of drug treatment programs.

Perhaps it is both wrong and irrelevant to attribute blame to the City government for not having made more of a dent in the heroin-addiction problem. Perhaps, as some analysts have suggested, it is the discontents of our society that lead to drug taking, discontents that issue from causes more fundamental than the Vietnam war or discrimination against minority groups. Graham Finney, in a paper written just after he resigned as ASA Commissioner, writes of addicts as one group of our society's increasingly numerous "superfluous people." He says, "The addict is a stark, warped mirror of the rest of us in an age of hedonism, instant gratification, the cutting of all corners, and a confusion of ends and means." Without basic cultural changes, then, Finney worries that an agency like ASA can never "go beyond symptomatology," no matter how competent its administration, or how generous its funding. If he is right, perhaps clear definitions of the addiction problem would make only an incremental difference in what local government could do about drug abuse.

4

The Sixteen-Story
Misunderstanding

I

From the beginning of his political career John Lindsay has
emphasized the importance of bringing government closer
to the citizen. While he was in Congress he spoke in general
terms of "humanizing" government, saying, "The task of
the future is to find better ways and means of bringing
government and its services close to home."[1] In his mayoralty campaign he sought to realize that ideal through his
plan to establish a system of Little City Halls all over New
York. Located in dozens of the City's neighborhoods, they
would be staffed by local residents who would answer people's questions and act on complaints—"like a one-stop seat
of municipal services," he said to an interviewer later.[2]
Their appeal lay not in their capacity for changing any
balance of power but in their value as a means of communi-

cation between the Mayor and the people of New York City. In his inaugural address of January 1, 1966, he reiterated the theme: "Together, we can open direct lines of communication between the people and their government."

By the mid-1960s, other Americans, prominent and anonymous, were also pressing for a different relationship with their governments. The civil rights movement had awakened the sense in many people that they had the right to demand attention from political leaders and to complain about inadequate services poorly delivered. The range of usual government responsibilities had expanded significantly in the previous thirty years, particularly at the local level; many Americans—professors of social work, mayors, neighborhood activists—were beginning to conclude that these new governmental functions could be performed sensitively and efficiently only if citizens played a more active role. They might merely require greater accountability, or they might plan, and even control, major local programs. Though the means for effecting a closer relationship between governments and their constituents were still to be worked out, the impetus for change seemed certain.

There was nothing new in the concern with the ordinary American's participation in public affairs. This nation was founded on notions of democratic self-government. Even the humblest of its early settlers could realistically hope to influence their leaders as they determined the location of highways or the sanctions for violation of sanitation ordinances. Thomas Jefferson's vision of the ideal political system stressed the formation of "little republics," local units where the citizens themselves would have charge of "the care of their poor, their roads, police, elections, and nomination of jurors, administration of justice in small cases, elementary exercises of militia . . . all those concerns which, being under their eye, they would better manage than the larger republics. . . ."[3]Alexis de Tocqueville, visiting the United States at the time of Andrew Jackson, found in the participatory nature of American democracy both its strengths and its weaknesses. He regretted its inefficiency, but praised its vigor and wished Europe could emulate it, saying that ". . . the most powerful way, and perhaps the only remaining way, in which to interest men in their country's fate is to make them take a share in its government."[4] The Progressives, too, aimed for "returning government to the people,"[5] with an emphasis on municipal reform to be undertaken by the middle class. The mid-twentieth-century surge of interest in citizen action and governmental decentralization, then, had strong American traditions behind it.

Historically, Americans have found several different values in a close relationship between government and citizens. We prize civic activity as an end in itself, considering participation in a political process to be healthy, virtuous, and often fun. In addition, we hope that the regular interaction of the governing and the governed will be a means toward many other individual and social ends. We presume that individuals or groups that can easily demand new and better services will be more likely to get them than the quiescent constituents of political leaders isolated from the public. We also presume that persistent pressure from even a few citizens may create social benefits for others. Complaints about the quality of merchandise in a ghetto store may result in increased overall enforcement of consumer protection laws, or demands from parents' groups may mean reforms that benefit teachers and children.

These different kinds of benefits have had varying interest throughout American history for those at the top and at the bottom of the social and economic spectrum. Jefferson thought all were important. He regarded the ordinary man's participation in political processes as valuable education; he also saw it as the best means of preventing dictatorship, and as a way of getting better performance of government's daily tasks. The Progressive reformer, usually a Yankee with secure upper-middle-class status, became politically active for the moral satisfaction it gave him, and because he believed that government could be directed to

produce a better life for all. Not so the poor immigrant of
the nineteenth and early twentieth century. The unskilled
Irish or Italian worker assumed that government was a
hostile force, dominated by the personal interests of men
far above him. He was interested only in the individual
benefits he might wrest from it. Richard Hofstadter describes the immigrant's participation in government:

> When he finally did assume his civic role, it was
> either in response to Old World loyalties . . . or to
> immediate needs arising out of his struggle for life in
> the American city—to his need for a job or charity or
> protection from the law or for a street vendor's li-
> cense. The necessities of American cities—their need
> for construction workers, street-cleaners, police and
> firemen, service workers of all kinds—often provided
> him with his livelihood, as it provided the boss with
> the necessary patronage. The immigrant, in short,
> looked to politics not for the realization of high prin-
> ciples but for concrete and personal gains. . . .[6]

By the mid-twentieth century the white working immigrant was no longer at the bottom of the urban heap. The
black migrant from the South—and, in Eastern and Western cities, the Puerto Rican and Mexican-American respec-
tively—had replaced him. Even more depressed and vic-
timized by discrimination than the ethnic worker before
him, the poor black evinced little interest of any kind in
building a close relationship with government at any level.
He remained the passive recipient of services until the
social movements of the 1960s aroused him. Then he began
to perceive the importance of putting pressure on government for both his immediate gain and the eventual betterment of his neighbors' condition. This impulse coincided
with a concern among some professional people at the top
of the heap that the poor might rise out of poverty partly
through a new involvement in government programs. The
conjunction of these interests in making government more

responsive to people's needs set a tone for much public discussion and political rhetoric.

It was natural that John Lindsay would be interested in forging closer ties between government and citizens. He came from an elite Protestant background which had imbued in him a belief in political action as every citizen's right and responsibility. As a congressman from the largest city in the country, a city teeming with poor and frustrated people, he had seen the consequences of mutual apathy in the governing and the governed. As he wrote in 1969, looking back on his perceptions of City government when he took office as Mayor in 1966:

> For a middle-class community, separation from government means discontent and delays. For a person dependent on government for every essential need, an unresponsive bureaucracy can mean eviction from his home, loss of work, loss of food to feed his child. All the frustrations that an ordinary citizen feels when he "fights City Hall" are multiplied by the stark fact that for an impoverished city dweller, indifference can literally be a matter of life and death.[7]

Lindsay's concern with bringing government closer to people did not automatically convey to him an understanding of the means of accomplishing it. He and his aides spoke often of the importance of people "having a say" in the workings of government, but they could not usually clarify how that was to happen, or to what end. Even with specific programs that the new Mayor had proposed during the campaign, like the Little City Halls and the board of civilians who were to review allegations of police brutality, he provided few answers to some very fundamental questions that would determine whether he could truly bring government closer to the people.

Lindsay and his aides framed their concern in 1966 within the issue of "citizen participation." They reasoned, as did the planners of the new federal anti-poverty program, that government programs should be not only efficient and comprehensive, but expressive of the needs and wishes of the people for whom they were designed. A glance at Lindsay's top appointments reveals how seriously he took the issue. Donald Elliott, chairman of the City Planning Commission, told a reporter in 1966, "It's possible, for instance, to create a program which will decide which roads ought to be paved, but then people in the various communities have to be given a voice in determining paving priorities. If the people in the neighborhoods don't have a say in what's going on, we'll have failed."[8] Frederick O'R. Hayes, Director of the Budget, came to New York from the Community Action Program of the federal war on poverty. Mitchell Ginsberg, the Columbia University School of Social Work professor who became Lindsay's first Welfare Commissioner, believed firmly that welfare clients had a legitimate interest in policies that directly affected them. Lindsay appointed Thomas Hoving as Parks Commissioner partly on the basis of his campaign white paper criticizing previous Parks Department administrations for having neglected community opinion in formulating park policies. Finally, the Mayor chose as his Human Resources Administrator—the man who would plan and coordinate the City's social action programs— Mitchell Sviridoff, previously director of Community Progress, Inc. (CPI), the local poverty program of New Haven, Connecticut. Sviridoff's first job for Lindsay was to oversee the preparation of a long report on new directions for welfare, employment, and community development programs. Issued in June 1966, it recommended that community groups be given some policy responsibilities in many program areas, and it included as one of four major overall goals of that branch of local government "increased participation of residents in poor communities in the development and operation of programs for their betterment."[9] The report was widely circulated, both in and out of City government. It added to the impression Lindsay gave his lieutenants that running a program with significant citizen involvement was, as one of his assistants put it later, "the way to catch the Mayor's eye."

Getting citizens to participate in government programs was only one element of effecting a closer relationship between the government of the City and its residents. Another was the negotiation of citizens and officials over the provision of additional or improved service. Then there was the possibility that actual control over some policies and/or services might be given up to residents of the City's neighborhoods. Or citizens might insist on monitoring City programs in controversial areas, like education and public safety. Or they could force employment quotas, so that minority group members and women would be more equally represented among public officials. But the new Lindsay administration could not separate these elements or analyze the problems they raised. "Citizen participation" was the watchword, and Lindsay officials focused on that to the exclusion of the others. Even there, they did not face such issues as what should happen when citizen involvement led to defiance of the governmental unit that had encouraged it, or whether citizen participation should seek to coordinate the resources of a community or celebrate the diversity of its residents.

Each dimension of the desired closeness of citizens and government had its own problems. To what extent could the public's demand for services be accommodated if it conflicted with rational program priorities previously set by the relevant City agency? At what point was giving up control of neighborhood programs likely to become politically unfeasible? At what point should the common sense of the citizen monitor be forced to give way to the professional expertise of school administrators and police captains? In establishing hiring quotas, at what point must the interest in representation give way to the interest in employing the most qualified workers? With each dimension, a spectrum of possible policies existed. Finding the proper point on that spectrum was a mammoth task which the

Lindsay administration, in its inexperience, could not undertake in advance of action.

The New York City officials were not alone in their uncertainty. These puzzles were plaguing every politician and planner trying to build a stronger relationship between government and citizens. A pair of distinguished sociologists have described the problem of policy definition faced by the foundation executives who sponsored CPI in New Haven and other "gray area" projects, private forerunners of the federal anti-poverty programs:

> The projects were, then, committed by the funding agencies to a democratic ideal of citizen participation, but were left with little guidance as to the form it should take, or even its essential purpose. They were bound to be held responsible for the consequences of any movement they stimulated, yet they were not, in principle, to defeat their own democratic idealism by controlling the direction which the movement chose. How the projects would come out, if the people of the neighborhood were drawn into conflict with civic leadership, remained obscure. Pledged to both sides, they could only hope to be allowed a benevolent neutrality.[10]

But neither Lindsay and his administrators nor the other politicians around the country struggling with the same issues could ever have the luxury of "benevolent neutrality." If conflict arose out of citizen participation, they were bound to be in the thick of the fray, at once both instigators and defenders. Failing to address the crucial questions in advance might well force the officials into positions where they would act, instinctively, in a manner at odds with their original aims. Reform could quickly become retrenchment, and the new policies would not then receive a fair trial.

The task was especially complex because of its double edge. The people were partners with their governmental leaders in working out new relationships. And the people were usually no better prepared to define their stance than were the administrators. They were ready to demand more attention from government, but they could not know what services would have greatest and most lasting value when they were finally provided. They wanted more control over public services, but how could they know at what point they could no longer use their new power effectively? They were eager to participate in the planning and operating of programs, but at some undetermined point that participation might limit their exploration of other means of advancement.

The following pages tell the story of one situation in which the New York City government tried, unsuccessfully, to forge a new relationship with a group of citizens on the Lower East Side of Manhattan. From May 1967 until October 1970 a shifting collection of residents negotiated with City officials—whose identities changed almost as frequently—for use of an immense, empty City-owned building, originally called Christodora House, at the corner of Avenue B and 9th Street. They wished to develop the building as a community center, housing a wide variety of programs and symbolizing hope and unity to a neighborhood of depressed and divided people. At first, it was a question merely of whether or not the City's stolid bureaucracies—notably, the Parks Department—could respond to the residents' wish for new services. When they failed, other City officials proffered—and the residents demanded —assistance of a less tangible kind, the help needed for a community-run, government-supported neighborhood center. That too proved impossible. Finally, the City tried to regain the trust of the community by making the greatest concession of all—granting to a group of residents total control of the building. The citizens had asked of their local government increasing amounts of responsibility and power. At each level the government failed them. The final blow fell when the City's highest legislative body, the Board of Estimate, refused to pass a resolution to grant the community group a thirty-five year lease of the building.

The seeds of defeat, however, had been planted in City offices and Lower East Side living rooms much earlier. Representatives of the Parks Department, the Mayor's Urban Action Task Force, and the Department of Real Estate had promised more than they could deliver and more than they really wanted to relinquish. They had discovered the bureaucratic and political implications of what they wished to do only after the community people had come to rely on their representations. On the other side, the Lower East Side residents had constantly overinterpreted those representations. They floundered in strange new seas, testing their abilities to participate in political processes as well as discovering the constraints that bound the government actors. Mutual frustration resulted, and stalemate, and finally a setback for both community services on the Lower East Side and the dream of fruitful joint action by the City's government and its residents.

Although causes of the failure were many and complex, one stands out. Neither the administrators nor the citizens were able to define, in advance, the potentialities and limitations of the new roles necessary to accomplish their ends. The two groups acted on each other in several different ways, reflecting the various dimensions of the task of bringing government closer to people: the attempt to provide services particularly suited to the needs of the neighborhood, an effort to create a community center with a high degree of citizen participation in the planning and operating of programs, and the negotiation of an administrative arrangement whereby local residents could acquire more-or-less complete control over the building and all the activities that went on inside it. Each of these problems entailed its own process of anticipation, conflict, and retreat—on both sides. The processes were concurrent, and the failure of one reinforced the failures of the others. As the citizens' impatience escalated into disillusionment and bitterness, the officials' simple ineptitude became resistance and cynicism. After the curtain fell, the actors viewed the drama in remarkably similar ways: a community leader remarked, "We should have known it would never work," and a Mayor's assistant said, "If anything proves that government doesn't work, it's Christodora House."

II

Towering over Tompkins Square Park on the Lower East Side is an empty sixteen-story building. Although scarred with graffiti and bits of old protest posters, it rises rather grandly above the surrounding slum. Its interior includes 240 light, pleasant rooms; an auditorium with fully equipped stage and projection booth; locker rooms and gymnasium; a paneled library with cork floors; a spacious sixteenth-floor dining room with spectacular views of the whole Lower East Side; several floors of office space; and a large swimming pool. Built in the late 1920s by a wealthy New York family to house the activities of a private social service agency, the building is very sturdy. Its mechanical systems are made of the best materials, and its cork flooring and acoustical ceilings attest to the builder's devotion to quality.

During the 1930s Christodora House provided community residents—predominantly poor, hard-working Eastern European Jews and Slavs—with many services. It housed a comprehensive medical and dental clinic and one of the first free birth-control programs. An amateur theater group flourished there for many years. Many of the area's teachers and social workers lived there in dormitory style, with rooms arranged in suites of three. Income from the residential floors ceased to support the service activities when rent control was introduced in 1947, and the City of New York purchased the building for over $3 million. From then on, the condition of the building declined. The oak paneling in the lobby was painted and repainted with institutional green. The swimming pool was almost irreparably damaged by disuse. The gymnasium was not maintained, perhaps because for much of the period it was used for storage, most recently for civil defense equipment. By 1967 the elevators no longer worked, broken risers made much of the plumbing unusable, and paint and plaster peeled from the walls.

During that same period the character of the neighborhood continued shifting in directions established before World War II. As the children of the original Eastern European residents moved out of the Lower East Side to more affluent communities, poor immigrants from Puerto Rico moved in. After the war the trend became more pronounced, and a number of black families diversified the neighborhood still further. By the mid-sixties, the Tompkins Square area was one of the most ethnically heterogeneous sections of New York City. At about that time the neighborhood began to absorb an influx of disaffected young people fleeing their middle-class upbringing in search of new life-styles.

Although a few professional families had renovated old buildings and moved into the area, most residents were poor or close to it. Welfare and crime rates were high, and many sophisticated observers felt that this part of the Lower East Side was second only to Harlem in the amount of heroin addiction. Despite dozens of community organizations, no central location existed where the area's residents could come for cultural, recreational, or educational programs. Tompkins Square Park provided only two small playground areas for children, and neither it nor the one other nearby park had any supervised activities for young or old.

The diversity of the area led to some strains among its residents. The flamboyant behavior and free wheeling views of some of the young people and blacks of the area often antagonized the working-class Italians and Slavs who still live in the neighborhood. Politically, Tompkins Square was hard to characterize. Nominally Democratic, many residents did not vote, and those who did often opted for conservative positions on such issues as welfare and crime.

By the spring of 1967 only a small portion of the Christodora building was being used. Because it housed a welfare center and office space for the Welfare Department, it was generally referred to in the neighborhood as "the welfare building." But it was not very satisfactory to the Welfare Department. The workers complained about the double fare necessary to get there from their homes outside of the Lower East Side, and the building's direct current was inappropriate for modern electrical needs.

Several Welfare Department employees working in the building perceived the community's need for the kind of facilities Christodora House had. They spoke to residents connected with nearby Trinity Lutheran Church, and they in turn began to talk with other neighborhood people. In mid-May a notice, in Spanish and English, appeared on tree trunks and lampposts around the park. It called residents to a meeting to devise a strategy for getting the Parks Department, which had jurisdiction over all recreational uses of City-owned property, to permit public use of the building's swimming pool. At the meeting, held on May 18, it quickly became apparent that many people wanted more than that. They saw in the building a potential community center that could house programs and facilities to develop the talents and interests of the area's residents, particularly the young people. Excited by the possiblities, they began to talk of athletic and cultural activities, of buying clubs and training programs. They knew they would need the City's help, but that did not seem overly unrealistic. After all, the building was almost empty, a waste of highly usable space. The group would go to the Parks Department, inform the officials of the pool's existence and the need for repair, and propose that Tompkins Square people would do the work of planning and executing the center's activities. They would begin modestly, with a recreation program. The group chose three of their number to represent the diverse interests of the community: a thirty-year-old black man then working as a tape cataloguer, a neighborhood Puerto Rican leader, and a white poet.

When the community residents phoned them, Parks Department officials had never even heard of the Christodora House pool. Before they could investigate, Tompkins Square Park erupted in a Memorial Day weekend riot. During a rock music festival put on in the band shell, a local resident complained to police about hippies sprawling in the park in open defiance of "Keep Off the Grass" signs. The police came in swinging, and a bloody confrontation resulted in thirty-eight arrests and many injuries.

Suddenly public attention focused on the area. Parks Commissioner August Heckscher asked his community relations officer, Courtney Callender, to talk to residents about the neighborhood's need for recreational opportunities in general and the use of the pool in particular. A young Mayor's assistant, Theodore Mastroianni, came to the Lower East Side to set up a task force of community people to help keep tabs on the area's problems and head off further disturbances during the summer. Deputy Police Inspector Joseph Fink, commanding officer of the Ninth Precinct, was assigned to examine the events that precipitated the riot and figure out possible methods for keeping the Lower East Side "cool" in the future.

Courtney Callender, a black man in his late twenties, had been on his job for only a few months. Parks Commissioner Heckscher's predecessor, Thomas Hoving, had felt that a new emphasis on making the parks more appealing for the people who used them would require more work with individual communities, so he had set up a new unit in the department to deal with community relations. Callender came to head that office after six years of working with schizophrenic children and two years with an anti-poverty program. Although he had gone to the City College of New York and spent most of his life in New York, his previous jobs had been in Westchester County and New Jersey, and he did not know the Lower East Side well. He came into the department without much idea of exactly what he was to do. Because his function was new, and because he reported directly to the Commissioner, he had unusual freedom, but this presented problems as well as benefits. He could be confident of support for his actions from above,

but he didn't know enough about the bureaucracy below
him to know whether and to what extent it could be bent
to accomplish the tasks he took upon himself. A sensitive,
intelligent man, Callender often seemed uncertain of the
powers and duties of his new position. He was excited by
his job, however, partly because he felt himself to be part
of an important new emphasis on making the City government more responsive to those it served.

After the Memorial Day riot, Callender invited Tompkins Square residents to a meeting at the Parks Department. Also present were Deputy Inspector Fink and a representative of Mobilization for Youth, one of the Lower
East Side's largest and most influential private social service organizations. Most of the discussion focused on ways
of preventing further trouble in the neighborhood. Callender reports that residents suggested using Christodora
House as a community center, but that it seemed to be
merely one rather casual proposal among many others.
That it was not so casually proffered seems clear from the
residents' reports of the Parks Department response; one
person says officials were "enthusiastic," another that
"they encouraged us." Callender invited the Tompkins
Square people to come back the following week to meet
with Commissioner Heckscher. This they did, bringing
with them a list of requests for City help, which included
repairing the pool and the gymnasium floor and providing
some paid personnel to help with the planned recreation
activities. Heckscher, who later called the area "a very alive
community that you wanted to work with," was accom-
modating; encouraging the work of this group seemed an
excellent way of helping the community to help itself.
Within a few days, he and Callender had been down to
Tompkins Square to inspect the Christodora House facilities. He promised the community group orally that he
would obtain the necessary funds for recreational help,
that the gym floor would be repaired immediately, and that
he would request pool repair funds—hastily estimated at
about $50,000—in the upcoming capital budget.

This expression of the City's interest in the project

stimulated further activity among neighborhood residents. They began to meet weekly, and the Committee for a Tompkins Square Community Center was born. Robert Collier, who worked as a tape cataloguer, emerged as the leader of the committee. Collier was a light-skinned black who spoke fluent Spanish and was close to many of the neighborhood adolescents, both black and Puerto Rican. Intelligent and intense, he understood and sympathized with the frustrations and animosities of the slum, yet was willing to talk with middle-class participants in the movement to start the community center.

One of Bob Collier's strengths was his ability to mediate skillfully among the various interests he represented. At an early committee meeting, a group of angry blacks tried to use the pool issue as a vehicle for raising political consciousness. Collier saw that such an approach would lose the support of more conservative citizens who simply wished to get better neighborhood facilities. He asserted the concerns of the majority of the group, but stressed that the more militant group was welcome to participate in the community effort.

City officials at first regarded Collier as a positive force in the community. Mastroianni from the Mayor's office found him "likable." Callender said later that his initial requests for use of the gym, the pool, and one room for a community center office were "quite reasonable." In a community where hostile neighborhood factions struggled for the City's limited resources, Collier seemed unique in that, in the words of one official, "He didn't turn anybody off." In late June Mayor Lindsay came to the Lower East Side to dedicate a new apartment complex with a private pool. When a group of demonstrators demanding action on the Christodora House pool threatened to disrupt the occasion, Collier stepped in and kept the situation under control.

Neighborhood residents began to work toward the building of a community center with great imagination and enthusiasm. A local artist planned to hold children's art classes in the building. A woman who had once been a circus performer was interested in starting a juggling and acrobatics program. The wife of a local doctor collected donations of paint from neighborhood hardware stores to brighten the inside of the building. Even an ex-prostitute helped, posting notices of committee meetings throughout the neighborhood. All of this was volunteer work, encouraged by Collier who felt that only spontaneous community effort would develop long-lasting dedication to the project.

Many neighborhood people pitched in to get politicians and bureaucrats interested in their cause. The doctor's wife wrote and phoned friends on Community Planning Board #3, the local advisory council for the City Planning Commission. Reverend John Puelle of Trinity Lutheran Church, among others, began to promote the community center among City officials who visited the area. Perhaps most important was Lorraine Miller, a local lawyer who had previously run unsuccessfully for the State Assembly from the Lower East Side. She drew up incorporation papers for the Tompkins Square Community Center, Inc., interested Manhattan Borough President Percy Sutton in the project, and brought the Lower East Side's City Councilman Saul Sharison to visit the building.

By mid-July the committee felt confident of realizing its dreams. Sutton had promised to request some aid from the Planning Board, whose members he appoints and which allocates small amounts of public funds for community use. Welfare commissioner Ginsberg had agreed to move his workers out of Christodora House and transfer total jurisdiction of the building to the Parks Department. Mastroianni from the Mayor's office put ten neighborhood youths—"community liaison workers"—on his payroll at $100 a week and assigned them to publicize the work being done to develop the community center. On June 30, Leonard Farbstein, Congressman from the Lower East Side, wrote to Mayor Lindsay expressing his hope that "prompt action will be taken to make the pool and gymnasium at Christodora House available."

But action was not taken promptly enough. Although

the Parks Department had promised to open the gym, no one had cleared the promise with the Welfare Department personnel still in the building. When community residents went to use the gym, the maintenance man refused to give them the keys. When this happened again, they marched on the building, 200 strong, armed with paint and brushes for painting interior walls. This show of determination produced hurried phone calls and eventually a promise to open the gym if the residents returned in a day or two. On July 15 Collier and his group were let into the building. They began to make superficial repairs and paint the walls of the lower floors.

Problems also arose over the pool. Parks Department engineers informed Callender that it would have to be virtually rebuilt, at a cost of at least $150,000. That kind of money would not be immediately available under any circumstances. Capital budget items had to be examined and approved by the City Planning Commission, the Budget Bureau, the Mayor's office, and the Board of Estimate. The Tompkins Square community would be lucky if it saw public money spent on the pool within two years. Furthermore, Callender had learned that general parks policy, set long before Heckscher took over, was to avoid spending money on indoor pools, because experience had shown they were underutilized. Callender could not get the Lower East Side residents to accept the bureaucratic priorities of the department or understand the delays inherent in the capital budget process. He also could not impress them by pointing out the senselessness of allocating scarce resources to this pool instead of to more basic projects such as the repair of existing playgrounds and parks. As Callender later remarked, "If you don't know how long things take, they [neighborhood people] think you are lying to them."

By now community residents had become determined to accept nothing less than the pool they felt they had been promised. Their rage increased when they discovered, in early August, that Parks planned to install a mini-pool for children in Tompkins Square Park. It seemed unfair to tell people that no money was available to repair the huge, year-round Christodora House pool and yet spend $30,000 to $40,000 on a shallow pool to be used by only a portion of the community for only the last few weeks of the summer. Why couldn't the Parks Department scrap the mini-pool and apply the money toward fixing up the pool in Christodora House? Local leaders told Heckscher and Callender that a private contractor they had called in had given them a $50,000 estimate for pool repairs. Why were the City's estimates so much higher? Callender explained that the mini-pool was part of a City-wide program, had been ordered over a year ago, and could not now be refused. Even if the pool could have been put in another community, it was bureaucratically impossible to transfer the money for it to another program category. As for the difference in the pool repair estimates, Callender believed it was because the City had to take public bids for work done inside City buildings. It was not a convincing explanation. The community would no longer listen to excuses. They felt that Heckscher had deceived them and that Callender had no authority to help. One worker says disdainfully, "Courtney packed no punch."

Bureaucratic problems also plagued the Parks Department's attempt to provide the Tompkins Square Community Center (TSCC) with recreation and maintenance workers. Callender had allowed TSCC people to appoint neighborhood residents to several Parks Department positions without regard to clear distinctions between those who were to sweep and those who were to supervise recreational activities. The two Parks Department unions, the Recreation Workers and the Maintenance and Operations Workers, felt that this merger of responsibilities threatened their structures. They attempted to subvert the TSCC by holding up salary checks in the payroll office or sending them to the wrong address. Callender says that for a couple of months he spent most of every other Friday trying to locate missing checks, with angry community workers sitting in his office.

Even the most patient members of the community

groups had become restless by late summer. It was not simply a matter of not getting the services they wanted, though that was paramount. The City officials seemed to them to denigrate their efforts and to assume that their demands were not to be taken seriously. Heckscher once fell asleep during a meeting with community representatives, an event that infuriated those who saw it and those who got the report second-hand, and third-hand, and fourth-hand. Ted Mastroianni was thought to be condescending and rude. Tompkins Square residents saw his hiring of neighborhood kids as a way of gathering intelligence on the relative unrest of the area; his job, they say, was to keep the city "cool," and he was simply faking interest in building the center as a lasting institution. People also thought the bureaucratic obstacles to meeting their demands had been utilized to obfuscate the City's real resistance to their desires to build the center. One middle-class member of the Committee for Tompkins Square Community Center says:

> At one point the community people were annoyed with something the City had done, so they marched up to the Parks Department and demanded to see Heckscher. He made himself available, with [Recreation Commissioner] Hayes Jones and several senior civil servants. During the meeting the civil servants could talk about nothing but the expense of doing the things the community wanted. For instance, the materials for the gym floor and the edges of the pool must be just right or a kid might cut his foot. The community people thought this ridiculous, since kids cut their feet in Lower East Side streets all the time. The City people said they wanted to help, but they continued to give all possible reasons why nothing could be done, unless of course money could be found in the Lower East Side to pay for thorough repairs.

In fact, the neighborhood people attributed guile to the Parks Department officials unfairly. Both Heckscher and

Callender shared the community's desire to redefine the department's role in providing recreation services to this particular community at this particular time. But their inexperience constituted a major bureaucratic sin. Neither of them knew enough about large bureaucracies in general or the Parks Department in particular to know how difficult it would be to get their agency to respond quickly to community demands that went well beyond the scope of usual recreation services. A black TSCC employee says, "The Parks Department was not responsive to our needs. They couldn't understand why we needed sophisticated materials like cameras and other photography implements. They thought all they had to do was give us a few basketballs and some pick-up sticks." And, commenting on the problems of trying to get pool table supplies for a table purchased with money raised in the community: "All we requested from the Parks Department were a few inexpensive items like cue replacements and chalk. But these kinds of things aren't listed on the standard requisition forms. It threw the department in a tizzy when we made the request."

The department was both financially and bureaucratically unprepared to meet the kind of demands which community people inevitably made. Most of its budget is tied up in capital projects, with little leeway for emergencies or locally determined programs. In 1967 its expense budget consisted of $5.2 million for personal services and its capital budget contained $21 million for everything else, divided among predetermined projects. In addition, the department had operated for many years in a very orderly, centralized way. All policy decisions had been made by the Commissioner, with a fixed chain of command to carry them out. Specific standards, difficult to modify, guided most of the department's operations. Parks could not be smaller than three acres, "comfort stations" could be of only one design, and playground equipment was completely standardized. Employees, many of whom had been with the department for twenty or thirty years, were used to this way of doing things. When Lindsay's new Commis-

sioners demanded greater variety in park equipment and
more flexibility in services provided, their jobs became
much more complicated.

The new kinds of parks administrators brought in more
than new designs and activities to disrupt the old bureaucracy. Their styles, values, and backgrounds contrasted
sharply with those of the maintenance men, recreation
workers, and clerks who worked under them. Some of
them were young and well educated, supervising middle-
aged workers with only high school educations. Some were
blacks who wore Afro hair styles and held strongly liberal
—or even radical—political views; most of the older Parks
employees were Irish or Italian, and their conservatism
embraced both dress and politics.

At the middle and upper administrative levels there were
also divisions between the old guard and the new. They
utilized very different strategies for providing park and
recreation services. Though the split was never explicit,
the "traditional" approach emphasized rational, centralized planning, with efficiency a primary value and technical expertise the mark of the successful administrator. Applying that strategy, one could not help but conclude that
the department's resistance to spending considerable sums
on an indoor pool was proper. But the newer administrators would not have applied that strategy. They were interested in adapting programs to the special needs of individual neighborhoods and in using the provision of services to
build community self-determination. Doing that required
sacrificing some rationality and efficiency, at least for the
time being. Unfortunately, Callender and Heckscher did
not know how much sacrifice either they or old-line
bureaucrats of the Parks and Recreation Departments
could tolerate. In effect, they challenged the traditional
strategy head-on by acting as though it did not exist and
appearing to accede to the residents' demands without any
thought as to how they fit into the larger web of policy.

Courtney Callender is very candid about the failures of
the Parks Department in meeting the residents' demands

for special services in Christodora House. He admits that he was guided more by his goodwill toward the group of eager, excited people than by his awareness of the Parks Department's limited capacity for supporting unplanned neighborhood capital projects. He now says ruefully that the approach he and Commissioner Heckscher took was "superficial and unsophisticated," that unwittingly they promised more than they could deliver. "We never said no in those days," he said later. "We wanted so much to be liked by the community."

III

Even without the facilities and services they thought they had been promised, the little band of community workers, high school dropouts, and housewives began to operate a variety of activities in the bottom floors of Christodora House. Basketball games and karate lessons took place in the gym. After school started in the fall, the auditorium was used for tutoring. Community meetings were held in the building during the evening. One night an informal gathering of Puerto Rican gang leaders, members of a hippie group called the Diggers, and heads of various community projects resulted in a "peace treaty" among the gangs and between the gangs and the hippies. At Thanksgiving TSCC made *The New York Times.* Local merchants and community organizations had contributed food for a free Thanksgiving feast held in the center. The *Times* noted that "Of particular interest was the fact that the hippies and Puerto Ricans, who have been antagonistic in this hippie enclave of the East Village, joined in the feast in apparent friendliness."

Bob Collier worked hard to hold the thing together, spending all his off-work hours at the center. The neighborhood kids loved and trusted him, and TSCC became a refuge for truants and dropouts who knew they would find sympathy there. "He had a very impressive sensitivity to

kids and their problems," says Donald Pace, a drama
teacher at Barnard College who served for a time on the
TSCC board of directors. "During TSCC board meetings,
if a kid came in to see Collier, he would always leave the
meeting to deal with his problem. This was annoying because it made meetings chaotic, but I liked the fact that
Collier felt it was important to attend to the kids' needs
first."

Putting the kids' needs first often meant, however, that
Collier's behavior contradicted conventional middle-class
standards for the proper stance of a recreational worker.
Lorraine Miller did not think he should allow neighborhood adolescents to use Christodora House while cutting
classes, and others objected to the occasional glue-sniffing
that reportedly went on in the basement. Deputy Inspector
Fink of the Ninth Precinct told TSCC workers that neighbors complained of runaways and muggers taking refuge in
the building. Collier agreed to be stricter with the kids, but
he thought reports of wrongdoing in the building were
greatly exaggerated. The complaints rankled, too, because
the center's failures seemed so insignificent compared with
its accomplishments. Ater all, hadn't TSCC already
brought neglected, undisciplined teenagers in off the
streets and united them in working to build their own
community institution? It seemed to Collier that neither
his community supporters nor the City bureaucrats ap-
preciated the importance of that. In November Heckscher
finally said that the Parks Department definitely could not
pay for repair of the Christodora House pool, and it turned
out that Percy Sutton had never requested funds for TSCC
from Planning Board #3 as workers thought he had promised to do. Collier began to express his bitterness by speaking of the City as if its interests were opposed to his—
bureaucrats on one side, "the people" on the other.

One reason the Parks Department said it couldn't repair
and support the Christodora House pool was that it would
entail regular janitorial and other maintenance service for
the whole building. But the TSCC people wanted to do this

themselves. The Union of Community Skills, an indigenous group of maintenance workers, could convert the building's current and put the elevators back in working order, they were sure. That the City would be liable for any disasters that occurred in the building when under community jurisdiction seemed essentially beside the point. The TSCC people were busy forging a new relationship with the City whereby they would plan and supervise their own neighborhood recreation services. They assumed, at first, that they and the Parks Department were partners in this effort. But the department was an old, encrusted bureaucracy, its mission buried too deeply in its procedures to be easily extracted and redefined. The naïve, new administrators had little chance of restructuring basic goals and activities through isolated pressures for the benefit of one community group.

At this point TSCC's ambitions had outstripped even the hopes of the Parks Department administrators. Heckscher and Callender had wanted to provide a limited range of services that would marginally increase opportunities for recreation in the Tompkins Square area. The TSCC workers now wanted help in building a permanent institution, a symbol of their dreams for the community. Unable to meet even the earlier, more limited demands of the residents, Parks Department officials looked to other City agencies for help.

More than any other office in the City, the Urban Task Force seemed to be working directly and primarily on forging a new relationship between government and citizens. Working out of the Mayor's office, the Task Force was originally a "fire-fighting" unit. At a time when parts of urban America exploded every summer, the Mayor was eager to establish contacts with residents who might know when a tense community could contain itself no longer. Walking tours through Harlem and Bedford-Stuyvesant might be effective as gestures of goodwill, but Lindsay knew they did not give him any real sense of the underlying volatility of the slums. He has written:

Early in my administration I had asked [Mayor's Assistants] Barry Gottehrer and Sid Davidoff to serve as troubleshooters to give me and the City a direct link with local communities. What they discovered was that communication did not exist—that we were reacting to events instead of anticipating them, and that it was only *after* trouble broke out that we became aware of what we did not know.[11]

In the spring of 1967 Lindsay formed the Summer Task Force to try to set up regular lines of cummunication between tense neighborhoods and City Hall. Almost twenty local units included community leaders of all kinds—clergymen, small businessmen, athletes, youths. Each was headed by a City official who was assured direct access to the Mayor's office. Essentially a means for gathering intelligence about potential trouble spots, the Task Force also tried to meet the residents' immediate demands for City services that might help ward off disturbances. Looking back on that first summer, during which the Task Force received "about a thousand" reports of trouble—none of which turned into a full-scale riot—Lindsay says:

The Summer Task Force met at 8:00 A.M. each Monday morning during the summer of 1967. Because it had representatives from virtually every City department, it provided a ready forum for specific neighborhood complaints, ranging from police to sanitation to parks to housing. In many cases, heads of agencies recognized for the first time the extent to which their programs overlapped and competed with others and understood how coordination could improve their programs. We found, too, that detailed information was coming to the City administration that would enable us to spot sources of potential trouble. We learned which individuals, which groups, which gangs were in conflict on which streets of the city. We found out specifically which kinds of summer programs would be dismissed and which kinds could actually enlist the support of neighborhood youth. And we learned, most of all, how to talk to communities that had never been reached by any City voice except that of the bureaucracy or a law enforcer.[12]

By the end of the summer it was clear that the Local Task Forces must continue to operate year-round. They enabled City Hall to identify failures in City service which residents felt most strongly about. Their access to the Mayor gave them leverage with which to pry new money and programs out of older, less flexible bureaucracies. They gave the citizen some sense of having an impact on the government closest to him. So over the next year Barry Gottehrer, a former *Herald Tribune* city reporter whose articles about New York's problems were viewed as helpful to Lindsay's 1965 reform candidacy, built up the local units and tried to expand their authority. They became less concerned specifically with riot prevention and more with facilitating the delivery of City services. They still functioned primarily, however, in response to crisis, whether it came in the form of the threat of bloodshed in the streets or of community indignation over the City's failure to clear out garbage-strewn vacant lots. And the Local Task Forces were still vitally important sources of intelligence about when, where, and how street violence might erupt.

By 1968 Lindsay felt the task forces had proved their usefulness sufficiently to make them permanent. Executive Order No. 73, dated April 22, officially established the Urban Action Task Force as

a mechanism which will: (1) open channels of communication between the members of a neighborhood and the City by providing a forum which will give residents of an area direct access, on a regular basis, to City officials; (2) act as a vehicle for coordinating City services at a local level; and (3) ensure that the agencies of City government are responsive on a direct and immediate basis to neighborhood problems.

The Local Task Forces were to include community members representing poverty organizations, religious groups,
merchants' associations, precinct councils, and block associations. Gottehrer became City-wide chairman, and Ted
Mastroianni, who had earlier provided "community liaison" workers for TSCC, became the official Lower East
Side Task Force chairman.

Superficially, at least, the Task Force had greater flexibility for adapting to a community's immediate needs than
did the Parks Department. In January 1968 an issue arose
that underscored the difference between the two governmental units. The previous autumn, the TSCC group had
submitted Bob Collier's name as their choice for the City-
paid position of recreation leader at Christodora House.
Approval of his appointment had gone unquestioned in the
administrative offices of the Parks Department, despite
Heckscher's knowledge that Collier had a rather dramatic
criminal record. Perhaps it slipped through because the
new Commissioner of Recreation was inexperienced and
eager to appoint community people to responsible City
jobs. The Mayor had previously approved the appointment
of blacks and Puerto Ricans who did not meet official requirements of education and experience for recreation job
slots. He had also, on several occasions, waived the prohibi-
tion on City jobs for those who had served prison terms.
But this appointment did not come from the Mayor's desk.
An irate civil servant within the department apparently
could not contain his anger that a $5,700-a-year job was
going to Bob Collier. On January 12 a headline in the *Daily
News* announced, "Statue of Liberty Plotter Hired by
Parks Department," and there followed the story of Collier's conviction for conspiracy to bomb the Washington
Monument, the Liberty Bell, and the Statue of Liberty as
a means of drawing attention to the oppression of blacks.
He had served twenty-one months in Lewisburg Federal
Penitentiary and had been released on parole in the spring
of 1967.

Heckscher tried to be supportive, releasing a statement
that said, in part:

Collier has paid his debt to society. He has never made a secret of his past to us, nor did he fail to include it in his application for employment. He has seemed to us in the Department who have worked with him to be a person who has grown day by day in his desire and ability to accept responsibility.

But Heckscher was the lone voice of support. Lindsay was angry that the issue had arisen and ordered Heckscher to back down. City Council President Frank O'Connor suggested sarcastically, "If the Lindsay administration is persistent in their efforts to hire this man, perhaps the Public Works Department could hire him as a demolition expert." City Councilman Matthew Troy introduced a resolution demanding Heckscher's resignation and calling the hiring of Collier "a personal insult to every City employee." The Civil Service Commission, after being asked to investigate, finally withheld approval of the appointment, allegedly because Collier "lacked the experience, education and training for this position."

That was not the end of it. A group of community people, including boys who had worked with Collier, businessmen who had helped put the center together, and heads of local service programs, visited the Mayor to urge him to carry Collier as a consultant so that his salary could be paid from private funds. A prominent citizen wrote to *The New York Times*, outraged that "outmoded civil service code requirements" should prevent Collier from giving his "leadership qualities" full-time to the community for which he had already done so much. The effective action finally came from Barry Gottehrer's office. Task Force efforts located a wealthy businessman willing to donate a year of Collier's salary anonymously. If the entire hiring process had been conducted by the Task Force, no large bureaucracy would have been involved, and probably no furor would have developed.

The apparent greater flexibility of the Task Force did not mean that it could respond much better than the Parks Department to many of the needs of the TSCC people.

True, it could grease the wheels of the bureaucracy a bit to produce relatively inexpensive goods and services with less delay. But during 1968 the issues surrounding the use of Christodora House became more complex, and the residents wanted not only attention, but autonomy and power.

In January the TSCC group finally heard that the Parks Department could fix only the gym floor and provide eight positions for recreation workers. This was distressing, but it did not defeat their other ambitions. Collier and his supporters had already become disillusioned with the City's ability to meet their demands for services. That disillusionment had become the root of a new, more intense concern that whatever programs went into the building would have to be run by community residents themselves. They now wanted the City's active support—through the Task Force, primarily—for that principle.

The Task Force, however, had divided loyalties. Its existence depended upon its ability to make information about local communities available to City Hall, but its credibility in the neighborhood rested on its devotion to the interests there. This dual allegiance broke down when citizen requests had political implications that were potentially dangerous for Lindsay. A widely diverse group of citizen-run programs in a City-owned building might well present substantial political problems for the Mayor.

To some extent, the different roles of people involved in the Task Force determined its different loyalties. The Director and the various City officials who headed the Local Task Forces were liaisons from City Hall, and as such their primary loyalties lay with the Mayor, though they tried also to represent the interests of people within the community they were assigned to. Community members of the Local Task Forces naturally felt their first duty was to represent the citizens, and sometimes they were particularly devoted to one segment or interest group within the area. Of course these lines were not always clear; some Local Task Force chairmen were closer to the Mayor than others, and some community members saw themselves as having broader constituencies than others.

More than any other person, the Local Task Force Chairman defined what action could be taken in any given situation. Although the views of community members might influence his initial reactions, they did not constitute an institutional force likely to constrain his individual decisions very significantly. This meant that local residents looking to their Task Force for help could predict the success or failure of their efforts only by knowing a good deal about their chairman—not only how deep his loyalties were to the Mayor, but also how much work he wanted to do in this extracurricular assignment, how many political chances he believed Lindsay could take, how much he supported the principle of "community control." Geoffrey Stokes, later to become Task Force Chairman for the Lower East Side, comments:

> The questions of loyalty lacked an institutional resolution, so they revolved around personalities. Ted [Mastroianni] was a Mayor's assistant and therefore very concerned with not getting him into trouble; my connections with City Hall were less close, and I perhaps pushed a bit harder for the Lower East Side—also because I lived there myself. It was confusing for the community. People had to figure out where everybody was, individually, before they could know what to expect.

For the City to have been able to support the independence the Tompkins Square residents wanted, the Task Force leadership—and ultimately the Mayor—would have had to feel that the TSCC people were a unified, competent group, broadly representative of "the community," and engaged in activities not inimical to the Mayor's political interests. This seemed less and less likely. For one thing, during 1968 the faith of many Lower East Side residents in the center eroded. Lorraine Miller, the lawyer who had gotten incorporation papers for TSCC, came to doubt that Collier and his followers could develop a program that would serve a broad range of Lower East Siders. In March she organized a party at the center to celebrate the acquisition of the corporate charter, but the kids who promised to help her did not show up in time, and the sandwiches and liquor vanished before the party really got going. Center staff allowed the building to be used as headquarters for the Poor People's Campaign, and during April and May they collected clothes and money for the march on Washington headed by civil rights leader Reverend Ralph Abernathy. This meant that unfamiliar black people were seen around the building at all times of day and night. Also, none of the clothing collected in the building was distributed to any of the poor people of the neighborhood. As the piles of clothing mounted, they had to be stacked in the gym, making it unusable for some planned activities. Community resentment grew.

Many of the center's troubles were attributed to Bob Collier. He had not taken into account the division between, on the one hand, the conservative white working-class families of the neighborhood and on the other, the young blacks, hippies, and middle-class professionals who made up the primary support of the center. Many of the activities which the latter group found constructive seemed wildly radical to the older residents, and Collier was seen as the perpetrator of evil influences. His charisma with young people made him doubly threatening. Strict Puerto Rican or Ukrainian parents could forbid their children to go into the building, but nothing guaranteed that they would not go anyway.

City officials also lost confidence in Collier and TSCC. As it became clear that the center's expanding program would require that it take over more space in the building, the City and the community group tried to work out a new administrative arrangement. Mastroianni and Gottehrer made clear to Tompkins Square residents that they would have to form a more broadly-based group to control use of a large portion of the building. TSCC and City officials agreed that the new Board of Governors, as it was to be called, would include both center people and representatives of the Northeast Neighborhood Association (which wished to use several floors of the building for a neighborhood health center) and the local YMCA. Bob Collier was in charge of organizing meetings to name the full Board and set up procedures for its operation. Both community people and City officials say that he did not send out notices of the meetings to those whom he had been requested to inform. Instead, he notified those closest to him. They were, of course, the people who had worked hardest and committed most to TSCC thus far.

By mid-1968 Gottehrer and Mastroianni felt that Collier as the leader of TSCC was a mistake. Gottehrer says, "Collier wanted to control everyone and everything in the building." Mastroianni adds, "Bob Collier wanted complete, supreme control." Community people devoted to Collier say that Gottehrer developed a deep personal dislike for him that affected his judgment on TSCC matters. Gottehrer says that Collier spread lies about him and undermined the community's trust in the City government. These personal animosities made it difficult for both sides to negotiate the already-complicated issue of who was to control what in Christodora House.

By late spring of 1968 mistrust between residents and City officials, and among various factions of residents, had brought negotiations over the use of Christodora House to a standstill. Part of the problem was that the Task Force, which had become the dominant City actor in the drama, proved to be no more effective at accomplishing many bureaucratic tasks than the Parks Department had been. Its power derived from the Mayor's office alone and was not sufficient to exert pressure for long-range improvements of the routine City services that Lower East Side residents found inadequate. Ted Mastroianni invited district representatives of several City agencies, including the Sanitation Department, to appear at Task Force meetings to hear citizen complaints. When the community's concerns were not met with specific promises, the meetings became very heated. Failure to follow up on complaints from one meeting to the next raised the community's ire still further. Finally, on June 12, a Buildings Department official came to talk to a Task Force meeting, and when people protested about a nearby residential building with a leaky roof, the official said he would have it vacated. This was not, of course, what the residents had in mind. In a fury they announced they wanted no more to do with the Task Force, and to this day they refer to that meeting as the night they "fired the Task Force." A newsletter put out by one of the community groups represented at the Task Force meetings expressed the community's disillusionment with the Mayor's attempt to reach people's problems on the most local level:

> Fifty of us showed up at Wednesday's meeting and were told that we must organize into committees to back up the Task Force in its work. But the Lower East Side is already the most organized neighborhood in the whole city and we know that when we tell the politicians what we need, they tell us that they would like to help but that the city bureaucracy ties their hands. . . . forming committees would only involve us in the same frustrations that the politicians say they feel and we are already frustrated enough at the way the city is ignoring our needs. . . . So, in spite of the Mayor's plans to bring the government down to us through the Task Force, he has only succeeded in bringing the city's red tape a little closer to the people who are most hurt by it. Let's go to the next meeting on Wednesday, June 12th at 7:30 pm at the Tompkins Square Community Center, 601 East 9th Street and give them the "little" jobs they have offered to do for us. Let us tell them of specific times and places when the garbagemen are sloppy in clearing our streets, about the cars that are abandoned and left for months in our streets, about the buildings which are left deserted and unguarded and the construction sites where our children are left to play. Come with specific grievances and maybe something will be accomplished.

Concern about Collier's leadership role, continuing rumors that drugs and revolutionary literature were being
distributed in the building, and the intractability of neighborhood residents' opposition to the Local Task Force
might have caused City officials to give up the whole notion
of encouraging the Christodora House project. But on July
21, the Lower East Side erupted again. A bar at Avenue C
and Ninth Street was fire-bombed, and the Tactical Police
Force (TPF), an elite corps of police trained to work in
rioting areas, moved in. For four nights youths started
trash fires in the streets, threw bottles at the patrolling TPF
men, and smashed store windows. Community resentment
of the presence of the TPF finally led to its removal, and
the City officials rushed to show new concern about the
lack of jobs and decent housing and adequate recreational
facilities for Lower East Side citizens. Plans for a neighborhood playground were speeded up, and TSCC people say
they were given reason to think that more help would be
given them in fixing up the Christodora House building.
But the help did not immediately materialize, and the
group's bitterness was reinforced. In September, the staff
handed out the following open letter on neighborhood
street corners:

TO: Community Residents
FROM: Tompkins Square Community Center
        601 East 9th Street

Dear Neighbor:

In mid-July, after the 9th Street and Avenue C community versus police confrontation, a meeting was
held with many organizations and community people
present. The City, at this time, said they would do the
job they were supposed to do; bring the building up to
safety standards!!

Barry Gottehrer and Ted Mastroianni from Mayor Lindsay's office are now saying they will not help co-operate to keep the building safe. When it comes to the helping of poor people it seems as though Lindsay's administration is always talking double-talk. Many organizations have said that the Mayor's office has broken its promises or just avoided them by not being in or not accepting phone calls from the people.

Look at the new emergency powers which the Mayor has *now* by law. Is this to surround and contain the poor people because they are tired of living in filthy homes, without jobs and receive poor education and educational materials? Look at the cut in the new welfare law, which saves the city money, as the Mayor says, but, what about that money? Will it be used to build more middle-income houses like Masaryk Towers, or East Village Towers? Will more be taken from the poor man? How much more taxes can the poor person stand? They lose their sons to fight a war, they come back and don't get any better treatment. Mothers weep when they hear hunger cries of children, mothers weep when they think of the poorness they suffer and raise their children in. And when they get mad because of these things they are run down by horses, arrested, beaten and their children hurt.

The community center has been trying to stay open and run programs for a year, with hardly any help from the city. The youth have been trying to make something for the people in the community to enjoy. The youth have stopped drinking, using dope, and are trying to find a better way to help their people. The youth have been learning their own country's history so they can talk to the people better. If nobody helps us, then, we have to help ourselves. If the Republicans and the Democrats are the same people in different uniforms, then, we better find someone else to represent us.

The community center has a water flood problem which could be dangerous if it hits the high-power electric lines in the sub-basement. We think the city is trying to stop us from building a community center.

Demonstrations seem to get our people hurt. Letters don't seem to have any effect. Phone calls they don't answer. Then what must we do? How do we fight for Human Rights and the right to live decently? How do we do it?

What do we have left?

This passionate, somewhat confused memorandum illustrates the continual problem of the City officials who made careless representations about what they would do—or try to do—for the TSCC people, and the community people who overinterpreted the representations, fixing them into firm promises. Although Heckscher never flatly stated he would fix the pool, the community residents felt he had made a promise. Similarly, when Borough President Percy Sutton retreated from his interest in supporting the TSCC's projects, the group felt that he had actively deceived them.

Perhaps the greatest of these gaps between implication and inference arose over negotiations that might have given residents real control over many of the Lower East Side's community services. By the fall of 1968 Tompkins Square citizens, with the aid of TSCC staff, had succeeded in putting together the Board of Governors that Barry Gottehrer had asked for some months before. This group included representatives of most of the Lower East Side organizations that would conduct activities in the building if it were to be repaired and dedicated to community use. On September 18 the new Board met with Gottehrer and Mastroianni—now conducting the Lower East Side's Task Force business in small meetings or at City Hall—and the Deputy Commissioner of Real Estate to discuss future uses of the building. Organizations represented on the Board included the large and well-established Mobilization for Youth as well as newer and less secure groups like the Real Great Society (programs for youth run by former gang members), the North East Neighborhood Association (eager to start a health center in Christodora House), and Odyssey House (rehabilitation for adolescent drug addicts). The Board and the City officials discussed the prospect that the Department of Real Estate, which had official jurisdiction over City-owned buildings not in active use by a City agency, could lease the building to the Board for a nominal amount. In return the Board would be responsible for correcting all building code violations—a job entailing major repair of electrical and plumbing systems and costing several hundred thousand dollars—and for maintaining the building and running programs in it. City agencies, as well as community groups, might rent space from the Board. Minutes of the meeting indicate that its aim was to develop firm plans for transferring the building and raising money to support it.

On September 25, a letter was sent out over Barry Gottehrer's signature to Welton Smith, a Parks Department employee at TSCC, setting forth the results of the September 18 meeting and outlining the planned duties of the two parties—the City and the Board—under the arrangement described above. The minutes of the meeting suggest that Gottehrer saw this letter as a "memorandum of understanding," not as a document having legal implications or inducing reliance on its representations in the Board. But its provisions were specific, and its readers interpreted them as binding promises, despite one of the final sentences, which read, "Finally, my involvement with the project is contingent upon the understanding that the Board of Governors is a functioning representative group from the Tompkins Square community that could supply the funds needed to maintain and operate the building."

It is impossible to know now how this letter was *meant* to be taken. Two years later Gottehrer did not even remember it, though he conceded the signature to be his. It seems probable that it was written without serious thought of the problems that might arise in giving up control of a City-owned building, even if the group assuming control was a "functioning representative group" from the community. Later events suggest that some of those problems occurred to City officials after the letter was written, but by then the credibility gap was enormous. The TSCC group read the letter as promising legal control of the building to the Board of Governors. When the building's violations were not corrected and no lease was forthcoming, they reproduced the letter many times and used it as evidence of the City's duplicity.

It is at least possible to conclude that the letter did not constitute a definitive statement from the City as to what should be done about Christodora House. On November 12, 1968, representatives of the Parks Department, the Department of Real Estate, the Department of Public Works, the Recreation Department, the Mayor's Task Force, and the Board of Education met to discuss the issue once again—this time without any community residents present. Alternative solutions, as described in the minutes of the meeting were as follows:

1. Close the building now. Tell the community that we will open the building in functioning condition when they come up with $100,000. (Some danger inherent in this plan involving, as it would have to, police enforcement.)

2. Close the building and put it on the market. (Tantamount to a complete rejection of the community by the City.)

3. Provide heat, light, water—bring building up to minimum standards as quickly as possible. Inform community that we will cease operation if they do not come up with funds. (Once we have shown that we can heat, light, etc., it would be almost impossible to pull out later, even without community funds.)

4. Go to the Mayor with a request for funds. City would assume full responsibility for operation. Turn building over to community group to run program. (Not to be mentioned as a possibility to the community.)

5. Provide heat, light, water. Bring building up to minimum standards. Give the community the first four or five floors and turn the upper floors over to another tenant who might be either a public or private agency. (Query N.Y.Y., HRA, Addiction Services Agency, State and Federal Government as to possible interest in space. Dormitories for social workers or students who might work in community programs. Possible use as artists' residences.)

Apparently no choice from among those alternatives was made at that meeting.

By mid-1968 the citizens' earlier demand for better services and some community participation in providing them had escalated. Now the TSCC group was asking for real control over valuable City property. Although theoretically these increasing ambitions fell on receptive ears— they presumably marked growing citizen involvement in government, a sign of a successful reform administration— in practice they stimulated a good deal of resistance from City officials. For one thing, each different dimension of what was intended to be a cooperative government-citizen relationship taxed the resources and capacities of City agencies almost beyond endurance. In addition, it could not be said that the TSCC group had demonstrated, in any of the usual ways, success in one kind of activity before requesting assistance in taking on another, more complex one. Finally, the City administrators realized that as the community group's ambitions expanded, so would the number and kind of political figures interested in and concerned about what was happening in Christodora House. As news of the likelihood of "community control" in this area spread to a larger public than just a few Lower East Siders, cooperation from prominent citizens and politicians outside the Lindsay administration would be necessary. And it looked as though many of them would not be sympathetic to the idea in the Tompkins Square neighborhood of extending the power and influence that the TSCC group seemed to symbolize.

During the last half of 1968 community tensions grew over the TSCC group's use of the building. The police received numerous complaints that muggers fled into it, and neighbors objected when their sons and daughters came home from TSCC activities with Black Panther literature and circulars recruiting cane-pickers for the Cuban Venceremos brigade. What had been described by staff members as karate classes appeared to many visitors to be paramilitary training activities for the angry young blacks in the area. Police and Department of Real Estate officials who were in the building regularly brought back reports that it was used for hiding loot and taking drugs. Some of the repairs made by community residents had not withstood hard use, and the superficial signs of further deterioration in the building did not engender confidence in its users. The elevators had broken down completely, the remains of clothing from the Poor People's campaign littered the gym, and messy piles of mimeographed handouts added to a general impression of disarray.

On February 11, 1969, the Department of Real Estate—without previous warning—sent an eviction notice to the Tompkins Square Community Center. On the 13th, an official telephoned Collier, explaining that the building would have to be closed because of its disrepair and chaos. At 1:30 the next morning, police from the Ninth Precinct raided the building and forcibly closed it. Substantial disagreement remains as to how this was done. Neighborhood residents maintain that twenty-four vehicles with eighty policemen were sent to do the job, while City officials estimate the numbers as twenty men in four or five cars. When the raid was over, little furniture remained and files had been confiscated. Community residents say the police broke chairs and smashed chandeliers. City people say the furniture had been burned by staff members to keep them warm in the unheated building prior to the policemen's entrance.

Even immediately after the raid, City officials and community residents agreed that it had accomplished very little. No one even pretended that concern about the mess in the building was the real reason for shutting it down. Both local residents and City officials hint that the FBI had informed several City departments that subversive and illegal activities were taking place at TSCC. But no drugs or guns were found. Although rumor had it that young people were "crashing" in the building, there was no one sleeping there when the police came. Some "revolutionary" literature was confiscated, but the rumors that the building was being used as an ammunitions storehouse were never substantiated. The building was occupied only by three TSCC staff members, working late to clear up files pursuant to the Department of Real Estate's eviction notice.

Community reaction to the raid was instantaneous. Even those who had not completely appoved of the activities going on in the building were horrified at this method of responding to them. The burgeoning distrust toward Barry Gottehrer became open hatred, the more intense when it came from TSCC staff members. In a newsletter widely distributed, staff members wrote:

> It is essential for all Lower East Side organizations to realize that these actions by the City are a most basic violation of community rights. The City is attempting to manipulate the Lower East Side as if it were a game of chess in which the City makes moves from both sides of the board. If past actions by the City have failed to make clear the base character of the City's motives, then this barbarous display of police power should make this abundantly clear.

The TSCC staff chose this moment when it had considerable community sympathy to air its version of the bitter history of the past few months. In another part of the newsletter it detailed "Unfulfilled City Commitments":

The memorandum of agreement with the city government reproduced on the last pages of this packet [Barry Gottehrer's September letter] specifies the following four-step program for transfer of the building.

1. Beginning on September 18, 1968, a survey of the building to identify existing violations was to be conducted by the City.

2. On completion of the survey the City was to begin removal of the violations.

3. When violations were removed (a deadline of December 31, 1968, was set for this) a $1.00 a month lease was to be made with the building's Board of Governors.

4. On signing the lease the Board of Governors would have ninety days to provide a suitable maintenance program.

Beginning with the survey which was never conducted to the lease which was never signed, the City has not met a single one of its written commitments. Not only has this delayed progress towards stablizing the building, it has also contributed to the deterioration of the building. The TSCC staff, assuming good faith on the part of the City, waited many months for the repair work to begin and only after all efforts to compel the City to meet its commitments failed did TSCC attempt to establish a repair and maintenance program of its own. In the meantime a chain reaction of mechanical breakdowns occurred which would not have occurred had TSCC known that the City would renege on its commitments.

Knowing now that we must rely on our own resources, a maintenance and repair program for the building is being provided. Heat has been restored to the building and other repairs made in a methodical and responsible fashion by neighborhood people working with the supervision of an experienced licensed engineer and with the financial assistance of the Lower East Side Civic Improvement Association.

It should also be noted that many other verbal commitments have been made by representatives of the Mayor's office including promises for new windows and a new floor for the gymnasium. Here too, in every single instance, the City has failed to honor its commitments.

The City's neglect extends beyond inaction. As a result of those few repair projects which the City did start but which were left unfinished, we have a disassembled summer boiler which is missing vital parts, inoperative ejection pumps and other essential equipment which is now in worse condition than it would otherwise have been had the work been completed or not even begun.

Most recently, when a main water feeder from Ninth Street burst due to freeze damage during the fuel strike, the City was asked to turn the water off from the street. This is a request that has been promptly met in the recent past by former tenants of the building. However, this time, after many hours and dispatching three trucks, the City sent a crew to rip up the street claiming that the Department of Water Supply, Gas and Electricity did not have the necessary tool to turn off the water.

Fearing that this would be another incompleted project for which the Center would be held responsible, two members of the Union of Community Skills (an organization formed for, among other purposes, maintaining the building) asked for a few minutes to try and solve the problem. Fashioning a wrench from three discarded metal bars, the two Union members were able to turn off the water.

Once again damage could have been avoided had the Center relied on its own resources instead of trusting the City. In the five hours that the City stalled, a serious flood developed in the basement.

As final evidence of the City's malfeasance, the TSCC staff circulated a memorandum recording a meeting Gottehrer had had with staff of the local YMCA, which was interested in renting space in the building, either directly from the City or from the governing board of a community coalition that would acquire a long-term lease. The memo said that Gottehrer felt there could be no effective coalition as long as Collier was the leader of TSCC. It reflected Gottehrer's view that Collier wished to use the Christodora House group as a personal power base, and that he would not advance the interests of the community as a whole. It stated, "Mr. Gottehrer is currently involved in conferences to deal with the situation. He will call us as soon as the future of Robert Collier within the Center has been clarified." To the already angry group of TSCC people this seemed the final insult. Meetings to which they were not party were apparently being held in the back rooms of City Hall to determine the fate of their director. This manipulation of their interests seemed the antithesis to the cooperative relationship with government they had been hoping to establish.

But Bob Collier was removed from the picture by forces far stronger than Barry Gottehrer. In April he was arrested with twenty others for allegedly conspiring in a Black Panther plot to bomb five midtown New York department stores. He was tried and acquitted two years later.

V

As soon as the building had been closed, the City set about trying to bind up wounds. On February 17, 1969, Barry Gottehrer wrote to Chet Mirsky, the attorney for TSCC, "It is my understanding that the Department of Real Estate considers the closing temporary and remains open to negotiate a lease to a broad-based community group representative of the residents of the Lower East Side, which would be able to provide funding for insurance, maintenance, and operation of the building for recreational purposes for the entire community." The letter went on to say that the question of the use of the property was now entirely in the hands of the Department of Real Estate.

When a City-owned building is empty, and has passed into the jurisdiction of the Department of Real Estate, the department has a responsibility to determine whether any further City usage is possible. It circularizes a notice of the building's availability to all City agencies and sometimes to community agencies as well. If no appropriate public use emerges, the building is offered for sale and put back on the tax rolls.

On February 27 Ira Duchan, then Deputy Commissioner of Real Estate, sent out a circular to agencies and community groups announcing that Christodora House was available for community use to "established organizations offering diversified programs, with adequate supervision. . . ." It also noted that "proof of financial capacity to meet both the cost of insurance and the annual maintenance will be required."

Duchan, a man with long experience in the City's bureaucracies, was interested in helping to bend them in the interests of new political and social imperatives. For several years he had tried to make the Department of Real Estate more responsive to the increasing demands for community control over local programs of various kinds. He had garnered some support for Mayor Lindsay in Jewish areas by renting City-owned space to synagogues for a nominal sum, and he commonly tried to modify City regulations to allow $1-a-month leases to established settlement houses and day care centers. But the groups he usually dealt with were middle class, with at least superficial internal unity, and not so scarred by earlier confrontations with the City as the Lower East Side group he met with concerning Christodora House.

The group that came to see Duchan in March 1969 was not the original band of TSCC supporters, nor was it the larger, more broadly based Board of Governors that had met with Gottehrer. Immediately after the February raid, the Board of Governors had collapsed, possibly because of the fear on some members' part of being associated with a building that was said to harbor drug addicts and revolutionaries. In its place a new board, calling itself the Coalition Group, arose. Formed of representatives from black and Puerto Rican organizations, it seemed to reflect more closely than earlier bodies the ethnic composition of those who would ultimately use Christodora House most. Two prominent local Puerto Ricans—one who was a City housing official and one who was considering running for Congress from the Lower East Side—participated in early Coalition Group meetings and pledged to try to get City support for the group's plans. But encouraging the new body had substantial drawbacks from the City's point of view. Its rhetoric was considerably more radical than City officials were prepared to swallow, and the image it projected had driven away some of the more moderate (and middle class) TSCC supporters. Furthermore, it did not seem to have contacts with established organizations or foundations which might help them raise the money they would need to make the building a viable enterprise. Vowing self-reliance, the Coalition Group maintained that most of the repair work could be done by the indigenous Union of Community Skills—self-taught, minority-group craftsmen who had already repaired leaking risers and broken toilets in the building.

While Duchan negotiated with the Coalition Group, uncertain of how much encouragement to give it, another community group became important. In April, a new Local Task Force chairman replaced Ted Mastroianni. Geoffrey Stokes had lived on the Lower East Side for several years and had been active in local politics, both informally and as president of a local reform Democratic club. He knew most of the leaders of the Lower East Side neighborhood organizations and had a good sense of community

problems through his job as Director of Program Development for the Addiction Services Agency. When Stokes first
began his work with the Task Force he was skeptical of the
Coalition Group's ability to unify the community behind
the Christodora House project. He advised Duchan against
developing any permanent relationship with the group,
saying that he feared they represented only the "radical
fringe" and that he believed Tompkins Square residents
could put together a sturdier coalition. He then met with
a number of those who had not become part of the Coalition Group, and Nueva Vida—Spanish for "new life"—
was born.

The first chairman of Nueva Vida was the Director of
the North East Neighborhood Association (NENA), Flor-
ence Parkinson, who was particularly interested in the
building as a potential site for a NENA health center.
Trained as a social worker, Miss Parkinson is an open,
articulate woman with a decisive, competent manner. Although not herself a political radical, she has tolerance for
many points of view. She set to work obtaining the broadest possible representation for the coalition, recruiting
members among the more stable social service organizations on the Lower East Side, but also leaving the door
open for participation by some of the groups that had cast
their lot with the Coalition Group.

For a time it looked as though Nueva Vida might not
survive. Commissioner Duchan, still discussing long-term
arrangements with the Coalition Group, gave it the building's keys "to go in and clean it up." This gave that group
its toe in the door, and its followers began to meet informally in the building. An article in the *East Village Other*,
an underground newspaper that later became defunct, presented the Coalition Group's view of its occupation of
Christodora House:

> The leviathans of finance and the guardians of political
> power in the City have capitulated. On July 3, a City
> honky ignominiously handed over the keys of the

building into the clenched fist of Tompkins Square Community Center brother John Wilson. The door facing the park, justly graffitied, "Why is this building closed?" is now open. People are inside; community people, black, brown, and white people. The latest battle in the war between community and City that began in 1967 has now been won.

But in this case possession did not turn out to be nine-tenths of the law. The Department of Real Estate, prompted by Gottehrer, Stokes, and John McGarrahan, the Mayor's assistant for housing, notified the Coalition Group that it would not negotiate a lease with it, that serious consideration for any permanent interest would be given only to a group representing a broader spectrum of the Lower East Side community. The prominent Puerto Ricans withdrew their support. Flo Parkinson used her diplomatic skills to persuade some of the leaders of the Coalition Group to join with Nueva Vida to present a united front to the City. Uneasily, the two groups merged, retaining the Nueva Vida name and structure.

In October Nueva Vida seemed stable enough for the City officials to be willing to make some commitment to its interest in the Building. The Department of Real Estate granted it a $1-a-month lease for eleven months, with the understanding that during that period the Department, the Task Force, and Nueva Vida itself would work toward a long-term arrangement. The new lease represented concessions on both sides: the community was accepting the City's failure to commit itself to fixing up the building, and the City was implicity endorsing Nueva Vida as representative of the interests of the Lower East Side.

It is interesting that both the City and the citizens seem to have experienced the sharpest internal discord during the period immediately preceding the giving of the short-term lease. Stokes spent several hours trying to convince an initially resistant Gottehrer that, as one memo put it, Nueva Vida had "as representative a body as is ever likely

to be assembled on the Lower East Side." When Gottehrer
was won over, Duchan had to be persuaded—a difficult job
in light of the fact that Duchan was eager to obtain money
for the City by renting portions of the building to "safe"
groups like the YMCA and the Silesian Fathers, and therefore resisted the notion of any written commitment to
Nueva Vida. The City people who pushed for granting the
lease felt it important to make some formal arrangement
before the 1969 mayoralty election. A new Mayor in 1970
would find it much easier to resist pressure for community
control of Christodora House if there were no written commitment. Stokes, at least, had arrived at a clear position on
the question of what relationship City government ought
to have toward this community group. He was convinced
that the City should relinquish its control over this facility
and any programs conducted in it. He managed to bring
other administrators along with him, to some degree. He
then set out to help the community find the massive financial support it would need to justify granting the long-term
lease.

The community residents had also had a moment of
truth. The more radical among them—especially those
who had seen the Christodora House issue develop over
more than two years—could not ignore the fact that their
troubles with the City had not been detrimental to all their
interests. Although they had initially intended only to find
a way to provide the area with better recreational programs
and facilities, they had quickly discovered in their bureaucratic tussles a source for raising the political consciousness
of many of their less radical neighbors. Settling down now
to raising money and establishing a permanent institution
would probably render them relatively impotent as radical
educators and instruments of revolutionary change. It was
a difficult choice. Finally the fear of being co-opted yielded
to the genuine desire of even the angriest young black to
see Christodora transformed from the symbol of frustration it had been in the past into the symbol of enterprise
it might become. John Wilson, a leader of the Coalition

Group and one of the angriest of the more radical group, became vice-chairman of Nueva Vida.

Resolving ambivalence was made much easier on both sides because this first commitment was so temporary and, in some practical ways, so unimportant. It turned out that an eleven-month lease was not a sufficiently sound anticipation of permanence to elicit solid promises of financial support from banks or foundations. Nueva Vida had also hoped to entice some large, secure Lower East Side organizations into committing themselves to renting space in the building, but they too were cautious. Potential investors and renters both pointed to major uncertainties about what the terms of the long-term lease would be, who would actually maintain the building, and how much repair and maintenance would cost.

Any lease of City property for one year or longer, or for which the monthly rental is $500 or more, must be auctioned publicly. A resolution to auction such a lease must be passed by a majority of the City's Board of Estimate, which is composed of the Mayor, the City Council President, the Comptroller, and the five Borough Presidents. A resolution can be worded in such a way that it amounts to a direction of the lease to a particular lessee. In this case the resolution was drafted with Nueva Vida firmly in mind. It resolved to allow the Department of Real Estate to lease the building for nonprofit purposes to a broad-based Lower East Side coalition of community groups. The time period of the lease was to be thirty-five years at a rental of no less than $50 per month. The lessee would assume all financial responsibility for repair and maintenance of the property and for acquiring liability insurance.

By January 1970 the lease resolution had been drafted and Mayor Lindsay asked the Board of Estimate to hold a hearing on it and vote its approval. The hearing was scheduled for Friday, February 13. The Board of Directors of Nueva Vida began to mobilize public testimony in its favor from community leaders, neighborhood residents, and heads of groups represented on the coalition. Barry Gottehrer was to appear, attesting to the Mayor's support for the project.

At this point Lorraine Miller, the lawyer who had originally incorporated TSCC, re-entered the picture. The disillusionment that had led her to disassociate herself from TSCC in 1968 had been reinforced by the rumors she later heard about the use of drugs and the distribution of "radical literature" in Christodora House. By early 1970 she had become convinced that the City had given the community residents adequate chance to "make good" with the building and that nothing had come of it. She therefore was convinced that granting a long-term lease to Nueva Vida would be a disaster.

Mrs. Miller's Lower East Side contacts made her a powerful enemy. She had worked closely with the City Councilman who represented the area, and she had some influence with the regular Democratic leaders from the area south of Tompkins Square. Furthermore, she was a member of Community Planning Board #3. In this capacity, she called the Nueva Vida leaders and asked that they present their plans for the building at the next Planning Board meeting. Mrs. Miller and several other members of the Planning Board found Flo Parkinson's presentation inadequate. They felt Nueva Vida had not demonstrated enough financial support for the project nor shown why it needed such a permanent commitment from the City. Mrs. Miller maintains that Nueva Vida did not provide a full list of thirty-five member organizations or a copy of the proposed lease, both of which had been promised the Board. Miss Parkinson felt that the Board, led by Mrs. Miller, asked for impossible specificity and had made up its mind to oppose the proposal before it was presented.

Shortly after the Nueva Vida presentation, members of the Planning Board went to see Duchan (now Commissioner of Real Estate) and Al Walsh, the Administrator of Housing and Development. They suggested alternative uses for the building—a YMCA center, government-run housing for the elderly, or the use of the top ten floors for people who needed temporary shelter while they were be-

ing relocated. Both Walsh and Duchan said thay they could
do nothing until the Board of Estimate acted on the Nueva
Vida resolution.

Undaunted by their lack of success with the two commissioners, Mrs. Miller and other Planning Board representatives met with Sanford Garelik, President of the City
Council and an influential member of the Board of Estimate. Garelik commands four votes on the Board of Estimate and a good deal of influence over several of the
Borough Presidents. Mrs. Miller says the Planning Board
members went to him "to see how he felt" about the issue.
It seems quite clear that they also expressed strong opposition to the Nueva Vida proposal.

Gottehrer, Stokes, and John McGarrahan, the Mayor's
former Assistant for Housing, all feel that Lorraine Miller's conversation with the City Council President was an
important influence. But Garelik was also probably predis-
posed to be skeptical about giving the Tompkins Square
residents any formal, permanent interest in Christodora
House. He had, of course, heard that the building had become a haven for illegal activities; as a former Chief Inspector of the Police Department he could scarcely ignore the
reports. He also has a reputation for being particularly
concerned about matters of loyalty. One City commissioner has said, "Garelik sees Communists under every
bed." A former Mayor's assistant maintains that at one
point during his police career Garelik supervised a secret
unit investigating "subversive" characters. Finally, Garelik
had shown some recent interest in disassociating himself
from the Mayor's positions, both to establish his independence—Garelik had been Lindsay's running mate in the
1969 City election—and to establish his credibility with the
City's more conservative Democrats.

Garelik also shared a major concern about Nueva Vida
with Abraham Beame, the City's Comptroller. Beame opposed the proposal because he felt that allowing community groups to use City buildings for a nominal rental was
against the City's financial interest, and perhaps even ille-

gal. A visit from Lorraine Miller and the Planning Board representatives only reinforced the reservations he already had about the appropriateness of the lease.

With the Mayor supporting the resolution, and the Comptroller and City Council President opposed, it began to seem clear how the Board of Estimate would decide. Each of these three officials has four votes on Board matters; the Borough Presidents have two apiece. Robert Abrams, Borough President of the Bronx, maintaining his liberal image, would go with the Mayor. So would Percy Sutton of Manhattan, since he could not lose credibility in his own borough by failing to support the residents in a community control issue. The other three were expected to go with Beame and Garelik. The vote would thus be 8 to 14, defeating the resolution.

This outcome became clear long before the matter ever came to a vote. Two days before the Board of Estimate hearing at which testimony was to be given for Nueva Vida, Garelik made his intentions very public indeed. In an executive session of the Board of Estimate, the City Council President voted against a $535,000-a-year appropriation for the office of Robert M. Morgenthau, the former U.S. Attorney for the Southern District of New York, as third Deputy Mayor. At the same session he questioned the suitability of the proposal to lease Christodora House to Nueva Vida. Public reaction to Garelik's position was generally favorable. In particular, the conservative *Daily News* lauded Garelik for his "show of independence." In a lead editorial, the paper exulted, "Garelik has at least served notice he will be no little Sir Echo for the Mayor. We hope he does not cave in under pressure."

On February 13, the Board of Estimate met and heard testimony from Nueva Vida people and community supporters on the uses to which the building might be put if the resolution was passed. Barry Gottehrer testified for the lease—the only time he had ever gone to bat publicly for a community program before the Board of Estimate or the City Council. Bertram Beck, Executive Director of the venerable and respected Henry Street Settlement and of

Mobilization for Youth, spoke movingly of the need for a social service center near Tompkins Square and of the confidence he had in Nueva Vida to meet that need. When the testimony was complete, the Board voted to postpone a decision on the lease resolution. Nueva Vida supporters were discouraged but perhaps also somewhat relieved. Having the matter put off gave them more time to drum up support for their project. They spent the next few months looking for money and allies.

Neither one materialized. Although one of Garelik's assistants tried to persuade him to approve the resolution, Garelik was adamant. When Nueva Vida representatives went to see him he voiced the opinion that City officials would be irresponsible if they allowed private community groups to manage City buildings. He said that he felt his accountability as a public official would prevent him from approving this kind of community control. When pressed, he admitted that he wanted the City to be able to screen the users of the building. He denied, however, that his oppposition to the lease stemmed from disapproval of any of the specific groups then interested in renting space.

During the next eight months, the Board of Estimate voted several more times to postpone final consideration of the resolution. (The City's cynics—both residents and officials—speculated that no vote could be taken during the warm weather for fear of a riot if the lease was defeated.) With each delay, Nueva Vida and its supporters lost confidence of eventual success. Funds were impossible to raise with no assurance that the building would belong to the community. Without the hope of a strong community program to hold it together, the coalition seemed likely to dissolve. In the early autumn Flo Parkinson, citing the pressure of other professional duties, resigned as chairman of Nueva Vida. John Wilson succeeded her, giving the radical wing more prominence. A number of supporters of the Christodora House project dropped out when Miss Parkinson resigned; they appear to have seen her action as evidence that the resolution was not likely to pass.

On October 29, 1970, the Board of Estimate quietly voted

to table the proposal indefinitely. The vote was as expected, with Lindsay, Sutton, and Abrams in the minority. Although the eleven-month lease had long since expired, the City allowed what remained of the TSCC to continue operating in Christodora House for another year. Various City agencies explored the possibility of taking over the building for their programs. In at least one case, the building's recent history helped an administrator to decide he did not want to have anything to do with it. As of the autumn of 1973, the building stood closed and empty, a sixteen-story symbol of the failure of the City of New York and its citizens to cooperate for the benefit of the Lower East Side.

VI

The escalation of the demands on the City regarding Christodora House is a familiar phenomenon. The revolution of rising expectations is as likely to be the result of disappointments as of successes. Kind-hearted reformers hold out hope to people who have had none. The hope generates pride. Forces unforeseen by the reformers and beyond their control stifle the hopeful initiatives. When the hope is dashed, the pride becomes outrage. Entreaties are transformed into demands, usually aimed at those same reformers who now realize their own impotence and respond with half-hearted, guilty attempts at partial solutions. The most far-reaching outcome of these encounters—and its importance should not be minimized—is often the heightened social and political awareness of the citizens who participated.

The various stages of the Christodora House situation illustrate the reformers' lack of clarity about both their effectiveness and their dedication. Heckscher and Callender didn't know how far they *could* go, and Gottehrer and Duchan didn't know how far they *wanted* to go. The questions got harder, of course, as time passed. Trying to respond promptly to requests for service was much less complex than relinquishing real power. Yet Lindsay's administrators were equally incapable of repairing a swimming pool, on the one hand, and leasing to a group of citizens a City-owned building, on the other.

The Parks Department officials' failures are attributable to innocence and vulnerability in the face of sophisticated bureaucratic resistance. The Task Force leaders and Mayor's assistants were less ingenuous. They certainly knew that giving the residents what they wanted could cause a shift in power relations on the Lower East Side. They either underestimated the probable resistance to that eventuality, or they did not care enough about victory to amass the kinds of support necessary to defeat the political leaders outside the Lindsay administration who were bound to take up arms and affect the outcome. The Mayor's men did not stimulate mass demands that might have aroused general public sympathy. Nor did they use the Mayor's influence to get support from large corporations, foundations, or City-wide private service agencies. The community people whose interests were at stake were not effective, either. Some of them did not have the experience in community organizing to get a wider spectrum of Lower East Siders behind the issue. Others let their fear of interference from outside the area keep them from modifying their aims and rhetoric in order to attract powerful allies.

Those who opposed the Nueva Vida lease had many reasons. They thought community control—at least in poor neighborhoods—was likely to threaten those other important governmental principles of efficiency and honesty. They did not have faith in either the competence or the political allegiances of Nueva Vida members. Most important, but always unstated, they feared that community control of such a large piece of property—a sixteen-story building filled with cooperating community services —might threaten the regular Democratic organizations of the Lower East Side; a new constituency of poor, angry people might develop to which the traditional leaders could not appeal. Some of the observers of the Christodora House situation maintain that the powerful local Democratic leaders of nearby neighborhoods pressured the Comptroller and City Council President to vote down the resolution.

A crucial question that remains about the Christodora House problem is whether, under any circumstances, Nueva Vida could have amassed the financial and managerial assistance to repair the building and carry on activities on all of its sixteen floors. By mid-1970 it was estimated that repair work would cost $750,000, an amount unlikely to be raised from donations. But John McGarrahan, Lindsay's former housing assistant, suggests that if Nueva Vida had held a long-term lease, the City might have subordinated its interest in such a way as to allow Nueva Vida to act as a first mortgager, obtaining a bank loan on that basis. Once the repair money was assured, however, enough tenants would have to have been found for the building to supply a rent roll of at least $18,000 a month. The Lower East Side has long been a haven of many small organizations, operating independently out of informal and accessible quarters. Getting many of those groups together in an imposing, centralized location would appear to be an almost impossible task under any conditions. A more feasible way to fill the building would have been to turn large parts of it over to a big organization like the YMCA, or to devote half of it to housing for the elderly or the dispossessed; but the TSCC people had resisted such notions before as too traditional and likely to dilute the authority of the community over the building. Perhaps a solution could never have been found. Certainly it was not likely without a determination by the Lindsay administration that this was a project worth more time and effort than merely giving official support to the Board of Estimate resolution.

Did the Christodora House situation teach either the Lower East Side residents or the City officials anything? For the Tompkins Square residents, the lessons have been mostly bitter ones. As the Mayor's statement said, delivered just before the final Board of Estimate vote, "Christodora House stands as a symbol to the community residents, a sign that the City does not care about them." Perhaps the Mayor's men learned more positive things. They may have learned something about the dangers of raising expectations. Surely they learned something about the difficulties of maintaining a long-term relationship with poor people, when both officials and residents change perspectives and identities many times within the time-frame of the planned project. These are important lessons to learn for the daily operation of local government. If learned well, they may contribute to a gradual improvement in the way officials and citizens communicate with one another. But they do not speak to the fundamental task of defining government's roles in new relationships with citizens. The Mayor's statement of support stressed the volatility of the neighborhood as a reason for allowing the residents to manage the building. To fund special summer programs for keeping restless youths off the hot streets may be effective riot prevention, and appropriate to that aim. To support a major community control effort for that reason seems, however, to have begged the question of how to bring governments and people truly closer to one another.

5

The Science
of Tunneling Through

I

Max Weber saw in technical knowledge the basis for administrative authority. It can also serve as a ground for resisting authority. A group of technicians may find that their common expertise binds them together in opposition to a directive more surely than shared work conditions, social attitudes, or backgrounds. Work-related bonds—like having gone to the same schools, or belonging to the same professional associations—may also be effective in holding off changes promoted by those with authority.

This is the story of an attempt by top New York City officials to get a group of professional workers—engineers at the City's Board of Water Supply—to implement a new mode of analysis in planning a major capital project, the third of the City's huge water distribution tunnels. It is another tale of reformers pitted against career civil service employees. Both sides maintained their positions in the name of science. But, as with many bureaucratic conflicts, its outcome was finally determined not by rationality but by organization.

Informed observers of New York City government often say, particularly in recent years, that the Budget Director is the second most powerful man in the administration. Not only does he hold the City's purse strings; he also exercises a great deal of control over the substance of programs' goals and activities. Even when he cannot defeat or stimulate a proposed expenditure, the Director may alter its scale so as to have profound effects on the delivery of a program. He has great discretion in determining what kind of analysis he will undertake on any project, either as part of the budget review process or pursuant to his role as an important policy advisor to the Mayor. His power often depends on how he exercises this discretion. It also depends on his relationship with the Mayor.

From his first days on the job, in September 1966, Frederick O'R. Hayes, the City's Budget Director, enjoyed the trust and confidence of John Lindsay. The Mayor wanted to attract men who were knowledgeable and concerned about the poor; Hayes came from the federal war on poverty, where he had been Deputy Director of the Community Action Program. At the same time, Lindsay admired the tightly analytical practitioners of modern systems analysis and management; Hayes had acquired technical skills in these areas as a senior analyst at the Federal Budget Bureau. To the Mayor, Hayes combined a vigorous social concern with a talent for efficient program planning, and his interest in developing a program-planning-budgeting system in New York seemed to bear that out. The two men also got along well personally. Hayes found the Mayor warm and supportive, and Lindsay responded to Hayes's obvious intelligence and quietly irreverent sense of humor.

Within a few days of Hayes's arrival in New York, members of the Budget Bureau's engineering staff drew his attention to a proposal from the City's Board of Water Supply (hereafter referred to as the Board) for the first stage of a new tunnel to bring New York City much of its water. The water tunnel was the first major capital project Hayes had seen in his Budget job. It was also the largest capital project in the City's history. Planned for construction in four stages over a period of twenty years, the tunnel would ultimately cost more than $1 billion. Stage One—a fourteen-mile stretch through three city boroughs—was budgeted at $238 million. When complete, the tunnel would stretch sixty miles, from the Hill View reservoir north of the City, down through the Bronx and Manhattan, across into Queens, and back up through the eastern reaches of the Bronx. It would distribute more than a billion gallons of water every day, about 40 percent of the water New York's eight million residents need to quench thirst, take showers, grow lawns, and run machinery.

The proposal made Hayes uneasy. In his view, it did not present sufficient justification for such an immense expenditure. He was not prepared to say that the tunnel was unnecessary. But he was concerned that the water distribution problem which the tunnel was to solve had not been properly defined. He thought the technicians should have presented alternative solutions, with their costs, so that he and the other policy-makers could have as wide a range of choices as possible. He expressed his doubts in a memo to his engineers, asking them to evaluate the Board's presentation:

> The engineering consultants [of the Board] are a little like my wife. They tell me we've got to have the facility—but they are not very interested in the right hand side of the menu. We need an economic analysis of options and costs. . . .

The memo went on to question the population assumptions on which the Board's projections of water demand were based. And Hayes thought the Board should have explained the reason for the tunnel size it specified, and assessed the effect of different tube sizes on the cost of the tunnel. He concluded:

> In sum, I am unimpressed by the engineering argument that we need the facility and this is the way to do it. There appear on the surface to be many feasible engineering options—and they are neither explained nor discussed in terms of cost to the City.

Hayes was not alone in having reservations about the proposal. Staff members of the City Planning Commission (CPC), which was responsible for the initial formulation of the yearly capital budget as well as for long-term physical planning for the City, shared his views. For months before Hayes took over as Budget Director, they had spoken out at meetings of the Mayor's Panel on Water Supply in opposition to the tunnel. Louis Schulman, director of the capital budget of the CPC, was deeply skeptical of the Board's planning standards and principles. He found its security measures for the tunnel overly cautious and its designs too expensive. Harmon Goldstone, one of the CPC's seven Commissioners and the one who assumed responsibility for water supply matters, shared Schulman's specific objections. He also distrusted the Board's tendency to expand its judgments from technical matters, where its expertise was unquestioned, into policy areas, where he felt the Board was unqualified.

The proposal, along with a request for design funds to be included in the 1967–68 capital budget, had been referred to the Budget Bureau by the Board of Estimate. This body, whose membership includes the Mayor, the City Council President, the Comptroller, and the five Borough Presidents, acts as a sort of upper legislative chamber for the City. It must approve both the substantive plans for any large capital project (usually called the "plan and profile") and all appropriations for its design and construction. The

Board of Estimate has no staff of its own to analyze proposals from City agencies, and it often relies on Budget Bureau opinions. In this case, the plan for the third City water tunnel, received from the Board of Water Supply in July 1966, was sent for review to all members of the Mayor's Panel on Water Supply. A committee formed during the drought of 1965 and reactivated primarily to consider the tunnel proposal, the Panel was made up of representatives of the various City agencies concerned with water problems—the Board of Water Supply; the Department of Water Supply, Gas and Electricity (hereafter referred to as the Department); the Health Services Administration; the Budget Bureau; the City Planning Commission; and the Office of Administration.

The reservations of Budget and CPC—along with others held by the Health Services Administrator—defeated all hopes that the Panel would immediately declare firm support for the Board's existing proposal. Plans for a letter to the Mayor reporting consensus on the need for the tunnel, its timing, and its costs were abandoned. Instead, the Panel's letter, dated November 14, 1966, agreed merely on the need for "an additional distribution facility." It also committed the Board of Water Supply to "promptly select and cause qualified experts, who have no connection with this project, to undertake a study in depth of all material questions raised . . . and to report thereon expeditiously." Appended to the letter were supplementary comments from each of the agency representatives, stating their individual positions.

By the time the Board's proposal was presented in 1966, planning for the tunnel had been under way for twelve years. During those years no objections had ever been raised. The tunnel project was generated and developed according to the same professional principles that had established the Board, many years before, as the builder of the most sophisticated municipal water system in the world. But now the planning process could no longer be an informal, in-house matter. The next steps would require review by a diverse group of agencies. Perhaps more significant, the Board would have to seek approval from the new Mayor's men, who might not know of the prestige and professionalism of the Board. When the Panel could not agree on the tunnel proposal, its proponents knew they could be in for a difficult fight in getting final approval from the Board of Estimate. Without that approval, design of the tunnel could not continue nor construction begin. But they were confident that opposition could be overcome. As the Board's Chief Engineer said later,

> We went straight on as though nothing could interfere, and it didn't. We didn't wait until we got everybody's blessing.

II

In the litany of "urban problems" that every New Yorker hears with numbing regularity, water supply and distribution are seldom mentioned. Occasional emergencies like drought or water main breaks do not seem to cause the same concern as school strikes, rising welfare caseloads, and air pollution. New Yorkers assume the availability of a safe, dependable water supply, and do not wonder about its source or its size.

The water supply and distribution network for New York City has three elements: collection and impoundment, primary distribution, and secondary distribution.

Raw water is collected in three watershed areas north of the City and stored in reservoirs not far from the City limits. Oldest is the Croton system, which now provides only 20 percent of the City's water. Some of the water impounded in the Croton Reservoir flows directly into the City and some into the holding reservoir (Kensico) about fifteen miles north of New York in Westchester County. The Delaware system collects water from the outlying Cannonsville, Pepacton, and Neversink reservoirs into the

Rondout Reservoir. From there the Delaware Aqueduct, 1,000 feet below ground at some points, carries hundreds of millions of gallons of water each day into the Hill View Reservoir, just above the northern border of the City. Hill View is the equalizing basin for that system and for the Catskill system, which brings water from Ashokan and Schoharie reservoirs through Kensico.

Primary distribution is carried out by two great tunnels carved into the rock hundreds of feet below ground. The tunnels begin at Hill View and carry approximately 1.2 billion gallons of water each day (more in the summer) to the five boroughs. City Tunnel #1, completed in 1912, comes down through the Bronx and Manhattan into Brooklyn. City Tunnel #2, built about twenty years later, extends from the eastern Bronx through the western edges of Queens and Brooklyn, where it joins Tunnel #1 and the new tunnel serving Staten Island. The tunnels run from 200 to 740 feet underground in order to avoid other borings for subways, utilities, and building foundations. They are sectioned by bronze valves which close automatically in case of a significant break and which can be operated manually if a section of tunnel needs to be inspected or repaired.

Distribution is completed by a system of vertical steel risers which carry water from the tunnels up to street mains. The mains in turn connect with narrower pipes feeding into virtually all New York business and residential streets.

Two City agencies—created at different times and with different administrative structures—share the responsibility for keeping New Yorkers supplied with clean, adequate water. The Board of Water Supply plans and constructs water supply facilities, while the Department of Water Resources (called the Department of Water Supply, Gas and Electricity until 1968) operates and maintains them. The two work closely together—"shoulder to shoulder," as the Board's Chief Engineer puts it. It is not surprising, therefore, that the initial conversations about the need for a new water tunnel took place between the Board and the

Department. In 1954 the Department Commissioner first formally notified the Board of his engineers' concern that severe problems of water pressure and distribution would develop if either Tunnel #1 or Tunnel #2 had to be shut down for repair. For the next four years the two agencies worked together on the problem, holding joint conferences and conducting preliminary field studies. From this work came the Board's first report, in 1960, which won approval from the Board of Estimate for $1 million over six years to conduct more detailed studies. The results of this work were embodied in the 1966 proposal that the Board submitted for Board of Estimate funding and approval.

Rarely can a large government project in New York City develop over a twelve-year period without coming to the attention of other departments. Usually the system of administrative checks and balances, combined with the natural competition among projects for scarce resources, ensures that an agency's plans will be subject to the scrutiny and criticism of other agencies with similar or supplementary program concerns. But water supply projects are quite special. Because the citizen's need for water was historically felt to be so essential, unique budgetary and institutional arrangements were created many years ago that protect even $1 billion projects from close observation until the planning process is virtually complete.

The Board of Water Supply was created by state legislation in 1905 in response to concern about the adequacy of the Croton supply and the possibility of private profit-making if the City should need to rely on the purchase of precious water from private corporations. Hoping to make it independent of partisan politics and above corruption, the legislature gave the Board unusual freedom and invulnerability. It can condemn land for water supply facilities, and it operates beyond most City administrative controls. Its three Commissioners, appointed by the Mayor, hold their tenure for life. The heart of its staff operation, the Engineering Corps, consists of about four hundred engineers and technicians who test materials, conduct surveys, prepare reports, and design all facilities. All staff members, including the powerful Chief Engineer, hold civil service positions; their status is not, therefore, affected by political changes in the City administration.

The Board's special independence extends beyond personnel provisions. Its projects, unlike most capital items, are not limited in cost by the state law that provides that bonds can be floated only in an amount that does not exceed a specified, but varying, percentage of the value of real property in the City. This exemption from the municipal debt limit ensures that water supply projects will not compete with other items in the capital budget—schools, hospitals, park equipment—for priority. Because Board projects are financed by bond issues, they do not affect the taxpayer's pocketbook except as his property tax rises to cover amortization and interest on the bonds. And a large percentage of this property tax bite is deferred for so many years that it does not generally arise as a political issue.

Only occasionally does the Board need to adhere to the usual administrative procedures. Before construction of its projects may begin, the Board of Estimate must approve a "plan and profile," as with the third City water tunnel. And capital funds for project design, and then for construction, must also be appropriated for the Board's projects. Once set aside, however, these funds may be expended without the item-by-item Budget Bureau approval necessary for most other agencies.

In the decades since its formation in 1905, the Board of Water Supply has added to its built-in institutional power. Its performance has been, by most technical standards, exemplary. As the daily water consumption of the City's residents has tripled, and water issues have become more and more complex, the Board has continued to rise to the tasks demanded of it. Tunnels #1 and #2 have been perfectly reliable, and water supply projects have been notably free from scandal. The Board has gained prestige as the most effective agency of its kind. Water supply officials from governments all over the world have come regularly to consult with New York's hydraulic engineers.

Loyalty to the Board and pride in its projects run very

high, particularly among the older men, many of whom have made life-long careers with the Board. Partly because the gestation of each project—a tunnel, a network of pipes, a reservoir—is so long, the engineers often develop an odd sense of personal identification with their work products. Chief Engineer Vincent Terenzio, in dating his tenure with the Board, says, with affection, "I came here in 1937, after graduating from City College. City Tunnel #2 was just a hole in the ground then."

Continuity and tradition also characterize the executive leadership of the Board. Edward C. Maguire, executive director of the Board, has worked in some capacity for every New York City Mayor since La Guardia. Appointed to the Board in 1951, he was president from 1965 to 1969. The current president, Herbert M. Rosenberg, first became a Commissioner in 1953.

The Commissionerships are usually patronage appointments. Rosenberg was appointed on the last day of Vincent Impelliteri's mayoral term. Robert F. Wagner chose to pay an old debt by filling a vacancy on the Board just three days before leaving office in 1965. And John Lindsay later appointed the national coordinator of his abortive 1972 Presidential campaign as a Commissioner. Because these men are generally lawyers or businessmen who know very little about water supply problems, they rely heavily on the technical expertise of the engineering staff to make policy judgments on the Board's projects.

The Board's engineers attribute the agency's success to its adherence to what they call, "conservative engineering principles." This means choosing construction methods that maximize reliability rather than economy. It also generally means using only technologies that have been proved through use in other projects, though perhaps not on such a large scale. Maurice Feldman, Commissioner of Water Resources from 1968 to 1971, says, "To call engineers conservative is not pejorative. It means that you don't fool around with something that might fail in a few years." Because of this concern, and because major engineering projects take so long to plan and build, conservative engineers often work with projections of demand fifty years into the future.

Both the justification for a new tunnel and its proposed design reflect the conservative orientation of the Board's engineers. The Board's 1966 report to the Board of Estimate indicated that Tunnel #3 would answer two needs—greater system reliability and increased water supply distribution to meet increased future demand. Tunnels #1 and #2 had never been shut down for complete inspection, and increasingly frequent repairs of the riser shafts of Tunnel #1 indicated that this might soon be necessary. The Commissioners noted that neither of the giant tunnels could be shut down for long without cutting sharply into the amount of water needed by the City's residents. In addition, the Board projected New York's population at about ten million by the end of the century and predicted that per capita water consumption would rise sharply as technology developed and incomes rose. Even if the population projection was wrong, the Board maintained that locational shifts of the present population would soon tax the water distribution system in outlying parts of Queens and Staten Island.

The details of the project plan also revealed the Board's professional caution. The tunnel was to be hewn out of deep rock, rather than constructed of pipes closer to the surface. This would protect it from jolts and cuts in the ground above and would maintain peak pressure for the water running through it. Its estimated growth also reflected the engineers' population projections. Whereas Tunnel #1 has a diameter from 11 feet to 15 feet, and Tunnel #2 from 15 to 17 feet, Tunnel #3 was planned for a diameter of 20 feet to 27 feet. And the proposal relied on the force of gravity to move water through the tunnel rather than on electrical pumps, which might not be reliable in a massive power failure. Board engineers reasoned that they should choose the system with the fewest moving parts, which would be easiest to maintain and most trouble-free.

Not everyone is sympathetic with this tendency to provide for maximum demand and guard against extreme disaster. Some City officials, including engineers who rarely differ publicly with other members of the profession, feel that the Board overlooks modern technological advances. They also feel that institutional self-interest may have as much to do with some of the Board's choices as a sound professional concern about security or adequacy. One critic maintains that the Board generally chooses construction techniques which, although they may entail the fewest risks, are always the most expensive and tend to require expansion of the Board's staff. Another alleges that the Board relies on extreme examples of disaster to bolster its arguments; he cites the Board's insistence on deep rock for the new Richmond tunnel when what he considers to be the best evidence indicated that a pipeline would have done the job much less expensively. The Board, in that situation, buttressed its position by showing the Mayor (then Robert Wagner) pictures of an anchor that had snagged a similar pipeline, and its argument won the day. A young City engineer from another agency, disenchanted with the Board's insistence on maximum security, says, "Those guys probably wear both suspenders and a belt."

Differences of opinion on the validity of the Board's project standards for City Tunnel #3 reflect rather clearly the differences in function of the agencies represented on the Mayor's Panel. The Board and the Department, operating agencies with engineers in most of the positions of power, were predominantly concerned with construction and maintenance problems. The Budget Bureau and the City Planning Commission, central offices of planning and review where the top officials were likely to be close to the Mayor, emphasized costs and the appropriate analytic techniques of project design. The Office of Administration, responsible for facilitating interagency coordination, limited itself at this stage to formulating areas of agreement and trying to get the other parties to reconcile their differences. The Health Services Administrator, concerned primarily with the quality and adequacy of the water when it reached City residents, was not a major figure in the dispute.

The history of relations among the various agencies also contributed to their differences of perspective. Lewis Schulman, the engineer who directed CPC's capital budget division, had dealt with the Board for twenty years and had come to feel that, as a general matter, its planning was undertaken with too much concern for system security and too little for project cost. He had opposed the new Richmond (Staten Island) tunnel for that reason. He had also helped to shelve a proposal for a bypass of the Rondout Reservoir. The Rondout bypass would have provided a backup link from the Delaware watershed to the City distribution network, to be used in the event that sabotage or natural disaster made the main link unusable. Now Schulman was certain that capital costs could be lowered if the Board would seek alternatives to a gravity flow tunnel, and he thought it had that responsibility. Harman Goldstone, the CPC Commissioner in charge of budget requests from the Board, had also acquired a skepticism about the Board's planning methods. He felt that in general the training and concerns of the Board engineers were too technically narrow to allow them to dominate policy decisions, particularly when they would have responsibility for implementing the outcome. He, too, had opposed the Rondout bypass. Both he and Schulman thought the Board had little basis on which to project substantial population increases. The CPC had its own figures which suggested that New York's population would actually drop by the year 2000.

Fred Hayes at the Budget Bureau had had no prior experience with the Board to make him doubt its judgment. He maintains that at the beginning of the dispute, "I was just being a good budget examiner, asking them to give us a better budget justification," but there were certainly other elements involved as well. Hayes was eager to apply a more systematic kind of analysis to budget problems than had been customary in the past. He thought the tunnel looked like an area where the alternatives to meet both the maintenance and distribution needs could be presented in easily quantifiable terms. He had explicit intentions of developing within his agency the capacity for the kind of cost-effectiveness study the Board had not done, but he had not yet had time to develop a staff to do it. He wanted to improve the Budget Bureau's analytical staff work so that on any given project the Mayor would be able to select from a number of options. He felt strongly that the Mayor's policy decisions should not be made on the basis of the skill in advocacy of technicians in the operating agencies. Judgment must rest on something rational, a balancing of interests whose dimensions were known. Hayes asks:

> Why do the experts say it must be done? When it gets to the point where they can only say "professional judgment" is the reason for doing something, someone has to step in. A project must be explainable to the intelligent layman. The professional must be able to communicate.

To him, then, the procedure of policy analysis was as important in this case as the substance of the policy.

The Budget Director's reservations did not convey themselves to the Board as real opposition to the tunnel. Hayes had said that he wanted to see comparative costs of alternative approaches to the one espoused in the current proposal. But he had also stated in writing that "this office is in complete agreement that this project should proceed with all dispatch." Since the Board had not really expected to get immediate approval of such an immense project, it accepted the delay necessary to get a report from an independent consultant, as promised in the Panel's letter to Lindsay. The Board at this point considered that its only real opponent was the City Planning Commission.

III

Neither the Budget Bureau nor the City Planning Commission made any attempt to influence the Board's choice of consultant. Hayes did not think of the project as urgent, and he was waiting to turn over most capital budget matters to his newly appointed deputy, David Grossman, who was to arrive in New York in December. A new CPC Chairman was taking over, too, and no one knew whether he would consider the tunnel to be a priority concern. Perhaps most important, neither agency had the right kind of staff person to work easily with the Board. Both agencies were divided between professional engineers, technicians who would be likely to make the same kind of consultant choice the Board would make, and program planners, generalists who were not qualified to judge the kind of consultant the Board would find acceptable.

The Board chose a large, well-known firm, the Parsons-Jurden Corporation, which had considerable experience in water supply projects. The firm had never worked under contract to the Board, though some members of the two organizations were acquainted. They attended the same conferences, read the same journals, and generally spoke each other's language. During January 1967 Board President Maguire determined that the firm was acceptable to the other members of the Mayor's Panel, and Parsons-Jurden engineers began work in the early spring.

Work on the tunnel did not come to a halt because of the requirement of consultant review. The fact that the Board of Estimate was not yet ready to approve the project plan did not mean that design funds could not be appropriated independently. Although the City Planning Council was unwilling to include the Board's request of $7 million of planning money in the 1967–68 capital budget, the Budget Bureau recommended the appropriation of $2.5 million, and the City and Council and Board of Estimate approved that amount.

During 1967, while Parsons-Jurden developed its reports

and the Board continued design studies for Tunnel #3, significant changes took place in the character and objectives of the Budget Bureau which were bound to sharpen its differences with the Board. David Grossman arrived to assist Hayes, and immediately took over responsibility for the tunnel project. As an architect and city planner, Grossman was particularly interested in physical planning problems. As a veteran of several government jobs, most recently working in the federal poverty program, he was convinced that a systems approach to policy analysis was the only way to evaluate all the possible programs that might meet a city's needs. He agreed with Hayes that the Budget Bureau ought to force the Board of Water Supply to assess quite explicitly the costs and benefits of each possible solution to the water problems it dealt with. Traditionally, new project proposals thrived or foundered because the proposing agency was skillful or awkward at promoting them, or because the policy-maker had general opinions, arrived at before the proposal was presented, as to whether the project was or was not a good idea. As one CPC staff member puts it:

> The operating agencies present a single concept, with no alternative, a take-it-or-leave-it issue. Then they push like hell for the project. The pressure comes because you [the planning agency or the policy-maker] are faced with a project you can't afford not to have. It was the issue itself, specially during the 1960's when there was a water crisis. Is the Mayor going to put off action on a water issue?

Hayes and Grossman hoped to inject into the capital planning process new methods that would enable the Mayor to make more informed and rational judgments than was possible when he was presented with only one option.

Of course, Grossman disagreed substantively with some of the Board's assumptions. From his reading, and from previous experience working as a city planner in New

England towns where sharp population decreases were the rule, he regarded the Board's estimates of population growth as "ridiculous." Skeptical about the possibility of ever achieving absolute security, Grossman was not willing to assume that the City should pay for whatever maximum could be attained. At any rate, he wished to see the comparative costs of several degrees of security. He knew that a deep rock tunnel would be more reliable than one powered by pumping, but how much more? At what added cost?

Grossman and Hayes had decided very early that they needed to develop a special staff in the Budget Bureau that could conduct cost-benefit analysis in many policy areas. Though the Budget Bureau engineers questioned the costs of the tunnel and some of the assumptions behind its design, they did so without challenging the Board's overall analytic approach. Hayes and Grossman knew they needed another kind of analyst to work on this problem—a person whose age and education would encourage him to fit the engineering and planning questions together into a context larger than one professional discipline could provide. So they asked members of the Budget Bureau's embryonic Program Planning staff to follow the development of the tunnel project.

But just as the Budget Bureau and CPC had not taken part in selecting consultants to review the Board proposal, so they did not participate actively in directing Parsons-Jurden's work during 1967. The consultants acquired all their information from the Board and the Department. They conformed to traditional engineering standards in their analysis and were never challenged in that practice by officials of the planning agencies.

During the summer and fall, Parsons-Jurden issued preliminary reports, and in November each agency on the Mayor's Panel received the consultant's "Final Evaluation." It validated the Board's estimates of future water demand, stressed the necessity for a water distribution facility that would allow complete preventive maintenance of the other tunnels, and found the proposed tunnel costs to be reasonable. On only one issue did Parsons-Jurden differ from the Board: the report suggested serious consideration of a narrower tunnel. This alternative would normally be powered by gravity, but water would be pumped through it at a higher velocity during periods of peak demand. The report did not emphasize the questions which Budget and CPC officials had asked. It did not assess the probabilities of various combinations of per capita consumption and population growth, nor did it analyze the sensitivity of tunnel costs to design changes which might result from new demand estimates.

Grossman did not think much of the reports. He thought Parsons-Jurden had not followed modes of analysis that would have facilitated and improved the policy decisions that had to be made about the tunnel. He wrote in a memo to colleagues at the Budget Bureau: ". . . my reading of the Parsons-Jurden reports leaves me—and most of the other people who've read them outside [the Department] and the Board of Water Supply—with reather queasy feelings." He began to think of other consultant groups who might do the analysis he found lacking in Parsons-Jurden's work. Nothing in the consultant reports had shaken Grossman's view that "considerable savings in construction and/or operating cost appear feasible if lower levels of security can be lived with—as I suspect they can."

Grossman also suggested that the Parsons-Jurden reports were somewhat "biased." By this he meant not only that the consultant might have been less than objective because it had relied so heavily on the Board as the source of much of its information about the City's water distribution system. He also, by implication, referred to the general influence the Board must inevitably have had on Parsons-Jurden even before the contract was let. The Board's fine reputation, as well as the twelve years of planning and study, had surely lent weight to the initial proposal.

CPC staff were also dissatisfied with the "Final Evaluation." Their objections paralleled closely those of Grossman and Hayes, and in addition they disputed the timing

of Stages One and Five as the Board planned it. The new
CPC Chairman, Donald Elliott, had accepted the views of
Schulman and Goldstone, as they briefed him on the tunnel proposal. The CPC was now prepared to recommend
only $2.5 million for design funds in the 1968–69 capital
budget, slightly more than half of the Board request.

The concerns of the planning agencies were not, of
course, shared by the Board. Its President, Edward Maguire, felt that the Mayor's Panel now had the clear responsibility to recommend to the Board of Estimate approval of
the tunnel plan. Parsons-Jurden had certainly vindicated
the design choices the Board had made, and further questions about methods and probabilities seemed frivolous and
arbitrary. The Board had fulfilled its obligations to have
the proposal reviewed by an independent group, and now
these nonexperts were insisting on something more.

And they did insist. At the meeting of the Mayor's Panel
convened to discuss the proposal's review with Parsons-
Jurden staff, Grossman and Schulman pressed their points
until the Office of Administration representative, trying to
mediate between the polarized agencies, suggested that
Parsons-Jurden might do an addendum to the report that
would provide more detailed cost analyses of the alternatives to a gravity tunnel. While this addition was being
prepared, capital funds would be made available for final
design work, so that delay would be minimal. Although the
agencies adopted this compromise, the superficial consensus only covered over a growing mutual resentment and
disdain.

IV

The tunnel dispute was based on many layers of difference.
First was the substantive issue of how City Tunnel #3
should be built. Making that difficult to resolve was the
conflict over what kind of analysis should shape policy.
Even more fundamental were some powerful and interact-

ing forces—both insitutional and personal—which diminished the likelihood that the disputants could ever agree on either the design of the tunnel or ways of arriving at an appropriate design.

By early 1968 the Budget Bureau had hired a number of bright young program planners who were intended to provide (or oversee) for many agencies the kind of analysis Hayes and Grossman had hoped to get from an outside consultant in the tunnel case. They tended to be generalists —lawyers or city planners—and even where they had special areas of expertise, they were generally interested in subordinating them to a broader concern with a systems approach to policy questions. These young staffers were often fresh from Ivy league graduate schools. They held only provisional civil service appointments, and they did not usually assume they would make a career of New York City government. They were eager to try to change the way the City operated, and the Budget Bureau promised an atmosphere conducive to that aim. If and when the atmosphere changed, in their agency or in City government in general, they would leave.

This spirit contrasted sharply with that of more settled operating agencies like the Board of Water Supply and the Department of Water Supply, Gas and Electricity. There the senior staff emphasized the acquisition of sophisticated technical skills, and professionalism was defined in terms of ability to perform highly specialized tasks. The engineers' mandate was maintenance of quality, rather than change. Civil service gave their jobs permanence and security, which they valued.

Not surprisingly, the two kinds of staff do not always appreciate each other's merits. While they often express recognition of each other's abilities in general terms, the particular observations they make of one another reveal important gaps in sympathy and understanding. Former Department Commissioner Maurice Feldman has said of Steve Disman, a young Budget planner assigned to water supply problems because of his background in engineering,

"He's a very bright kid, but what kind of help can he give us if he never took the basic course in water supply at his engineering school?" To which Disman's reply is, "Why should I take such a course? That's the sort of thing you can look up."

The mutual suspicion was certainly heightened by disparities of personal style. Take David Grossman, Deputy Budget Director at the time of the tunnel dispute, and Vincent Terenzio, the Board's Chief Engineer. Terenzio is thin and straight, rather formal and precise in both dress and vocabulary. Grossman is compact and vigorous, with a talent for choosing pithy phrases and moderately colorful ties. Where Terenzio is guarded and cautious, Grossman can be arrogant and expansive. Terenzio values the loyalty, consistency, and dedication of his engineers; Grossman is most interested in the young program planners who show imagination, confidence, and a dash of irreverence.

The institutional stakes of the principals varied as much as their professional standards and styles. Hayes and Grossman had been hired as innovators, and their success was to be measured at least partly according to their use of modern management methods which improved the products of City government. They were expected to shake things up a bit, so they did not fear its consequences. They answered only to the Mayor and had no larger constituency to satisfy. Their positions gave them much greater freedom than most City employees, even those at the Commissioner level.

Board officials were in a very different position. The faultless operation of earlier Board-constructed water facilities had shaped their success, and they hoped it would continue to do so. Their mandate was reliability, not change; safety, not improvement. They were not close to, nor protected by, the Mayor. (Board President Maguire did not even meet Lindsay until 1968, more than two years after he had become Mayor.) Those who understood and evaluated the Board's performance were members of the engineering profession outside the agency, friends at the Department, and the water supply bureaucrats with whom the Board staff often worked in Albany.

To Hayes and Grossman, the Board's insistence on the necessity of an expensive, deep-rock gravity tunnel seemed like "hot, sweaty-palmed lust," as Hayes once put it. As the conflict developed between the planning and budget agencies, on the one hand, and the Board and Department, on the other, Budget Bureau and CPC staff members began to wonder if the Board had overdesigned the tunnel in bureaucratic self-justification. They suspected that protection of the City's water supply might be less immediately important than maintaining the agency's annual expenditure and employee levels.

The Board could not help but have a strong vested interest in the proposal it had developed. For one thing, the third City water tunnel would soon be the Board's only big job. By 1967 the two major projects it had been working on for many years—the Richmond tunnel and the last stage of the Delaware supply system—were complete. The Rondout bypass proposal had been at least temporarily shelved. The state had primary responsibility for the development of future watershed areas upstate, outside of the Board's operating authority. And the very nature of the Board was changing. It appeared that the Board's traditional autonomy would soon be curtailed by its proposed absorption into Lindsay's new superagency, the Environmental Protection Administration.

In early 1968 Maguire began to think that extraordinary measures were necessary to get the tunnel moving. He let it be known that if the Budget Bureau and CPC delayed much longer, he would write a public letter to the Board of Estimate setting forth as strongly as possible the Board of Water Supply's view that the tunnel project must proceed immediately if the public's water was to be safeguarded. At least partly in response to this veiled threat, Grossman restored to the 1968–69 capital budget the $2 million in design funds deleted by the CPC. Although he intended to proceed with an independent systems analysis of the project and hoped it would provide usable alternatives to the Board's plan, Grossman felt he had to allow design work to continue. The Mayor could not then be accused of delaying on a matter as vital to public health and safety as water. But Grossman balked at Maguire's proposal that the Board of Estimate be requested to pass a resolution that would approve the Board plan but leave open the size of the tunnel diameter. More was at issue than just the width of a hole.

A number of consultant groups had by now submitted applications to the Budget Bureau for a systems analysis of the water problem. In March, Grossman sent Maguire copies of the proposals for comment, indicating that he favored the paper sent by the Hudson Institute, an organization performing policy analyses on such disparate problems as nuclear deterrents and heroin addiction. Maguire replied that all the proposals seemed to suggest a duplication of work already done by Parsons-Jurden and that most were deficient in understanding basic problems of tunnel design. At the end of the month Grossman wrote to Maguire defending the proposals and reasserting the Budget Bureau's interest (with CPC concurrence) in retaining the Hudson Institute. He also reported that the Corporation Counsel had advised him that the Board of Estimate could not legally pass a resolution adopting the "plan and profile" but leaving the tunnel diameter unspecified.

The various bureaucratic players did not align themselves in this stalemate as unambiguously as one might have expected. Agency loyalties were not the sole determinant of the various positions in the tunnel dispute. The division between engineer-types and planner-types which defined the relationship between the Board and the Department, on the one hand, and the Budget Bureau and CPC, on the other, also existed, to a lesser degree, within each of the latter agencies. Although it had been the Budget Bureau's engineers who had initially expressed doubts to Hayes about the proposal, they focused on cost-cutting questions—the diameter of the tunnel and the timing of the stages. Because Hayes and Grossman viewed the principal issues as resource allocation questions, they came to rely more on the program planners to work on the tunnel. At the CPC much of the work was also assigned to the young planners, for the same kinds of reasons.

This arrangement had some practical disadvantages with respect to promoting a proposal counter to the Board's. The young BOB and CPC planners were closer to their agency heads than the older engineers, and they worked on the issue as their chiefs worked. They made it a high priority item when their bosses were concerned about it and slacked off when they were not. The trouble was that the top officials at the Budget Bureau and the CPC never gave the tunnel the attention it received from the Board and the Department. They had too many other projects to evaluate. For Grossman, at the Budget Bureau, the tunnel did not seem of first importance because it was outside the debt limit, and therefore did not compete with other expenditures. And CPC Chairman Elliott frankly admits he never completely understood the technical issues that dominated the tunnel controversy. Without presenting a practical alternative, how could he effectively oppose what the Board wanted to do?

Elliott also hesitated to resist the Board aggressively for another reason. A new actor had entered the drama—Merril Eisenbud, head of Lindsay's new superagency, the Environmental Protection Administration. Elliott respected Eisenbud's need to orient himself on the stage.

John Lindsay's goal of making urban government work better centered partly on the notion that loose, functional federations of agencies might comprehend the interrelation of many City problems and deal with them in a more unified way than the sixty-odd separate bureaucracies of the Wagner era. To that end, he had combined the Bureau of Water Supply (part of the old Department of Water Supply, Gas and Electricity), the Sanitation Department, the Bureau of Water Pollution Control (part of the Municipal Services Administration), and the Department of Air

Resources into the new Environmental Protection Administration (EPA). This superagency would be overseen by an Administrator who would take charge of policy and program planning for all programs affecting New York's physical ecology. In early 1968 this superagency was born, not without agonizing labor pains. Its intended Administrator, the former Department Commissioner James Marcus, was indicted in December 1967 for receiving kickbacks, two weeks after he had resigned from his City job. Eisenbud, formerly Director of Environmental Studies of the New York University Medical School's Institute of Environmental Medicine, replaced Marcus in March 1968. At that time, no system of priorities had been set for the Administration's member agencies, and no structure supported the administrative umbrella that EPA was intended to provide.

One of Eisenbud's first problems was how to integrate the Board into EPA; another was how to deal with the Board's frustration over the tunnel issue. Perhaps he thought he could further the former by helping with the latter. In any case, he reviewed the proposal and the Parsons-Jurden report and decided that the Board's complaints were justified. As a trained engineer, he felt he could assess the issues—and the Board's ability to handle them—better than the planners at the Budget Bureau. The Board had "a fine track record," whereas Hayes and Grossman had never built anything. He determined that this issue must hold the highest priority for him in his new job; people could go without clean air or clean streets far longer than they could without adequate water, he reasoned. He also saw in the tunnel problem a chance to ascertain whether his program responsibilities as EPA Administrator were actually matched by the authority to carry them out.

Eisenbud immediately assumed a dominant position in the controversy. He increased the Board's access to City Hall by getting Maguire included in the Mayor's cabinet. As Administrator of City agencies dealing with environmental problems, he had coordination functions that seemed to supersede the responsibilities the Office of Administration had exercised for the Mayor's Panel. So in early April Eisenbud called together the agencies involved in the tunnel dispute to try to get the project moving.

Not surprisingly, this meeting was no more successful than previous gatherings of the now-inactive Mayor's Panel in arriving at the consensus. Supposedly the Budget Bureau and the Board agreed to work together in drafting a resolution for the Board of Estimate that would authorize design work on the tunnel without finally endorsing the "plan and profile." But Grossman seems quite deliberately to have avoided that task, fearing that once a resolution had passed, the Board's proposal would have gathered momentum difficult to overcome with a later plan. Eisenbud appeared at the meeting to find the Hudson Institute acceptable to do a systems analysis, as long as it was limited to examining the social and demographic considerations relevant in projecting New York City's water demand. But in later, private conversations and memos he opposed the choice so strongly, maintaining that the Hudson Institute was simply not qualified to do the job, that Grossman finally backed down. Grossman reasoned that work done by the Hudson Institute, no matter how competent, would have no chance of getting EPA support.

Eisenbud did not need to rely entirely on his own persuasive powers to apply pressure on the Budget Bureau and the CPC. In May the awaited Parsons-Jurden addendum came out, concluding that its original speculations about the possible advantages of a pumping/gravity tunnel had not been borne out by further study and generally reinforcing the Board's conclusions. In addition, the Mayor's Science and Technology Advisory Council, a panel of eminent university and industry scientists, had reviewed the Board proposal at Eisenbud's behest and with his participation. In June it submitted a report to Mayor Lindsay, recommending strongly that a tunnel be built without further delay. Furthermore, it criticized the Budget Bureau and CPC as having exceeded their authority:

Budget reviews will not, and in the opinion of the Council, should not, place technical and direct management responsibility and authority for the project in the Bureau of the Budget and Department of City Planning. The Council believes that such responsibility and authority should remain with the Board of Water Supply and the related technical agencies.

With the Council report and the Parsons-Jurden addendum to buttress his concern, Eisenbud went to the Mayor to urge him to help expedite the tunnel so that it could not become an issue in the following year's mayoralty election. Lindsay agreed to a July briefing on the tunnel and several other EPA issues.

By now fourteen years had passed since the first field studies for the tunnel had begun. It was almost two years since the "plan and profile" had been submitted for approval to the Board of Estimate. Yet, no public attention had focused on the project. As one CPC staffer remarked, "There was more fuss about police stables in Central Park than about a billion-dollar tunnel." If Maguire had carried out his threat and made public complaints to the Board of Estimate, a Councilman or two might have picked up the issue and made the Lindsay administration look obstructionist. But even that wasn't very likely. The planning money allocated in the capital budget did not draw attention to the tunnel; no holes in the street announced its coming. Basically, the issues were too complex, too technical. Only engineers were likely to understand, and they do not generally constitute a vociferous public where local issues are concerned. At the later public hearing on the tunnel—held as a routine matter on all capital projects—the only opposition testimony came from a citizen who mistakenly thought its construction would disrupt a park.

Past experience, however, did not necessarily dictate future events. Projects that would normally go unnoticed might make great political capital in an election year. To be sure, the tunnel issue was not easy to encapsulate in a headline. As CPC Chairman Elliott explains it:

It was such an incredibly complex issue. For the papers to pick it up, they would have to run headlines
like "CPC Endangers Safety of City Water Supply."
Before they could print something like that they
would have to come to us and we would give them the
issues. They would find out that it was complicated.
Then they wouldn't print it with that headline. No
paper is really going to believe that the CPC would
subject the city to risk of disaster.

But suppose there was a drought, and it became known that
the administration had stalled on building a new tunnel?
Few people were able immediately to distinguish between
water *supply* and water *distribution*. Or what if Tunnel #1
should break down when City agencies were still squab-
bling over how to build Tunnel #3? The issue suddenly
appeared to City Hall strategists to be potentially explosive.

Although Eisenbud conducted it, the Mayor's briefing
turned out to advance the positions of the Budget Bureau
and the CPC. The Board presented its proposal and the
assumptions behind it, and Grossman immediately challenged the presentation. (Observers in attendance at the
meeting, according to their predispositions, describe
Grossman's behavior as either "heckling" or "asking
pointed questions.") Mayor Lindsay was troubled at such
high population projections, reportedly turning impa-
tiently to a CPC staffer and demanding, "This goes against
all the figures you guys have been giving me since 1966.
Who is right?" Grossman and Maguire argued about
whether the Board could legally spend design funds already appropriated in the capital budget but not yet expended because the Board thought it would be illegal to do
so without overall project approval by the Board of Estimate. Grossman appeared to have persuaded the Mayor
that the Board should authorize only further design work,
reserving approval of the "plan and profile" until after
further analysis had been done by an outside consultant.

Lindsay asked the Budget Bureau and EPA to prepare summaries of all the issues for discussion at a September meeting of his Policy Planning Council (PPC). This committee included the Mayor, Deputy Mayor, City Administrator, Budget Director, and CPC Chairman and served as the Mayor's closest advisors on controversial policy matters. The Mayor and his staff were pushing for a speedy resolution of the conflict, but without taking a stand yet themselves.

During the summer the disputants prepared the documents for the PPC meeting. The Budget Bureau turned to the Urban Systems Laboratory at the Massachusetts Institute of Technology, hoping that Eisenbud would find it a more acceptable consultant than the Hudson Institute. MIT's credentials in general were impeccable, but a problem still existed with the Urban Systems Lab. It excelled less in the areas of social and demographic analysis that had been agreed upon as the scope of a new consultant study than in the analysis of engineering issues that would influence tunnel design. A contract between MIT and Budget would surely cover areas of the Board's greatest expertise. Eisenbud objected to MIT's proposal, saying that the suggested computer analysis of the City's water distribution impinged on the Board's jurisdiction and accusing Grossman of allowing MIT to plan work agreed upon as the Board's responsibility. For his part, Grossman refused to approve EPA's draft of a resolution to the Board of Estimate. He felt the language granted a degree of authority to the Board that would make any later design changes impossible to impose.

The memos for the PPC meeting, prepared in the form of letters addressed to the Mayor, did more to record the mutual scorn of the disputants than to add anything new to the controversy. Hayes's letter, drafted by Grossman and Steve Disman, the young program planner who was doing most of the Budget Bureau staff work, concluded that "Parsons-Jurden, however competent they might be as design engineers, were either not interested or not competent in these areas [where analysis had been requested]." It added that the Budget Bureau had been frustrated for four months in its attempts to get agreement on the scope for another consultant study and the group to do it. Eisenbud's responding letter stated firmly that both Parsons-Jurden evaluations had supported the Board's plans, and equally firmly asserted that the problems raised in Hayes's letter could best be handled by the Board, not by another outside consultant. Eisenbud's deputy, Matthias Spiegel, who had formerly worked on the tunnel issue in his post at the Office of Administration, added his own views to Eisenbud's. In a memo he stated that Hayes's letter "continues to obfuscate the decisions that must be made with respect to the Third City Tunnel," and went on to suggest that the agencies' struggle had ramifications that went far beyond the project at issue:

> One may ask . . . why has there been almost two years of wrangling and no movement with respect to the first stage of the tunnel. The answer is who shall control the project—the operating agencies trusted with responsibility or the staff agencies who do not have operating responsibility. This is a battle which has been fought in the City for many, many years. It has frustrated and delayed the decision-making process. It is larger than this specific project and illuminates the necessity for a revamping of procedures and controlling interrelationships between BOB, City Planning Commission, and operating agencies.

Spiegel also wondered "whether the reason for [the Budget Bureau's] conclusion that Parsons-Jurden is not competent stems from the fact that its report fully supports the conclusions of the operating agency."

Once again a meeting that was to have determined the parties' future behavior led to confusion and antagonism. Though both Eisenbud and Grossman thought they had gained significant victories, they came away with very different notions of what they had won. And the Mayor's assistants who were present remembered a still different outcome of the PPC meeting. No stenotypist recorded the event, and not everyone involved was present for the entire meeting. What is clear is that Grossman and Eisenbud clashed openly on the questions of what level of approval should be requested of the Board of Estimate and whether further consultant evaluation was needed. City Hall representatives intervened and suggested a compromise, which was apparently accepted. The Budget Bureau was to recommend Board of Estimate approval for final design plans, with the understanding that those plans would be subject to later PPC review. In exchange, EPA and the Board were to cooperate fully with the MIT study. Eisenbud saw no problems with this result because the Board had maintained all along that a final figure for the tunnel's diameter could evolve only from final design studies. Grossman, too, was pleased because he assumed the MIT study would lead to a full-scale policy review before final approval for the project was given.

The PPC meeting probably shifted City Hall's view of the problem somewhat. The Mayor had initially been sympathetic with the concerns of CPC and Budget Bureau officials. They were, after all, his appointees, whom he trusted and regarded as smart, modern administrators. The Board, by contrast, was an annoyingly independent entity which had presented him with an immensely expensive project, more or less as a *fait accompli.* But he was beginning to lose patience. He had given Budget two years to come up with convincing evidence that the project should be delayed or altered; so far he had not seen that evidence. As one assistant states:

The Mayor's attitude toward the tunnel was that this was an area where the choices ought to be quantifiable. He felt he was getting only mushy stuff from the Board and other agencies. He said, in effect, you do the technical work, and I'll make the decision.

By late 1968 the Mayor and his staff opposed any further delay of the project. But, just in case the MIT study turned up important new information, they felt the PPC compromise left them the option to reconsider the Board's plan.

On October 18, 1968, after some further argument between Eisenbud and Grossman about whether the Board of Estimate should reserve the right of final design approval for a later date, a resolution was passed by that body. It approved and adopted "the said report, map and plan, and profile submitted by the Board of Water Supply on July 19, 1966" for the first stage of City Tunnel #3. It was understood that design work would be done out of the $7 million appropriated in the 1967–68 and 1968–69 capital budgets.

V

Looking toward a PPC review of the final design, Grossman was still hopeful that the MIT analysis would present cogent reasons for scaling down the size of the tunnel. With this in mind, he and Steve Disman worked out a study plan for MIT which covered a much broader range of questions than those of population and demand which the Budget Bureau had originally wanted answers to. The research team was to examine

> different means of improving the existing primary water supply system, evaluate the merit of alternative schemes under a range of future demands, and rank these possibilities according to relevant figures of merit.

Board and EPA officials bridled at what they felt was both a deceptive expansion of the agreed-upon scope for the MIT study and an infringement of the Board's areas of expertise. Eisenbud asked Maurice Feldman, who, though only recently appointed as Department Commissioner, had been a City engineer of excellent reputation for many years, to evaluate the MIT work program. Feldman reported of the proposed study:

> It is understood that the Board of Water Supply has planned all along to make this type of computerized study preparatory to sizing the tunnel diameters. This proposal also indicates that judgment will be the main element in selecting tunnel diameters from capacities and costs. Judgment is best exercised by those with the greatest experience and with the responsibility for performance following construction.

Differences over what MIT was to do did not hold up design work. While Budget officials were negotiating the contract with MIT, the Board hired the engineering firm of Charles T. Main to help it complete the tunnel design as quickly as possible. Speed had become more and more imperative to the Board. Inflation clearly affected construction costs—the Board estimated the escalation at a rate of $3 million per month, though Grossman called that "nonsense." Equally important was a provision in the 1969–70 capital budget, arrived at after more dispute between the Board and CPC. If the final design were completed before the end of the fiscal year, the budget, which provided for only about $3 million of design money, would be amended to grant almost $250 million of additional funds for construction. And once that step had been taken, there was no turning back. Not even the Board of Estimate could then delay or modify stage one of the tunnel.

That assurance did not mean total confidence at the Board. The MIT report might still sway the PPC, and if that happened, the Budget Bureau was not likely to recommend full funding for the tunnel. Tensions between the Board and the MIT people mounted. Each group tried to limit access to information the other requested. Board officials construed the MIT contract to provide that the consultant could evaluate the Board's work, which angered them. MIT hastily responded by denying such an intent and saying that it would, in fact, be contrary to professional ethics. Communication did not, however, improve.

By June, when MIT's interim report came out, all the City actors knew that it would at least partially bear out the Budget Bureau's contentions. As a City Hall assistant put it in a memo to the Mayor: "The report takes issue with the Board of Water Supply's Third Tunnel proposal essentially on the same grounds that the Bureau of the Budget has been pressing." It predicted steady or decreasing population and only a slight increase in consumption. MIT recommended a narrower tunnel with the water flow powered by a combination of pumping and gravity.

Initial reactions to the MIT report were expectable. Hayes wrote in a memo to Grossman, "Generally, I feel that MIT has made my 1966 objections respectable." And Grossman reported to CPC Chairman Elliott that the MIT paper was

> a first-rate job of technical analysis that suggests what many of us have long felt is the case: that there are options that would meet either the supply or reliability requirements of the City's water distribution rather less expensively than the Board of Water Supply.

But Eisenbud, Feldman, and Maguire were, as the City Hall observer noted, "very unhappy" about the report.

> They feel that it is inconclusive, that it presents no truly workable alternative, that it misconceives the Board's plan, and relies upon irrelevant and incomplete information.

Next came preparation of the report into a form that could be presented to the PPC. For this purpose Hayes and Eisenbud called upon two men who seemed particularly skilled at interpreting the technicians and the generalists to each other. Carter Bales, an Assistant Budget Director (unpaid), was also a promising young partner at the prestigious management consulting firm of McKinsey and Company. A Harvard Business School product, he had long experience and considerable talent at reducing complex issues to simple, graphic presentations. Maurice Feldman had known many of the disputants for many years and understood both the City's water distribution system and the bureaucracies that operated it.

As Bales, Feldman, and some of the more active parties examined the report carefully, they grew more and more uncertain of its value. The Board contended generally that it was "trivial" and "prepared by professors who have never tested their theories," while Eisenbud called it "without merit." Even Budget Bureau and CPC staff conceded that it was "too academic," that it had "a snotty tone" and "no good grasp of the social and demographic factors." More specifically, City engineers alleged that construction cost estimates had been based on equations from a project undertaken in California not applicable to conditions in New York. MIT also projected water consumption figures based on data collected at the end of a period of drought when City water engineers say demand was abnormally low. And—perhaps the feature that drew the most scorn—MIT suggested a tunnel route that was geologically unsound. ("They wanted the tunnel to go along a fault!" said one engineer in astonishment.) Grossman and Hayes felt some of these errors were matters of detail that did not nullify the basic points of the document, but they had to admit that a coherent presentation of alternatives to the Board proposal, based on the MIT report, seemed difficult at this late date.

A small flurry of new information and analysis complicated the final resolution of the issue. A young CPC planner infuriated the Board and EPA by presenting the outline of a two-year maintenance study that would examine ways of rehabilitating Tunnels #1 and #2 so that a third tunnel would not have to be built. The proposed solutions seemed farfetched—they included making re-

pairs from a submarine and sealing off sections of the tunnel with inflatable materials—and they reopened the question of whether there should be a tunnel at all. In the face
of what the Board and the Department considered to be
firm commitments to move without further delay, the in-
troduction of the maintenance study seemed outrageous.

From July to September Carter Bales worked hard on
pulling together and analyzing the opposing recommendations of the Board and MIT. He prepared a simple, graphic
issue paper to present to the PPC. He met regularly with
Maurice Feldman, and together they narrowed the issues
to the question of whether to build a 15-foot pumped tunnel
or a 20- to 24-foot gravity tunnel. Bales reported that he
found "major gaps in information and understanding" in
his discussions with Feldman and the Board. Nonetheless,
Feldman ultimately agreed that if the Charles T. Main cost
figures showed a pumping tunnel to be much less expensive
than a gravity tunnel, he would support the former.

That did not happen. Charles T. Main's cost estimates
showed less of a differential between the two types of tunnels than the MIT paper had. At a crucial late September
meeting, Budget people pushed the Main group on their
figures but were unable to shake them. After that meeting,
Grossman finally gave up. He just did not have a strong
enough case to persuade the Mayor to reject the Board's
proposal. He called off plans for another PPC review. On
October 7 he wrote to Maguire

This is to inform you that we concur with the current
plans of the Board of Water Supply for the first stage
of the Third City Water Tunnel. Accordingly, we will
recommend to the Mayor that he advance the budget
amendment requested by Merril Eisenbud on July 31,
1969. This should enable you to proceed on schedule
with your bidding plans.

I want to express my appreciation to you and your
staff, as well as to Maurice Feldman and his staff, for

your cooperation with us and with the MIT Urban Systems Laboratory during our review of planning for the tunnel. I hope that we will be able to introduce this type of analysis into the planning for future water resources projects at an earlier stage.

One month later the City Planning Commission held a public hearing on the capital budget amendment, and on December 10, 1969, adopted a resolution to increase Project W-10, "City Tunnel #3, First Stage," from $2,925,000 to $252,425,000. Bids for construction of the tunnel were opened on the same day, and the digging began in February, 1970.

VI

During the three-year period of the water tunnel dispute one of the often-cited advantages of a systems analysis over the traditional "professional" engineering approach was its greater rationality. Its advocates argued that since it took into account a greater range of considerations, systems analysis provided the basis for more rational and comprehensive policy-making at the top. By elucidating all the alternatives, planners could give the Mayor much more complete information on which to base important final decisions. But the attempt to inject a new kind of policy analysis into City government became a struggle in which internal politics, not rational analysis, dominated the choice of outcomes. And the Budget Bureau officials who fought hardest for the systems approach were as quick to resort to political tactics to make their points as those who resisted the technique. The actors on both sides hired consultants whom they trusted to conduct analyses that would support their conclusions as to what kind of tunnel was appropriate. Personal animosities influenced the planning process as much as analytic studies. And the proposal for the smaller, cheaper tunnel finally died not because the top decision-makers rejected it on its merits, but because its supporters could not come up with studies which justified it.

Much of the difficulty in persuading the Board of Water Supply to alter its planning methods came about because the City's reformers underestimated its organizational strength. The Board had both independence and status. It also had strong professional traditions that sustained it in the face of attack from the Mayor's men. The advocates of a systems approach had many other pressing matters to attend to, and they could not spend enough time on the tunnel to learn about the institutional resources the Board could mobilize to resist change. Perhaps, even if the Board's strengths had been clear, Budget Bureau officials would not have cared. They might have assumed that the superiority of their methods was obvious enough to make a compelling case in any competition between them and the Board. In any case, the tunnel now being built represents a victory for the continuity and durability of bureaucracy. Those who advocate more systematic, scientific analysis as a major cure for our urban problems may learn something from this history of institutional triumph.

Not surprisingly, the various actors in the drama of the tunnel have done a good deal of speculating since its end as to whether construction was actually affected by the dispute and delay and, if so, how. The MIT group maintains that its work was responsible for narrowing the tunnel diameter by four to seven feet for a not inconsiderable savings. Budget officials agree. The Board and the Department label this claim as untrue, insisting that their original, larger diameter was merely the most extreme possibility, set forth to keep the cost estimates conservative. The engineers say that the tunnel diameter was never fixed during the period of the dispute, that it could not be determined until the final design parameters were fed into the computer. But Hayes and Grossman question whether a difference in magnitude of 20 percent between the original diameter estimate and the final choice is not too large to attribute simply to the normal range of estimates.

In any case, Budget Bureau and CPC people seem not to have changed the Board's analytic approach. The Rondout Bypass proposal, blocked in 1963 by the City Planning Commission's refusal to approve design and construction funds in the capital budget, became once again in 1972 the subject of active policy debate. The Board maintained that the bypass was essential to keep the City supplied with water in the event of the sabotage or pollution of the Rondout Reservoir. The Budget Bureau asked for plans and cost estimates of alternative ways to protect the reservoir. The City Planning Commission asked for an analysis of the timing of the project and demonstrations of the size of the risk and the potential extent of water loss. The Board found these requests obstructionist. It presented basically the same proposal in 1972 as was presented for inclusion in the 1963–64 capital budget.

It is not surprising that the Board could not—or would not—implement the change to systems analysis of water projects. To begin with, the staff does not see how the systems approach is really any different from what they have been doing all along. One official says, "Those systems guys are just restating the obvious in polysyllables." At most, the new analysis is just an embellishment of the old kind of plan or design. An unofficial Board document describing the tunnel dispute says, "The basic design work, including systems analyses of a complexity and depth never envisioned by the MIT researchers, was completed early in October 1968."

The planning agencies were never really in a position to force the Board to understand systems analysis or consider using it. BOB and CPC had the power to withhold approval of the Board's work up to a certain point. But that was a very limited power. It was not likely to stifle institutional defense against change. It did not include the authority of Grossman or Elliott to give orders or assignments to Board staff members. The Board lost none of its independent power to line up influential allies in support of its proposal.

Lacking coercive powers, the central agencies had to

reply on persuasive appeals to the Board's professional pride to bring about what they saw as a professional improvement in the agency's operation. Relying simply on persuasion, they could not possibly have swayed the Board. Traditional engineering methods have served the Board well in the past. Now those methods were under criticism only from nonprofessionals whose judgments about professional issues could easily be dismissed. (Perhaps if this kind of dispute repeats itself ten years from now, this will not be the case. Some of the most prestigious engineering departments in the country, including MIT's, are beginning to train their students to be systems analysts, and the force of this influence may soon reach the profession in general and the Board staff in particular.)

The story of the tunnel reveals conflicts over more than just substantive professional judgments. Also important were considerations of style and association. The lack of common reference points and vocabularies made it difficult for those on one side of the dispute to identify with those on the other. The loyalty of some of the actors to their own backgrounds widened the distance between them. Both Grossman and Disman of the Bureau of the Budget had gone to MIT; Terenzio, who had gone to City College, chose a City College professor to do hydraulic designs for the computer's final calculations on the tunnel diameter.

Profound issues of institutional jurisdiction also play a part in determining a professional stance. Government agencies, no less than old schools, generate loyalties that influence the views of even the most sophisticated actors. Carter Bales, the Budget Bureau Assistant Director who came in at the end of the tunnel dispute to try to mediate between the parties, wrote to Hayes after working with Board Staff and Maurice Feldman, "Clearly, the Board is too far away from the control of City government." Eisenbud, after working with the Board for a time, reversed his original position that it should be incorporated into the Environmental Protection Administration and now asserts that it is vital for the Board to be independent from City

Hall and the planning agencies. When such jurisdictional questions become important, they cannot help but detract from substantive matters also at issue.

Looking at all the influences on the tunnel dispute, we may ask: does government by rational policy happen at all? Could the decision about what kind of tunnel to build, even if backed up with good systems analysis, ever have been determined solely by rational calculations? Probably not. No matter how serious the reformer, how objective the official, or how scientific the planner, policy development is a political process. It involves the shifting of power relations, particularly when substantial change is imposed on large groups of people or organizations from above. People or institutions who resist the change will do so by manipulating the formal rules and relying on customary practices about which the agents of change may know nothing. Knowing those practices and paying attention to the institutional assumptions that guide that staff in working on any important problem is essential for the administrator who wants to know what he can accomplish and what strategies he will have to follow.

The recognition that government decisions are usually based on a mixture of substantive and political issues suggests another conclusion. Since the nonrational forces are often deeply embedded in the organizational life of the bureaucracies working on a problem, they do not change quickly, certainly not generally in a four-year mayoralty term. Perhaps, then, the political positions of our elected officials are not always as important as their ability to understand and work with government organizations whose goals and practices render them inherently resistant to change.

6

Locked In

I

On August 8, 1970, thirty-five black prisoners took over part of the ninth floor of the Manhattan House of Detention, better known to prisoners and public alike as "the Tombs." They were rebelling over the treatment of a fellow inmate who had been accused of striking a guard. They seized two white inmates and held them hostage for several hours. New York City's Correction Commissioner George McGrath stated that the Department of Investigation would look into what was termed an "incident." The matter was relegated to the back page of the next day's *New York Times.*

But the "incident" turned out to be the preliminary tremor to a major earthquake. Two days later, on Monday, August 10, the same floor erupted again. This time inmates subdued five Correction Officers and held them hostage for eight hours. By midafternoon the rioting had ended. The guards were released only after inmates had given reporters a "petition of grievances" and exacted from Commissioner McGrath a written promise that they would face no reprisals.

The protest was not over, even temporarily. As Mayor Lindsay was holding a press conference the following day to announce a "corrections crisis" in New York City, an aide handed him a note telling of more trouble. Inmates on four other floors of the Tombs were rioting, taking hostages and destroying bedding and furniture. The rest of the week was tense, not only in the Tombs—where prisoners retained partial control of the prison—but at other City penal institutions. On Wednesday prisoners at the Brooklyn House of Detention refused to return to their cells and demonstrated for forty-five minutes against conditions there. On Sunday the inmates at the prison on Riker's Island threw coffee and meal trays in the dining area. And the following week, for two days running, Tombs prisoners—most of whom were being detained pending disposition of their cases—refused to appear in court for the bail hearings or other court appearances previously scheduled.

The prisoners' "petition of grievances" set forth a clear and comprehensive picture of the immediate causes of the riots. It described both prison conditions and other aspects of the criminal justice system. It inveighed against the overcrowding in the Tombs, the brutality of correction officers, poor prison medical care, roaches and rats in the cell blocks, and bad food. As one inmate told the *New York Post*, "We rioted because of the stink and the stench and the roaches and the ants and the fleas." They also rebelled against "the injustices we suffer in the courtrooms of the Criminal Courts and the Supreme Court": delays in trial scheduling, the denial of preliminary hearings (or their superficiality), excessive bail, denial of hearings on writs, and pressure from Legal Aid attorneys to offer a guilty plea in exchange for being charged with a lesser offense than what they were originally arrested for ("copping a plea").

Publicly at least, no one blamed the riots on the inmates. Commissioner McGrath announced immediately that those who participated would not be punished. In a press conference he said, "The ironic thing is that most of what they say I have said many times over in the past months. The institution [the Tombs] is abominably overcrowded." And Mayor Lindsay promised to investigate charges of guard brutality. Other official reactions passed the buck. Mayor Lindsay and Governor Rockefeller traded accusations over the issue of who was responsible for the overcrowding in the prison and the backlog of Criminal Court cases that contributed to it, while the Mayor and State Senator John R. Dunne squabbled publicly about the usefulness of a proposed state investigation of the New York City Criminal Court system. The Mayor announced that he would ask the Bar Association of the City of New York to investigate the inmates' charges that Legal Aid was forcing defendants to enter guilty pleas in order to speed up trials and minimize sentences. In return, the Legal Aid Society announced it would sue the City, charging that conditions in the Tombs violated the constitutional bar against cruel and unusual punishment. Manhattan Congressman Edward Koch said he would conduct a survey of prison conditions. Leo Zeferetti, head of the Correction Officer's Benevolent Association, was the only official who avoided laying blame at all. He said simply to the press, "Let's not kid ourselves, we're not correcting anybody in there."

At the heart of the bureaucratic and political conflicts was the question of whether the state or the City was primarily responsible for the troubles of the City's courts and jails. Criminal cases are heard in both the City's Criminal Court and in the State Supreme Court (not an appellate court, as its name would indicate). Also, both City and state institutions house prisoners arrested and convicted in the City, though the usual pattern is that inmates with longer sentences are sent to state institutions and detainees remain in City jails. The day after the first riot Lindsay sent a telegram to Governor Rockefeller requesting that the state prison system house 4,000 sentenced prisoners presently in New York City. A day later he said, "It is imperative now that 1,000 more inmates be removed to state institutions." Rockefeller promised that the state would take 300 prisoners now and 350 more in November, but he also stated that overcrowding was due primarily to local inefficiencies. The acrimony and confusion of the state-City conflict was perfectly exemplified by the reactions to Senator Dunne's proposal to the City, made on August 23, that 2,000 inmates then awaiting trial for nonviolent misdemeanors be released without bail. A City Councilman and a retired State judge declared that such an action would be dangerous to the public. Two State Supreme Court judges asserted that City officials had no administrative authority to implement such a policy. And a Criminal Court judge maintained that such defendants were already being released.

Behind the public furor of the riot was the chaos within the City's Correction Department. A week after the initial riot, correction officers (COs) threatened to strike unless they were allowed to search the Tombs for weapons, repair the broken locks, and tighten general security within the jail. Commissioner McGrath averted the threat by allowing a weapons search of the fourth floor of the Tombs and by promising the COs prompt payment of overtime pay, an in-service training course, and new riot control equipment. But it was clear to correction officials that the respite might be only momentary. COs testified repeatedly at Senator Dunne's hearings that they agreed with the inmates' grievances—with the obvious exception of the charges of guard brutality—and the conditions they objected to were not likely to be improved immediately. Furthermore, the department was badly understaffed. Everyone was edgy about prison security when the ratio of COs to inmates was less than 1 to 100. Dr. Violet Stevenson, the department's Director of Psychiatry, resigned on August 27 after only three months on the job, pointing to the inadequacy of prison medical care and hinting at serious internal tensions in the department. In announcing her resignation, Dr. Stevenson vigorously criticized the bureaucratic rigidity of the department and assailed the agency as "phobic about any program which represents change."

Before the City had a chance to settle down and address itself to correcting at least some of the prison problems, more rioting broke out. This time the action was not so spontaneous, nor the grievances so specific. Although differing as to how the new riots actually started, all reports —including inmates' newspaper articles and letters to the press—emphasized that the riots were planned. And the prisoners' demands spoke more directly to large political and systemic problems than they had in August.

The trouble started in the Long Island City branch of the Queens House of Detention on October 1. Rioting inmates seized seven hostages and took control of the entire prison with the exception of the warden's office and the visitors' lobby. At 3 P.M. the next day Tombs inmates rioted, seizing eighteen guards. That same evening inmates at the Queens House of Detention in Kew Gardens refused to be locked in for the night, seized a number of hostages, and took over four floors. At the Brooklyn House of Detention on the following day, three more hostages were taken. Negotiating sessions at the Long Island City jail and special bail hearings held to meet prisoners' demands seemed to be having little effect, and at 6 P.M. on October 3 Mayor Lindsay announced that he would retake the prisons by force, saying "we cannot and will not be powerless in the face of this disorder." Sunday was a day of battle, with prison guards using tear gas grenades and clubs to quell the uprisings in Brooklyn and Kew Gardens. Mayor Lindsay warned the rioters in the Tombs and the Long Island City jail that if they did not give up their hostages, the prisons would be taken by force. In both cases, the inmates surrendered rather than face attack.

The events of the October riots expressed a sense of

urgency and fury far greater than in August. This time every major penal institution in the City, with the exception of the Bronx House of Detention, had participated, with approximately 2,000 inmates of the total census of 12,000 involved. Twenty-eight people were held hostage during the four days of rioting, and close to $2 million worth of damage was done. Even in the fall of 1972, some badly needed cells in the Tombs still went unused because they had not been repaired. Although not all prisoners who rioted held radical political views, many justified their actions as—in the words of one Black Panther inmate—"a political act of rebellion, brought about because of the oppressive and inhuman conditions prevalent in this dungeon. . . ."[1] At Long Island City, the negotiating committee called itself the Inmates' Liberation Front, and when special bail hearings were held there, some of the inmate observers were dressed in Arab garb and identified themselves only as "revolutionaries."

Official reactions to the riots were also more intense and often indicated great confusion. Though some guards allegedly beat prisoners in the two Queens jails, many others supported the inmates' complaints. A number clearly agreed with their colleague who said to a newspaper reporter in August, "It's an inhuman situation for all of us. It's too crowded, it's filthy, and the prisoners are angry. There's racial tension. And we're the ones who have to contend with this every day. We've got to be for reform." Then there was the report of the hostage at the Tombs who —during debate about whether to release the hostages in answer to Mayor Lindsay's ultimatum of surrender or attack—cried, "Don't let us go. You've got them by the balls. Keep negotiating." No more of a consensus existed at higher levels. Immediately after the riots, Lindsay issued a statement to the Administrative Board of the State Judicial Conference in which he described the overcrowding of the jails as "inhumane" and proposed six major reforms. Though the reforms included emergency court sessions to clear up the backlog of criminal cases and the merging of the New York City Criminal Court into the state court system, both judges and other officials said that Lindsay had never really been interested in court reform or the improvement of the related offices of Probation, Correction, Legal Aid, and the District Attorney. A *New York Times* article reported that "Some of the top-ranking judicial officials in the city" believed that the Mayor "wanted the court crisis to reach such a point that the only remedy would be a complete takeover by the State."

It may be that there *is* no remedy for the conditions of our criminal courts and prisons, that our social need for coercive restraint of those who violate certain norms will burden us forever with a series of public crises. But after the 1970 prison riots in New York City both politicians and citizens demanded a new focus on what penologists call "the back end of the criminal justice system." They pressed for more equitable and humane treatment of criminal defendants in courts and penal institutions. Perhaps even more important, they began to work on making correction more accountable to the general public. This chapter looks at the problems of imposing penal reforms on the men and women who may risk their lives—and certainly must alter their attitudes—in carrying them out.

II

The deluge of proposals and counterproposals set forth by politicians and judges in the aftermath of the riots—as well as the indicators of impending trouble that had been ignored for several years—reveal much about American society's general attitudes toward those who break its rules. To understand the situation and determine the validity of these responses, one must look at the wrongs and suggested remedies individually.

On the surface the principal immediate problem seemed to be the terrible overcrowding of the City's penal institutions. Commissioner McGrath stated, shortly after the riots, "If I can just get this albatross of overcrowding off my neck, we'll start to move." And Warden Arthur J. Singerman of the Bronx House of Detention said to an interviewer many months later, "Problem number one is overcrowding, which keeps us from solving all the other problems." On August 10, the day of the first riot, 1,959 inmates occupied the Tombs, which had a planned capacity of 932. On October 1 the Long Island branch of the Queens House of Detention, designed to hold 194 inmates, had a census of 338. The press reported a shortage of mattresses, and in some institutions as many as three inmates occupied one cell. Unquestionably, the cramped quarters contributed to the indignities of prison life in 1970 in New York City. (It is interesting to note, however, that in the long, detailed, and extremely articulate petition of grievances submitted by the August rioters, no mention was made of the overcrowding problem. And two of the observers closest to the correction system—the head of the correction officers' union and the president of the Fortune Society, an organization of ex-inmates—commented to the press that overcrowding was of far less concern to the prisoners than other problems.)

The political solutions proposed were of two kinds. Once again the Mayor urged the state to take more of the City's sentenced inmates and to assume responsibility for all inmates given sentences longer than ninety days. In addition, political figures at all levels raced to propose new facilities to relieve overcrowding. McGrath asked the City Planning Commission to approve $43 million worth of buildings and equipment, the Board of Estimate authorized an $18 million expansion of one of the Riker's Island institutions, and Governor Rockefeller promised to ask the legislature to authorize special, low-interest loans for building more prisons.

Inmates' complaints during both riots often emphasized court delays, which resulted in many months of pretrial detention. And the men had reason to complain. As a general rule, two-thirds to three-fourths of the City's inmates were detainees, prisoners being held pending a trial or sentencing. After the October riots Lindsay stated that in 1968 43 percent of the detainees were held for more than a year awaiting trial. Detainees were often the youngest and poorest of criminal defendants, those who could not raise even $50 or $100 bail. In the City's Houses of Detention, there were no education or work-release programs to mitigate their enforced idleness and isolation. For many, the detention period provided only an education in crime and an exposure to violent homosexuality.

A number of proposals sought to speed up case disposition. Mayor Lindsay appointed David Ross, former majority leader in the City Council, as Administrative Judge of the City's Criminal Court in the hope that he could increase the court's efficiency by developing longer court sessions, assigning judges to the kinds of cases where they had most expertise, and prodding the judges to put in longer work days. (Ross met, or perhaps exceeded, the Mayor's expectations. On January 1, 1971, the Criminal Court had a backlog of 59,000 pending cases; on January 21, 1972, it was down to 22,000 cases, a number that could be disposed of within a month.) Several political figures had differing proposals for streamlining the disposition of felony cases handled by the State Supreme Court (the trial court in New York), and they were debated in the daily press. Experts of various sorts suggested that more defendants should be released on bail, that "victimless" crimes should not be tried in the criminal courts, and that it should be made illegal to detain someone more than a set number of months. A civic group proposed that one hundred volunteer lawyers be deputized immediately as judges for misdemeanor cases. And of course there were the inevitable poverty pleas, voiced by both State and local officials: if only the federal government would provide more money for courts, judges, and programs. . . .

Jail conditions and guard brutality, though perhaps easier to improve—at least partially—than either overcrowding or court delays, got very little immediate attention. McGrath pleaded for an increased budget for the Department of Correction so that he could care for the inmates better, and within two or three months mail and telephone privileges had been extended, additional medical personnel had been hired, and there were fewer complaints about the food. But the riots worsened conditions in some ways, too. Security was tightened, and for the two weeks right after the riots family visits were not allowed, religious services were curtailed, and inmates could not take showers. In February the State Correction Commission, after inspecting the Tombs, reported, "The compressed and depressive living in the present Manhattan House of Detention for Men under existing conditions is conducive to mental, moral and physical deterioration and thus a further threat to public welfare and safety." As for guard brutality, Mayor Lindsay promised to launch an investigation of reported incidents. That study, completed the following spring, confirmed the beating of prisoners by guards in both Queens institutions. Charges brought by the department against a number of uniformed personnel resulted in some suspensions without pay. More than two years after the October riots, eleven guards and a warden were indicted for brutality.

An issue not raised by the rioting inmates, but which obtained some prominence after the August disturbance, concerned better protection of the COs. To some extent a trade-off existed between improving conditions for the inmates and making life easier for the COs. The temporary limitation of visits to inmates and the general tightening of security represented a resolution of that conflict in favor of the officers. But not all the measures proposed to protect them were inherently costly to the prisoners. In September the Board of Estimate approved funds for three hundred new COs, and the department announced in October that it was buying more riot equipment for the men. An in-service training program for officers was proposed so that the men might learn to be both more efficient and more humane.

Most of the individual proposals were intended to make

the system operate more efficiently. They aimed at swifter processing, tighter control, greater productivity in the task of sealing off criminals from the rest of society. They spoke to the punitive impulse that most citizens feel toward criminal offenders and still guides much of the policy-making in the corrections field. And if those proposals had all been implemented, they would surely have provided at least a momentary respite from charges that the City treated its offenders like animals.

But improving the efficiency of the system does not ensure its effectiveness. Speedy trials may better enable defendants to see the connection between the offense and their punishment, but will probably not contribute to their positive functioning in society once the trial has been held, the sentence pronounced, and the term served. Furthermore, the sealing-off process, which is usually approved by the public when the inmates get restless, appeared on closer reflection by liberal government officials to lead nowhere except to greater repression and greater expense.

The dead-end quality of usual prison reform proposals helps to explain why, for many years preceding the 1970 riots, experts, legislative committees, and even tourists had sounded ineffective warnings about New York City prison life and its potential explosiveness. Numerous reports had been submitted to the City's politicians and administrators documenting the overcrowding, the court delays, and the oppressive jail conditions, usually with no effect. When Karl Barth, the famous Swiss philosopher and theologian, came to visit the city in 1962 he remarked, "The jails in Switzerland are a paradise to what I saw here." In the same year the then Commissioner of Correction, Anna Kross, stated in her request for funds to improve medical care in the penal institutions:

> Except in rare cases, the only physicians that can be hired at the present rates are those too old for active office practice, those with unfortunate personalities, and those physically or mentally handicapped.

Although she was widely criticized for the statement and argued in defense that she had been quoted out of context, she never retracted the remark.

Other reports had more official sanction. During 1968, a state senate investigating committee conducted a study of penology in New York City and warned of the problems of overcrowding, inadequate funds, and uniformed personnel resistant to change. The following year witnesses at the Joint Legislative Commission on Penal Institutions decried the overcrowding and oppressive conditions of the Tombs. In 1969 Senator Dunne began to probe the City's jails with his State Commission on Penal Institutions and made a special issue of the causes of the rising suicide rate within the prisons. A Commission report released in November found the jails of New York City and some upstate counties to be "more fertile breeding grounds for crime than the streets," "settings less humane than our public zoos." Finally, people who had contact with the prison system during the first few years of the Lindsay administration continually warned his City Hall aides of the indecent and potentially explosive conditions of the jails. One knowledgeable and concerned observer, a man with several years of experience in helping criminal defendants find and hold jobs, wrote in a long 1970 letter to a mayoral assistant that the situation had eroded during Lindsay's first years

> for at least two reasons: the inmate population has been steadily growing (increased numbers of arrests and backlogged courts causing larger delays between arrest and disposition) and the total failure of the Department of Correction to produce ideas, programs, change the atmosphere, improve recruitment, rethink objectives, etc. The administration and staff have contributed *nothing* during this period to alleviate problems or improve programs—their total effort has been expended toward custodial efforts and warding off criticism with time-tested defensive comments about money, staff, facilities, etc.

Summing up the problems, he noted, "The New York City correctional system is the stuff of a large scandal."

And, indeed, the reports and testimony and criticism did not retard the growing crisis. On August 11, 1968, *The New York Times* reported that on August 2 there had been 50 percent more men and women in detention in the City's facilities than on the same day in 1967. When McGrath took office in 1966, he noted that the occupancy rate of the City's jails had risen from 93 percent in 1954 to 122 percent in 1965. In 1969 the Tombs population rose above 200 percent capacity, and the jails' overall census was 150 percent of capacity just before the 1970 riots. Whereas suicides in the City's jails had averaged fewer than ten per year during most of the 1960s, Senator Dunne announced in August 1969 that so far that year there had already been ten suicides.

Clearly, the Lindsay administration had, until late 1970, been unable or unwilling to consider seriously effecting the reforms indicated by official and unofficial studies of the City's penal institutions. There were probably several reasons for this. For one thing, to take aggressive action would entail a major reallocation of resources within the City's labyrinthine criminal justice system. In 1967 less than 14 percent of total monies spent on criminal justice in New York City went for criminal courts and corrections combined. The police received about 84 percent. As one official put it, "The emphasis is always on the front end of the system." Changing that emphasis substantially would fly in the face of more than just tradition. A healthy majority of New Yorkers appear to believe that effective foot patrol is the front line of defense against crime, and the public plea for more police is hard for any local politician to disregard. Conversely, many people wish to blot out the necessity of any kind of support for those they regard as criminals and hoodlums, even if the support is limited to guaranteeing basic constitutional rights.

This fact helps explain the second cause for political inaction on the City's penal problems. The City was not likely to allocate scarce resources for more humane jails and rehabilitation programs when there was no outside pressure on it to do so. And prisoners have no effective constituency, no articulate spokesmen or powerful allies to counteract the prevailing political distaste for criminals' welfare. As Congressman Koch remarked, "Time after time there have been exposés about the City's jails, but those guys can't vote, so nothing is done."

But after the riots something *was* done, though it took a couple of years to have any effect, and it met with much bureaucratic and political resistance. The measures taken were of two different kinds. Some followed proposals made over and over in the past, proposals for more efficient and humane means of making judgments and sealing off criminal justice functions from the rest of community life. Others pursued different goals. They emphasized rehabilitation (which has supposedly been official policy among American penologists for the past one hundred years) and the connections of prison life to the outside world. The first kinds of reform measures were easily implemented—given adequate funds and a few efficient administrators—but did not reach the fundamental problems of the isolation and hostility of prison life. The second kind, though aimed at more basic problems, were bound to encounter strong resistance from people who derived both their livelihoods and their views of the world from the penal system as it was before the riots. The remainder of this chapter focuses primarily on these latter reforms and the difficulties of implementing them.

The intrinsic conflict in these two directions of reform partly explains Lindsay's initial foot-dragging. On the one hand, he initially resisted the shifting of City tax-levy funds from other areas into courts and corrections. It became widely known that he would continue to support Commissioner McGrath, even though that official had made fewer and fewer attempts to improve the system the longer he remained in office. (When McGrath came in, in 1966, he had professed himself to be a strong proponent of incarceration as rehabilitation. Yet during his tenure the department had

made very little progress in adopting the work and education programs that were generally held to be the best
preparation for an inmate to return to the outside world
and make himself a productive citizen in it.) Furthermore,
Lindsay's rush to blame the state for the more obvious
defects of the system caused a good deal of skepticism that
he intended to try to use local authority and local resources
to improve matters.

The press attention given to the riots did not necessarily
mean that Lindsay would suffer politically if he did not
lobby immediately for improvement of prison conditions.
As a short-term matter, ignoring prisoners might, at that
time, have been politically less harmful than fighting for
their interests. Although Jack Newfield launched articulate
attacks on City officials in *The Village Voice*—much like his
muckraking on the lead-poisoning issue—that kind of article was not as likely to create a secondary constituency for
inmates as it had been for lead-poisoned children. And,
although the criticisms of State legislative committees and
lawyers' goups were annoying, they did not necessarily
reflect the voters' concerns. They would surely subside—
or at least be taken off the front pages of the newspapers
—if the rioting diminished. That could be accomplished at
least partially by heeding the correction officers' requests
for tighter security. Detailed news stories about the penal
institutions could be suppressed to some extent by maintaining the policy that barred reporters from touring jails
and interviewing inmates.

On the other hand, pressures to begin reform also
affected the Mayor. Though the issue of prison conditions
may not have had great local political significance in and
of itself, to ignore it would surely have tarnished Lindsay's
national image as a reformer. He must have taken that into
account in a year when politicians and journalists all over
the country were eyeing him as a dark-horse Presidential
candidate. In addition, reliable sources within his administration report that he was truly disturbed by the conditions
and attitudes he saw when he went in October to negotiate

in some of the City's prisons. These mixed motives help explain (with the advantage of hindsight) the character of the actions the Mayor took.

By and large Lindsay continued to demand attention for the issues that had already become matters of public debate —overcrowding, court delays, and the like. In the aftermath of the riots, he could not deal immediately with the lack of rehabilitative programs or, indeed, examine the question of whether rehabilitation was possible at all in the existing penal system. He had to speak to the pressing need for a return to quiescence, the adoption of procedures that would remove from the nightly news the terrifying picture of criminals on the rampage.

But the Mayor also knew that prevention was the best treatment in the long run for inmate discontent, and that effective prevention would have to include an observance of the department's professed aims of rehabilitation. To this end, he needed a group that would report regularly to him on department activities and plans, but would be separate enough from it so as not merely to represent its momentary bureaucratic interests. For many years the department had had a "watchdog" group of citizens appointed by the Mayor—the Board of Correction—and empowered by the City charter to inspect all department facilities, study its plans and programs, and evaluate its performance. In 1967 Commissioner McGrath had requested the board's dissolution, saying that

> The Board is a group of lay people who get involved in matters that are none of their business. . . . The City charter provides for a built-in Board to frustrate a City function. I am suggesting that those are citizens with no expertise. This city is full of people who are running around with badges and shields interfering with the orderly process of government. I think it's abominable.

Although the Board was never officially abolished, the Mayor did not fill its vacancies or attend to its reports, and it became moribund. But on October 18, 1970, Lindsay appointed William vanden Heuvel, a New York lawyer formerly associated with Robert F. Kennedy and prominent in reform circles, to head a newly activated Board of Correction. Vanden Heuvel says Lindsay "gave us carte blanche," and the group rapidly became the principal public critic of the courts and jails. Its first report, investigating the suicide of a Young Lord in the Tombs, concluded that "the intricate system which we have designed to protect the community and the individual succeeded only in deranging him and ultimately, instead of protecting him, it permitted his destruction." It went on to recommend reforms to make prison conditions better known to the public and more humane for the inmates. In February 1971 it issued a fifty-one-point critique of prison conditions, and vanden Heuvel announced that in one hundred days he would assess progress made toward improving them. Later reports, given considerable play in the local press, focused on such matters as detailed criticism of medical care in the prisons. Perhaps more than any other group looking at the prison system, the board concentrated on instances of what a leading sociologist calls the "mortification of the self," the inevitable daily humiliations of involuntary confinement.[2] It protested with equal fervor the neglect of individual inmates who were addicts, diabetics, or psychotics and the lack of work and literacy programs for all inmate groups.

III

Over the two years following the 1970 riots, a number of recommendations put forth by legislators, judges, and local politicians were at least partially put into effect. Judges in the City's Criminal Court now sit on an average of over five hours a day, twice the amount of the previous year; low bail and probation cases have increased; and as of the end of November 1972, the jails' occupancy rate had dropped from 150 percent to 123 percent. More City inmates now go to less crowded state institutions to serve their sentences. The

State Administrative Board of the Judicial Conference has ruled that most charges against a defendant must be dismissed if his trial is not held within six months, and he may not be held in detention more than three months without a trial. (It is still too early to tell whether this rule can be an effective stimulus to speeding up the processing of criminal court cases.) The Correction Department expense budget has increased by 50 percent in two years. Among other things, the extra funds have bought better food and medical care, more items of personal care (soap, sheets, and underwear), and more counseling for youthful offenders. Repair of the old Long Island City branch of the Queens House of Detention—where the trouble started in the October riots—make it more bearable; the new Women's House of Detention on Riker's Island is, in most respects, a vast improvement over the dark, crowded jail in Greenwich Village that it replaced.

The toughest problems, however, have often remained resistant to even partial solution. Many, if not most, of the heroin addicts who come within the arm of the law—and they comprise more than half of the prison population— still get no treatment beyond the assistance of methadone in detoxification. The State Supreme Court remains as inefficient as ever. A prison psychiatrist testifying in November 1972, in a case brought to close the Tombs because of its "cruel, unusual, uncivilized and unlawful conditions," stated that both guards and inmates were in a constant state of "intolerable" anxiety. There appeared to be no appreciable drop in either the prison suicide rate (twelve in 1971 alone) or the recidivism rate. Though there had been marginal improvements in the details of the system's operation, no one would have said that the two years after the riot gave hope that criminal justice in New York City would become, in the words of one federal judge, "a model of communication and cooperation." A *New York Times* editorial in late 1972, noting that the criminal courts were "hopelessly undermanned and overwhelmed" and that there were "shocking disparities in sentences for rich and poor, black and white," found in the court system only "chaos [that] has paralyzed the system in some cases, made it a dismal instrument of injustice in others."

The improvements that had taken place appeared to many to be largely attributable to the tactic of riot. The sudden injection of local and federal money and the decrease in the inmate census after the fall of 1970 seemed undeniable evidence that the riots and their publicity had led to at least some of the reform that the many groups of legislators and experts had failed to generate. But the public officials often would not, or could not, make the connection between the riots and the reforms. Perhaps they feared that doing so publicly would make it seem that they endorsed violence as a catalyst for social change. Or maybe it was a more ego-centered calculation: if I could not improve the system with my professional dedication to the public good, how can I admit that crude demonstrations of misery and deprivation have been a more effective prod? For whatever reason, it was difficult for those most responsible for the changes to acknowledge their origins, and the closer they were to the criminal justice system, the more likely they were to equivocate. John Lindsay, commenting on improvement in prison conditions during the spring of 1971, would not concede that the riots had had a beneficial effect. "I've never seen violence help anything," he told reporters, while Commissioner McGrath pointed out the riots' costs in terms of injury to hostages and property damage. At the same press conference, however, vanden Heuvel—whose function was to monitor the penal system rather than to operate it—said, "I believe the riots played an overall healthy role. The grievances of the prisoners were legitimate and valid." Perhaps the most trenchant observation about the effects of the riots came from Jack Newfield, who wrote in *The Village Voice* that they "catch the public's fickle attention" but do not, in and of themselves, stimulate basic institutional change.

In a national climate of inmate unrest, however, even the momentary public attention generated by one riot may contribute to the development of a general social impulse which eventually leads to substantial change. The newsmakers pick up the issue of "prison reform," experts are forced to reassess their analyses of a status quo that no longer exists, and pollsters ask the man in the street to evaluate public policy in an area he is only beginning to think about. In the wake of prison rebellions in New York, California, New Jersey, and many other places, a Harris poll found that many Americans have become sympathetic to the needs of inmates and, indeed, believe that their goals in taking over jails and holding hostages are reasonable ones. During 1972 a number of prominent Americans, including Tom Wicker of *The New York Times,* began to wonder about whether as a society we ought not simply to abolish incarceration as we know it today.

Most of the public attention after the riots focused on objective, visible conditions like prison overcrowding and court abuses. But Newfield, vanden Heuvel, and others also stressed the less tangible problems like the fear and hatred that often define the relationships of both guard to inmate and inmate to inmate. These matters of atmosphere were, of course, intricately tied in with the dismal physical conditions of imprisonment; ensuring that each man had his own cell would probably reduce the terrors of homosexuality, and providing inmates with recreational and educational activities might defuse some of their resentment against their jailors. But officials within the Lindsay administration knew they had to try other short-range means of relieving, for staff and inmates alike, the psychic pressures of incarceration. The long-range, tangible improvements might never come, and even if they did, nothing guaranteed that they would induce greater understanding among the occupants—voluntary and involuntary—of the City's penal institutions.

It was no easy task to introduce new programs for inmates and guards into the department. No recent programs for inmates existed, and the "pilot" programs of a decade earlier had soon withered and died, leaving the old-timers in the department even more cynical about reform than they might otherwise have been. Although McGrath had come into the department as a reformer, he had never taken much initiative in promoting special programs. (Perhaps, as he hinted in 1970, he was always waiting to get the over-crowding problem solved before he turned to education and other rehabilitation experiments.) In 1967 he had publicly pressed for a work-release program for inmates, but nothing materialized—observers say because he wasn't convinced enough to buck the opposition of the wardens. The special training program for guards begun that same year was limited to teaching them how to recognize potential suicides, and the high school equivalency program never reached many inmates. Federal funds for a Manpower and Development Training Act program ran out in 1969, and nothing replaced it. For much of McGrath's tenure several of the major administrative posts in the department remained vacant, including those of Deputy Commissioner and one Assistant Commissioner. One warden, interested in reform, explained the consequences of that situation: "Until recently, the central office was one man, and one man only. You can't start anything new that way. Most of the initiative for special programs has to come from the central administration. The warden has all he can do to keep the institution running."

Even if administrators in the department's central office had considered it important to improve the atmosphere of the jails, members of the uniformed staffs would have resisted most experiments. For them anything that might bring people closer together held the very real threat of making it harder to contain the angry mass of humanity in their charge. For most of them—particularly the officers and wardens who had been in the system longest—good personal dynamics prevailed within the jails when matters of security and discipline were handled with a minimum of friction or violence. They could see little possibility for the improvement of human relations in what one reporter has called "the emotional boiler factory" in which they worked.

The Mayor had several ways to pressure the department

into improving attitudes within the jails. Vanden Heuvel was interested in this aspect of prison reform, and one of the first things the Board of Correction pressed for was extended visiting hours for inmates; another was the provision of phones, so that inmates could talk to their families between visits. Lindsay also had a valuable resource in his Criminal Justice Coordinating Council (CJCC). Formed in 1967 as an advisory group of citizens and officials who would help the Mayor set policy in criminal justice areas, CJCC had just begun, earlier in 1970, to develop a professional staff headed by Henry Ruth, formerly a planner of criminal justice programs in the Justice Department of the federal government. This group was responsible for developing projects dealing wich such problems as crime prevention, correction, and drug addiction and submitting them for approval and funding to a State agency, which in turn received money from the federal Law Enforcement Assistance Administration. Although Ruth and his assistants had already recognized the need for many new kinds of programs in the corrections field (he noted with horror shortly after he came into office that less than one-half of one cent of every dollar spent on criminal justice in New York City went for inmate rehabilitation), they were spurred into actual planning and negotiating with department officials by the 1970 riots.

Two of the new two-year programs planned and approved in time for mid-1971 funding were a human relations training program for correction staff—COs and commanding officers, new recruits and experienced men—and a project for hiring and training paraprofessional correction aides to work in the penal institutions. Much of the rest of this chapter illustrates the difficulties of implementing these projects, which were aimed, not principally at improving physical condition in the jails, but at easing the tensions there.

Another step the Mayor took was to make some important personnel changes in the department. Aided by Mayoral assistant Michael Dontzin, Henry Ruth, and some ad-

visors outside City government, Lindsay found a new
Deputy Commissioner and two Assistant Commissioners.
The former, a black ex-parole officer named Bernhard J.
Malcolm, was to backstop McGrath in administering the
department, and the latter two were to develop and run
reform programs. These men were appointed during mid-
1971, and many observers expected that their arrival would
mean the imminent departure of George McGrath, who
had come under heavy fire after the 1970 riots. All three of
the new appointees were eager to institute many reforms
and to make the penal system more accountable to the
public. McGrath admitted that many changes were necessary, but by not pressing for them earlier, he had earned the
reputation of supporting the status quo. Against the urg-
ings of many advisors, Lindsay did not immediately ask
McGrath to leave, and it was not until November 1971—
after it was widely known that Lindsay was shopping for
a new Commissioner—that he resigned. In January 1972
Ben Malcolm became Commissioner of Correction, and
after that the new program, born shortly after the riots,
swung into full operation.

There has been much private and press speculation
about why Lindsay did not call immediately for the resignation of McGrath. After all, McGrath had known of the
worsening physical condition of the institutions over
which he had jurisdiction; he was on notice of the rising
suicide rate; he could not claim ignorance of the increase
in the jails of persons who had not yet been convicted of
the crime for which they were being detained. But he had
been a loyal employee, if not an aggressive reformer. He
had never blamed the Mayor for short-changing his agency
during budget season; he had managed to soothe his employees on several occasions so that embarrassing strikes
had been averted; he had done the dirtiest job in town
without complaint. After four years of predominantly unsuccessful reform battles, Lindsay must have been grateful
for having been spared, for a time, what appeared to be a
particularly hopeless one. In addition, the Mayor seems

truly to have believed, before the riots, that all was as well
as could be expected within the prisons. In February 1969
he said, speaking at the Riker's Island Adolescent Remand
Shelter:

> Far from being inadequate, the programs of the De-
> partment of Correction are exemplary. They reflect an
> enlightened recognition of all that is desirable to effect
> the rehabilitation of the deviant. There is no emphasis
> on punishment. There is an intelligent effort to effect
> rehabilitation consistent with necessary custody.

With such recent confidence in the rightness of the department's efforts, perhaps he did not relate the riots to any
failures on the part of the Commissioner.

When he finally began to search for a successor to
McGrath, the Mayor appears to have been profoundly ambivalent about what he wanted to find. On the one hand,
he considered appointing two or three men who would
have turned the system on its head. (Apparently they all
either failed to pass the inspection necessary to be offered
the job or, as one informant put it, turned it down as "too
much of a can of worms.") On the other hand, a reliable
source reports that when the Deputy Commissioner was
being considered for promotion, Lindsay asked at least one
of his colleagues in the department if Malcolm would "keep
the lid on."

IV

Of all the new programs, perhaps the human relations
training course for COs held the greatest potential for
creating better understanding among staff and inmates.
Vanden Heuvel expressed eloquently in *The New York
Times* the essential aim that program hoped to achieve:

> The tone of a prison is set by the men who administer
> it. Skillful correction officers are much more impor-

tant to the success of an institution than its newness in architecture. They combine discipline with kindness. They sense the vulnerability of a man in a cage. They speak quiet words, listen to problems, and then try to make the days and the nights more gentle. Normal prisoners invariably respond generously. Personal respect is the foundation of prison reform.

Administered by the Urban League, the project brought trainers to the Correction Academy to provide COs with an opportunity to learn about and discuss such matters as the race and class origins of inmates and the psychology of incarceration. It was hoped that the officers would become more sensitive to the inmates and learn new ways of relating to them.

As soon as the project plan for the training program was completed, its troubles began. For once in the City's history, the money for a new experiment came through immediately. Although the Urban League trainers were not yet themselves really prepared for their task, the Correction Department asked them to conduct human relations sessions as part of the training program planned for two groups of new COs during the summer of 1971. They agreed but did not have time to work out comfortable relationships with the correction staff with whom they were to work. (In addition to training COs, the trainers were to teach department staff to conduct similar sessions as part of the regular Correction Academy program.) Furthermore, 200 trainees showed up, instead of the expected 120, so the Urban League had to find more trainers and throw them in, quite unprepared, to what was already a touchy situation.

Despite these problems, the summer session convinced department personnel that they wanted more of the training. No way was yet available of measuring the change that might have come about as a result of the summer's work, but officials in the central office were willing to keep the experiment going. Even some of the personnel in the penal institutions were getting interested. One of the wardens served on the training committee that was developed to advise the program, and during the fall of 1971, when a course for experienced officers was being devised, other uniformed personnel were occasionally heard defending the program against the less sympathetic. One professional consultant to the program, when asked to explain the occasional interest of usually hostile program critics, remarks, "Even those who resist will reach for something which might conceivably ease their burden."

By January 1972 week-long sessions were being held for COs who had been on the job for up to twenty years. Many continued to believe that, as one put it, "A good smack in the mouth never hurt nobody; it's better than all the theory put together." Others were probably not much affected by the attempts to sensitize them, because they already understood more of the subtleties of the human relations problems of their jobs than did their trainers. But a sizable group in the middle did seem to gain a better understanding of the complex motivations of both the inmates and themselves as they struggled to survive the agonies of prison life.

To understand the problems of producing atmospheric change in the Department of Correction, one must look carefully at the structure and content of the lives of the human beings who are asked to implement the changes. I spent a full work week in February 1972 at the Correction Academy on Riker's Island, listening to COs in the human relations training program talk candidly about themselves, their supervisors ("the brass"), their jobs, the inmates, society, and "the public." Their observations help explain the cynicism that pervades the whole uniformed force over the possibilities of improving life behind the prison walls. By the end of the week I thought it extraordinary that they were not even more opposed to the initiatives for changes that were being pressed upon them by the vigorous new group of reformers downtown.

Of 3,800 department employees, more than 3,000 are members of a uniformed force administered according to

military traditions. At the bottom rung are correction officers (COs); above them are captains, assistant deputy wardens, deputy wardens, and ten wardens. The Director of
Operations is a uniformed man of high rank who acts as the
liaison with the central administrative office. Entrance into
the force and all promotions (with occasional exceptions at
the top) are by civil service examination. An officer may
retire with half-pay after twenty years of service, with full
pay and medical benefits after thirty-five. In 1972 an officer's
base pay was about $10,000 a year, with 5 percent extra for
night work (which rotates so that everyone gets some), and
time-and-a-half for overtime (which may amount to as
much as twenty or thirty hours a week if the department
is very short of staff or the institutions are tense). The
officer's functions include maintaining security (locking
inmates in and out), supervising recreation (when there is
any), serving food, providing personal supplies, and over-
seeing visiting hours. For these tasks he receives anywhere
from one week to four—depending on how understaffed
the department is and how important the current Commissioner considers it—of training at the Correction
Academy. Recently a group of COs wrote out the following
description of their role for some outsiders:

> The job standard of the Correction officer is to provide
> inmates with the following services: care, custody, and
> control, to provide an atmosphere of rehabilitation,
> and to encourage necessary communication between
> Correction officers and prisoners, so as to fully utilize
> the various institutional services provided for his or
> her benefit.

Virtually every correction officer has contradictory feelings about his job, many expressed in a number of different
ways. Some feel proud that they are protecting the public
but are disgusted at the idea that their principal function
is to restrict the physical freedom of other human beings.
They hate to be called "guards," but are hesitant about

assuming tasks like social service or counseling the inmates, because they feel unprepared or frightened of an inmate disturbance. There is widespread annoyance that COs are not paid as well as policemen, but also a pervasive feeling of inferiority to them. Many COs failed the policemen's exam and came to correction as second choice. An unkind department joke says that the initials D.C. on the collar of a CO's uniform really stand, not for Department of Correction, but for "Disappointed Cop."

The CO's job conditions are often terrible. Alone on a cell block with a hundred inmates, he may have to withstand unbearable tension. He may have to watch several directions at once, and if he lets down his guard long enough to perform some service for an inmate, he may lose control of security in the area for which he is responsible. The tensions take their toll. High blood pressure and ulcers are occupational hazards, and signs of mental strain are obvious even to the least sophisticated officer. One says, "There's floors in every institution where, when you go home at night, you're talking to yourself. I do the best I can, but I don't tell my wife I love my job." They are aware that the tensions, increased since the riots, separate them from one another. "Everybody is so eager to get out of here [the Rikers Island institutions] they don't stop for anything. It used to be that if you couldn't get your car started, several guys would stop, bring jump wires to help you out. No more." They vie with one another for the "tit" jobs—clerical positions or others removed from the cell blocks. (The job of guarding inmates is a "wheel" job, one which rotates regularly, making you feel as though you are spinning on a wheel.)

Almost without exception, the COs feel for the inmates a complicated mixture of hatred and respect. Many think they are "society's misfits" and agree with their colleague who said, "They're not good guys or they wouldn't be in here." The same CO said in one afternoon, "Inmates look forward to coming to jail," and, "Those guys may not be book smart, but they're plenty street smart. They don't

miss anything. They make a profession out of watching."
The guards are very aware that intelligence is often a function of necessity and role. One said, "They [the inmates] are
more observant than officers. They look at you and see who
you are, what you look like; we look at them and see only
inmates." The grudging respect COs have for the inmates
often comes out in unfavorable comparisons with themselves. They say, without irony, that they wish they could
use the techniques the inmates do—riots, refusals to eat—
to improve their lives in the jails. And they occasionally
admit to learning from the inmates. One said thoughtfully
to the others in his training session:

> When we had the riots, the inmates said to us that we
> were "computerized human beings," pushed around
> by the bosses, not acting according to our own im-
> pulses. I thought that was wrong at the time, but later
> I began to think about it. We *were* acting as the bosses
> wanted us to.

Much has been written about the common values and
backgrounds of prisoners and the men who guard them. In
New York City this is perhaps true only between inmates
and some of the younger black officers. By and large, even
where inmates and officers have similar origins, the fact
that they have taken different roads in life is enough to
erect great barriers to communication. COs listening to a
lecture about social and economic deprivation do not see
any connection between that and their own backgrounds.
The only obvious sense of identification between prisoners
and COs comes from their similar situation in having to
spend much of their lives behind bars. That identification,
however, is very strong: "We're more institutionalized
than the inmates; the prisoners come and go, but we stay
on."
   Even when officers do not sympathize with the inmates
and are terrified of allowing them more freedom or greater
privileges, they are quick to perceive the injustices of the

system and the ways in which it penalizes the offenders beyond what is reasonable. They are indignant about physical conditions ("If I had to wait in those court pens all night, I'd never be the same"), and their criticisms of the medical treatment of prisoners are even more harsh than those of the Board of Correction. In one of the human relations training sessions a burly CO who thought the course was "a bunch of baloney" and had announced loudly on the first day that he wasn't gong to participate in any of the discussions, suddenly burst out:

> Those doctors care much less about the inmates than most of us. I've seen a doctor come out and look at a bunch of guys waiting to see him and say, "What are you guys waiting for?" When they said, "To see the doctor," he said, "Well, you're seeing him," and walked away.

Not surprisingly, the black officers often seem most sophisticated about the lives of the inmates, most of whom are black or Puerto Rican. They see the cyclical effects of poverty and crime. As one said, "You have to put yourself in the position of the inmate. If I were an inmate and someone knocked me down, I might get a gun when I got out. I'd want to be treated like a man. I'm still a man even if I'm incarcerated." The white officers, though they know intellectually that the inmate comes from a world where standards of conduct are different from his own, often cannot easily incorporate that understanding into his daily dealings with a ghetto black man. One middle-aged white CO said, "I treat an inmate like a human being, but when he calls me 'motherfucker,' it's hard to keep from hitting him." The young black officer quoted above began to laugh. "You can't knock an inmate down for calling you a motherfucker. That's what's been wrong all along. You have to let him know he's still human, all the time."

As one listens to both the officers and the inmates, their psychic energies seem consumed by a perpetual struggle to maintain their humanity, to preserve a sense of self in the midst of an environment that renders them personally powerless. I found virtually none of the sadism or bigotry among COs that the popular press has described—only extreme frustration as to their lack of control over their own lives and work conditions. Again and again, they expressed their interest in changing the prison system, but simultaneously came doubts that they would ever have sufficient personal security to face the demands of change. A typical CO remarks:

> With one officer for four hundred men, you need to have complete physical control. If you *have* the physical control, you have more time and opportunity to handle complex problems. Without it, all the time is spent trying to regain order.

The pervasive sense of their own powerlessness is especially apparent when the officers speak of their superiors. Repeatedly, the CO said, "It's not the inmate who gives you the biggest problems; it's the brass." Almost to a man, the group I saw felt that supervisory personnel in the uniformed force were out of touch and unsympathetic with the COs' daily work problems. (They were also antagonistic to the civilian administrators, but in a different, less intense way, to be discussed later.) Furthermore, they described the faults of "the brass" as oppressive to all attempts by COs to assert their concerns and ideas about the penal system. Typical comments were:

> If you do something that the brass thinks is out of line, you may not get disciplined for it right away, but you'll be watched. Observation is an easy way of taking care of a person who doesn't conform.

> They say they are open to suggestion, but if you go into a warden's office, he says, "Get out of here before I kick you out."

I worked the bing [solitary confinement], and we had
a guy go crazy. It took us three hours to get a captain
down there. That guy had been here almost twenty
years, he was waiting for his pension, and he didn't
want to get involved.

Once I made a suggestion, and the dep turned to the
warden and said, "Give that man fifteen cents for the
Staten Island ferry."

Whether the supervisors are really as unresponsive as
this is not the principal issue. I have had neither the time
nor the access to study their behavior. What does matter is
the extent to which these views of "the brass" contribute to the feelings of isolation and dehumanization of
those who are most immediately responsible for implementing change. Self-respect and confidence are necessary
concomitants to taking personal risks. These qualities may
spring from internal or external sources, usually a combination of both. The CO's usual ambivalence about the fundamental nature of his job diminishes self-generated confidence. The order and discipline of a paramilitary system
focuses the external source for that confidence and security
on a man's supervisors even more than in most job situations. If a CO feels that "As soon as a man puts on that
white shirt, he forgets," he is surely unlikely to feel supported in any action he takes that does not follow exactly
the pattern he has established in the past.

The department's incentive system does not seem to
work well for most COs. The structure does not reward
men sufficiently for superior performance, and moving up
in the system does not generate respect among one's fellows, as it does, say, in the City's Police and Fire Departments. There is no gradation between correction officer
and captain, and most COs feel they are stuck forever in a
dead-end situation. The captain's test seems remote and
unrelated to job performance; it is given only rarely, and
only a fraction of the eligible men take it. One CO reflected
a widely held view when he said:

In most cases you find it's the guy who goes into the corner and reads the books who makes captain. The guy who does the extra things on the job, who tries to make the inmates a little more comfortable than he has to—he doesn't have time to read the books and pass the exam.

Even if that is principally a rationalization for not making the effort of studying for the test, it does not mean the officers would be unwilling to make another kind of effort for a reward that they found more meaningful. Several men suggested that the department should have "something like the detective squad in the Police Department, an incentive for a job that's in between the regular guy and the supervisor, for the guy who can't put it on paper." And there is evidence that some men do work that they are not required to do, usually involving more personal contact with inmates.

A leading sociologist holds that in institutions like jails and mental hospitals an "institutional perspective" usually develops which frames and justifies all the measures taken by staff for and against the inmates.[3] It also helps explain the behavior of inmates. Thus, a man who comes to jail must be a criminal, and criminality is whatever brings one to jail. Though circular, this reasoning is functional for maintaining the staff's sense of control over the inmates. It would appear that at least some New York City correction officers do not adopt an institutional perspective, and that their jobs are more difficult because they do not. They are too aware of the hypocrisies of the system. Every officer has a story like the following:

Last week the dignitaries came down. They took pictures and observed the conditions, but they made one mistake. They informed the brass before they came, and that facility was cleaned and fixed up beforehand. Man, they waxed floors that hadn't seen any wax for years.

They see that white middle-class youths who commit crimes do not come to Riker's Island, but black poor ones do, and with that knowledge they cannot comfortably accept the legitimacy of the institutions they work in. The lip service given to rehabilitation rather than punishment as the purpose of incarceration gives COs another source for doubt; they are simply not gullible enough to swallow the notion that anything done in the New York City Houses of Detention will teach an inmate to live a better life when he leaves. In their dealings with inmates, some officers may assert the ostensibly rehabilitative objectives of the prisons. But paying half-hearted and cynical lip service to the system does not provide much psychic sustenance.

Perhaps one reason the COs fail to apply more of an institutional perspective in their dealings with the inmates is that they receive inconsistent messages from above as to their roles and functions. A great gulf divides the civilian administrators in the central office and the supervisory personnel of the institutions. The latter tend to define the department's role as purely custodial—not necessarily because that is the way they believe it should be, but sometimes because they are more cynical about other possibilities than "the men who sit at desks downtown." They also hold on very hard to the old ways of doing things, because those traditions have advanced them within the system. Their careers are tied much more confiningly to the department than are those of the civilian administrators; it is rare for a warden or deputy warden to leave the department for a similar job in another city, and the skills acquired in an institutional career are not easily transferable to other lines of work. The central administrative staff, however, generally holds tenure only for the term of office of the current Mayor and has more complex views of the goals and functions of the penal system. If the wardens do not like a Commissioner's approach, they (and the COs) often correctly reason that he will move on before they do, and they can safely continue to do things as they have done them in the past. Commissioners generally have very little power over the wardens, who have civil service appointments and can be disciplined only by being shuffled from one institution to another. Regulations provide that Commissioners can pass over one out of every three deputy wardens who qualify for promotion, but until Malcolm took over, no one exercised this privilege.

The COs are aware of the cleavage between the central office and the institutions. Although they resent the dominance that institutional supervisors have over them, they do not see guidance from "downtown" as a preferable alternative. The civilians seem to them generally well-meaning but powerless. As one CO said of the new Assistant Commissioner who had set up the human relations training program, "Jack Birnbaum may be fighting for us, but he doesn't count for shit. It rests with the Mayor, and he doesn't care."

The total effect of the COs' cynicism about themselves, their bosses, and the system they work in is to make them feel powerless to an extreme degree. Despite working conditions worse than those that have caused other municipal workers to strike—for a while the department was a year behind in the payment of overtime for some men—they do not have an effective union, and the group I saw had little interest in more militant organization. They feel themselves too insignificant in the total scheme of things to believe that they can effect change either for their own benefit or for that of others. They see change being worked *upon* them, not *by* them, and they resent that.

Yet for all their resistance, many officers are troubled by a sense that the prison world *must* change, that the societal ferment outside the institutions has seeped in willy-nilly and requires a response. A few think that response must involve a return to the time when corporal punishment was standard recourse for a CO faced with an unruly inmate. One man summed up this view by saying:

The rules and regulations have been relaxed more and more in the fifteen years I've been in this job. If we had enforcement of the rules, we wouldn't need to be here [in the human relations course]. They've been relaxed by the brass. The inmates notice that, and they make our job harder. People used to be afraid to come to jail. Now they look forward to it.

But this is a minority voice, and it is heard chiefly from men who will retire soon. The majority feel that strict observance of the old rules that made the inmates walk in step and forbade unnecessary conversation between COs and prisoners serves no purpose. Director of Operations Joseph D'Elia, the uniformed man who works as liaison to the central administrative staff, represents the general view, at least of the younger men, when he says, "Taking a man out of society is enough punishment. We're not there to add to the punishment. . . . It used to be unfashionable to show that you cared about the inmates. That's not true any longer."

Despite the COs' widespread belief that "even if we get together, nothing will happen," they are ready with suggestions, if asked:

We need after-care programs. It's ridiculous to send a guy out with a few bucks and one set of clothes. It's not surprising that he comes back in two weeks.

We should knock out the old slogan that the time should fit the crime. We could take the uneducated prisoner and hold him long enough to give him a high school diploma.

You can't rehabilitate anyone this way. We should segregate the guys you can help and, say, all the first-time offenders. Then you should teach them, let them go to school inside the institution.

Although the men sense that something must be done, they can not quickly or easily adapt to the new, more relaxed routines imposed on them in the name of penal reform.

They cannot easily rid themselves of the fear that a more permissive atmosphere will increase the physical risk of their jobs. They find it difficult to internalize new rationales. And, accustomed as they are to a paramilitary command, they find it confusing that the new way provides at times only imprecise guidelines instead of exact orders.

The problems of implementing the human relations training program and the correction aide program illustrate very well the COs' ambivalence about change, as well as the resistance of the supervisory staffs to reform programs. At first the officers and staff almost universally regarded the Urban League program as "subversive" and alleged that the principles it propounded were "something from Hanoi." At the opening session I attended, one of the first questions asked of the Urban League trainer was "Are these brainwashing sessions?" The deputy warden who was then head of the Correction Academy gave an orientation speech to officers which described the program as "a fine opportunity" and justified its existence by saying, "Times are changing on the outside, and the changes filter into the prison." But away from that setting he let it be known that he approved the program only under duress. During the first few months of the program's operation, the trainers were subjected to a good deal of harassment, not so much in class as out of it, from officers who had not been in the program. Occasionally their admission into the Riker's Island complex was held up because they were accused of having inadequate identification. At least once the same objection kept two men from going in to the dining room for lunch, although a visitor with no obvious identification at all was allowed to pass through without so much as a glance. An unverified but oft-repeated story tells of plans made in the Supervising Warden's office by suspicious COs not in the program to plant "contraband" (probably drugs) in the thermos bottle of one trainer.

As the program has widened its focus and used more correction personnel in planning curriculum and giving lectures, much of the hostility to it has vanished. The Urban League trainers have prepared correction officers to take over their roles in leading the small group discussions that supplement lectures and encourage the COs to endorse, with group support, new ways of behaving toward inmates. A new head of the Correction Academy fully supports the program, and all new COs now get a substantial dose of it upon entrance into the department. By now almost one-third of the COs have had the human relations training course. Furthermore, where newly promoted captains and assistant deputy wardens used to have no formal preparation for their positions, they now spend a full four weeks in the Academy. Much of that training period is devoted to the same kinds of exchange that the COs have, and department administrators are very hopeful that communication between officers and supervisory staff in the institutions will improve as a result. Supervising Warden Francis Buono, who strongly opposed the program at first, now gives a popular lecture about leadership to the new commanding officers.

Adjusting to the correction aides has been more difficult. Funded with more than $1.7 million of federal funds, the program pays the salaries of "paraprofessional" personnel and their supervisors, who help the COs bring certain services to the inmates. The 1972 Criminal Justice Coordinating Council report describes the aides' role as follows:

> Their job is to assist the correction officer in providing the inmates with basic services, assist the inmate in maintaining contact with outside family members and in some cases serve as interpreters for Spanish-speaking inmates. By assisting COs in a number of basic service functions, this program will allow the officers to begin more specialization in program skills to work with the inmates. This development of CO personnel will enable many to assume greater functions than maintenance of order and providing basic living needs.

The CJCC description of the aides' activities fails to suggest a vital aim of the program: to make the inmates feel that they have friends among the prison staff and thereby to reduce the tensions. For this reason, the first groups of aides were deliberately chosen for their ability to relate to inmates—a criterion that meant, among other things, similarities of background and attitude. Of the 213 aides, 90 percent are black and Puerto Rican, and they come, by and large, from the same neighborhoods as the inmates. Perhaps one-fourth of the aides have been criminal offenders themselves. They are paid $6,700 a year, work in six of the City's penal institutions, and spend a day or two a week as students at John Jay College of Criminal Justice.

The early months of the program, in the fall of 1971, were beset with problems. Many COs felt extremely threatened by the aides. They reasoned that the new workers would ultimately take over all their functions, that gradually the uniformed men would lose all influence in the institutions and be left simply "manning the gates." The aides were supposed to be able to relate to the inmates. To the COs this meant that they might align themselves with the inmates against the rest of the prison staff. Then there was the problem of the aides' benefits. To the COs it seemed grossly unfair that the aides, some of whom seemed like hoodlums from the streets, should get a paid two-year college education while they did not. (Although efforts are being made to make some educational opportunities available to COs, budget constraints make it unlikely that they will be as extensive as those of, say, policemen in the near future.) Finally, there was a racial issue. To many COs, this program seemed like another example of "giving everything to the blacks," and they rebelled.

Resistance to the aides program showed itself through many incidents of confrontation and sabotage. On a number of occasions officers have falsely accused an aide of bringing drugs into the prison, and they have objected to the use of ex-offenders in the program. Aides who arrived promptly at the institution's main gate were sometimes kept waiting by the CO who let them in and out so that they would be late reporting for work. In one "rap session" for aides and officers, a CO asked an aide what he thought of him and received an insulting reply. When the aide refused to apologize, he was harassed with threatening phone calls and personal abuse. In another meeting of inmates, led by aides, the group was discussing their reactions to putting an inmate in "the bing" (solitary confinement) for a minor infraction. Some inmates felt they should protest the punishment, others that they should ignore the incident. When the aides seemed sympathetic to the angry inmates, the attending CO reported to "the brass" that the aides were organizing inmates to strike.

The problems of the first group of aides, assigned to the Tombs, encapsulate all the stresses of the first few months of the program. There the warden and the institution's program director came into almost immediate conflict, with program staff lining up behind one or the other. The warden's complaints emphasized the fact that the program director was a woman, but observers of the conflict maintain that a more important problem was the warden's inability to release some authority within the institution. Some of the tension was undoubtedly caused by the program's failure either to involve the institutional personnel in planning or to make explicit what the aides were to do. The inmates were also not told who the aides were, and at first they made life hard for the new workers, threatening them physically and asking them to bring in contraband. The aides were often hostile to the COs, perhaps because they had not really been trained to understand the COs' functions and predispositions. Eventually the crisis passed, and with some shuffling around of personnel that group of aides has become more or less accepted within the institution by both COs and inmates. Though some COs still resent the program, others feel it has made their job easier and, therefore, approve of it.

The COs' most effective weapon against the aides has been the law. Almost as soon as the program began, the Correction Officer's Benevolent Association obtained an injunction against the appointment of a new group of aides, pending a determination whether the department could hire aides who were not subject to civil service regulations.

The case was settled out of court, with the program's administrators agreeing to hire only aides chosen from the top of the list of those who passed a specially designed civil service examination. Although none of the civil service aides had actually come to work as of November 1972, department officials thought they could predict ways in which the new mode of selection will change the program. The new group will probably be older on the average than the first aides, perhaps more traditionally middle class in attitude, "more 'family people,' " as one administrator put it. The proportion of whites will probably be somewhat higher. What the officials do not say is that they fear the new aides will relate less well to the inmates, but that is surely a concern.

The aides, too, have had some complaints about the program, though in general they regard it as an important personal opportunity. The new policy of providing access to phones for inmates has created a new need for people to dial the phones and supervise the calls, and a substantial amount of the aides' time has been spent on this menial task. Performing similar functions, like handing out sheets and towels, has kept the aides from providing the social services that they and department administrators think appropriate. Assistant Commissioner George Camp, whose jurisdiction includes the aides program, hopes to put the aides into functional units and train them to give tutorial assistance, job counseling, and advice about court problems. He believes that many of the more menial tasks that aides and COs have been doing can be done by inmates, freeing staff for more meaningful tasks and giving inmates more responsibility.

To some extent, the civilian administrators understand the threats that the new programs pose for the correction officers. Assistant Commissioner Camp admits that some of the COs' objections to the aides program are justified:

For a long time the officers and staffs in the institutions had been told that they had been doing a pretty good job, and the agency rocked along, a sleepy dog before a fire. . . . Then the riots came, and the finger pointed. People who had been praised were now being told they were terrible: "You haven't been doing your job; we've got to get someone in there who can." The COs said, "We agree we can't do everything we should, so why not get more COs and trainees?" We said, "No, we need street people, people who can rap with the inmates." . . . Quite frankly, the COs were right. . . . By bringing in this program, we slapped them in the face. It's wrong both programmatically and strategically. A balance could have been struck. . . . We should have moved some COs into the new programs.

Both Camp and Gwen Goree, the program administrator, say that making the aides program part of civil service has helped to dispel some of the opposition to it: "Everyone is part of the same club now." Camp also thinks that making clearer the different assignments of COs and aides will reduce friction.

But one wonders if the goals of the aides program are not inherently opposed to the interests of the officers in such a way as to increase the latter's sense of powerlessness and hence their resistance to change. One officer in the human relations training group voiced the sentiments of many when he said, "The CO is caught between the inmates and the brass, the inmates and the public." By introducing into the prison a group that is closer to the inmates than the officers can even be, will the COs not feel more isolated, more impotent? Or will the program seem a benefit to the CO because it lightens the load he carries? Time works to the advantage of the latter possibility, simply because it may heal some of the personal antagonisms between officer and aide that have underscored the structural problems. In any case, serious consideration of the effect of the program on the COs is important.

Perhaps the answers to questions about the success of implementing a new program in the department lie not simply in the operation of the program itself but in the totality of the changes that are under way in the City's penal institutions. Commissioner Malcolm has made a conscious attempt to open the correctional system up to public scrutiny and, simultaneously, to protect the interests of those within it. Interviews with inmates and visits to the institutions have increased. Various special-interest groups run counseling and education programs inside some of the prisons. Attempts are being made to increase library resources for inmates, including legal reference works. For the COs, overtime is down slightly, and the delay in getting paid for overtime work has been reduced to about three months. A new group of promotions has increased the ratio of captains to officers, and the new captains have been trained to be more sensitive to the officers' needs. A general feeling pervades the department that finally—whether as a result of the riots is irrelevant—someone cares. Although resentment against Malcolm and his reformers in the central office persists, many COs feel that the new Commissioner is helping to maintain the current public interest in improving prison conditions, for their benefit as well as for that of the inmates.

And what of the actual results of the programs instituted to improve the atmosphere of the penal institutions? It is too early to make definitive pronouncements, and perhaps the long-range changes, if they occur, will not be quantifiably measurable. It appears at this time that the new training programs have had some sensitizing effect on the 725 COs and 135 commanding officers who had been through them by the end of December 1972. Program personnel say they have heard COs rebuking one another for harsh or insensitive handling of particular situations with the admonishment, "We learned about that in training." Department officials think the effect is greatest among the new officers, who participated in human relations groups as part of their initial training course at the Correction Academy; but that seems a dubious conclusion, since there is no way of assessing the attitudes or behavior of these men before they came into the department. It may be that the new groups are simply more flexible, because they are younger and not yet hardened to prison life, or because they have grown up in a more permissive and introspective time in American society than their older, more experienced counterparts. And it may be that they are a brighter, more capable bunch than the department has attracted for some years. One experienced correction administrator says that the caliber of job applicants for CO positions improves noticeably in times when the national economy is slack.

As for the correction aide program, there is virtual unanimity within the department that it has succeeded in making some of the inmates feel that they have friends in the system. In general, inmates no longer look upon aides as cops, and it would seem that inmates will profit greatly from the social services provided by aides, if the program can be modified to put more emphasis on that role. Success is more partial with regard to making the life of the CO easier, but that too may improve.

The new programs have provided important lessons for the civilian administrators. They have learned that implementing reform proposals of this kind requires breaking down the strong resistances to change that are inevitable in people who work continually within a closed system like that of the Department of Correction. Perhaps they have learned, too, to listen more intently to the people whose lives will be immediately affected by anything new—to involve them in planning, to respect the imperatives of their jobs, and to recognize the sources and extent of their fears.

If penal reform in this country is to mean anything at all, it must go beyond attempts merely to make incarceration more tolerable. It will have to find ways of reintegrating criminal offenders into society at large. This will mean loosening up the penal system—developing alternatives to large gloomy prisons, taking inmates out of institutions at least for jobs and schooling, and bringing the public into the prisons for many different purposes. The changes will inevitably create conflicts between the individual needs of

workers within the prisons and the demands the changes
make on these workers. The men and women at the bottom
layers of the prison hierarchy see the deficiencies of prison
life at closest range; they often have the most intense awareness of the need for substantial change. But they cannot
usually afford to support that change because the tensions
of their daily work lives permit little more than conservative efforts to protect their own turf. If reformers above
them cannot, as a general matter, increase the incentives
for risk-taking at this level, the initial steps so important for
launching full-scale overhaul of the prisons will fail. New
York City's top Correction Department officials are beginning to recognize this, and they are working to improve the
lives of the COs as well as those of the inmates. But the
changes are still as marginal as the reform efforts, and one
wonders if anything can ever make the job of the guard
tolerable for enough kind, sympathetic men and women to
staff our prisons. Perhaps the ultimate answer lies in phas-
ing out the job as we phase out traditional incarceration.
Until that is possible, both inmates and officers will have
to bear the fundamental alienation of being locked in.

7

A Hotel
Is Not a Home

I

Housing the poor has confounded political leaders for centuries. Shakespeare's King Lear, wandering in "this pitiless storm," thinks of the "houseless heads" of his subjects and bemoans, "O, I have ta'en/Too little care of this!" The City of New York—and the United States—has always ta'en too little care of this. Since World War I—when the rental market went so high that New York State legislated the first modern urban rent control laws—competition has been fierce for living quarters with light and space and cleanliness. The losers in that competition have, of course, been the poor. They have continually been forced to occupy the deteriorating central-city housing left to them by the middle-class movement to the suburbs.

Low vacancy rates and lack of money have not been the

only problems poor families have faced in finding housing. The problems of addiction, crime, and disease which often accompany poverty have made landlords leery of renting to those most obviously poor—recipients of public relief. Even before the caseload was predominantly black, welfare families faced substantial discrimination from both private landlords and the City Housing Authority. Once housed, welfare clients also were often the first to lose their housing. They were identified as "problem families," and landlords were often eager to evict them on any pretext. Moreover, their living quarters were far from fireproof, and fire can evict tenants faster and more efficiently than landlords can.

For both rich and poor, the housing market was unusually tight during the period immediately following World War II. Developers were waiting to begin new construction until wartime rent controls were lifted, and in the meantime, veterans were returning to New York and hunting for housing that was not there. On October 14, 1945, the *New York Herald Tribune* reported, "With 500 discharged service men returning here daily, New York City's record housing shortage is becoming steadily worse. Thirty thousand families are already doubling up, according to Joseph Platzker, Commissioner of Housing and Buildings. Under the best of circumstances, a survey indicated yesterday, the crisis would last at least another year and probably two." And indeed it did. On January 1, 1947, the chairman of the Citizens' Housing Council emergency housing committee announced a rental shortage of over 250,000 units and stated that, although six public housing projects were currently being constructed, "the prospects for the citizens of modest means are actually less promising now than the hope held out to them by public officials last June."[1] Legislative recognition of the housing squeeze came when New York City instituted its own rent control system that same year.

What do you do with people who must have housing when none is available? There are always hotel rooms that are temporarily unoccupied. Because they are temporary, and often empty, hotel rooms are relatively expensive. They solve an important problem, but at great cost.

On May 9, 1947, the front page of the *New York World-Telegram* announced that "Family's Ritzy Relief Cost $500 in Month" and went on to describe a family's stay in a West Side hotel, where the Department of Welfare paid $9 a day for their three-room suite and $1.50 per family member for meals. Two weeks later a rash of angry articles in the *World-Telegram*, echoed by more sober pieces in *The New York Times*, turned the housing of welfare clients in hotels into a major scandal. Mayor William O'Dwyer ordered Welfare Commissioner Edward Rhatigan to rehouse the hotel families "as quickly and humanely as possible."[2] The City Council and the New York State Department of Welfare demanded that the situation be investigated. Public indignation focused on the injustice of placing welfare families in "luxury" hotels while many returning veterans could not find anything but cold-water flats to live in. One paper printed accusations that the hotel situation was yet another example of Communist influence at work in the Welfare Department. The *World-Telegram* presented the problem as a contributor to other social injustices. On May 24, it reported indignantly:

> Without an investigation of the case, the City Department of Welfare recently denied a teen-age girl relief money needed to maintain a home for her ailing, widowed mother, it was learned today. Rejection of her application for aid came while the Department maintained other families in hotels, some at costs in excess of $500 a month.

City officials reacted to the unfavorable publicity with both concern and self-contradiction. Commissioner Rhatigan initially justified using hotels on the ground that they were the only emergency facilities available when a family had been turned out or evicted precipitously; a few days later, he promised that no more families would be placed in hotels unless it was a serious emergency. The New York City Housing Authority Chairman admitted that many public housing projects discriminated against relief clients and implied that he could not change that practice. But he tried to meet the immediate crisis by pledging that twenty apartments for the hotel families would be made available during the next week.

City officials were in a bind. In pointing out that the temporary use of hotels was the only way to provide for poor families who suddenly found themselves without a home, Charlotte Authier, the Welfare Department's Director of Public Assistance, commented:

> The only other alternative left open to the Department for handling this type of case is to break up the family, refer the children to a shelter and the man and woman to the Municipal Lodging House. Under current standards this would be a more costly plan.[3]

The pressure from newspapers and the Mayor's office did, however, develop a third possibility. Welfare and Housing Authority officials found a solution that was speedy but not very humane. *The New York Times* reported that homes for all but one of thirty-seven hotel families had been found between May 20 and May 26, but it turned out that these families had been sent to dilapidated, rat-infested apartments, many without gas, electricity, or hot water. Some were Housing Authority apartments that had previously been condemned by the Health Department. Mayor O'Dwyer was forced to modify his previous stand and order families back into hotels if no decent housing could be found.

Two steps that seemed to promise immediate relief for the problem at least succeeded in killing the adverse publicity. The Housing Authority found adequate apartments for many of the families, and Commissioner Rhatigan announced that a new family shelter would be opened, run by the Department of Welfare for temporary housing of homeless families. The subsequent months saw little of the public furor of the month of May. In September a department spokesman announced that there were still twenty families in hotels, but there was little public reaction.

The "solutions," however, did not accomplish much except to deflect public attention. The Housing Authority's restrictions against most relief families were not eased by the need demonstrated during the hotels crisis. The crisis did not stimulate the construction of new low-income units in the City. And the emergency shelter turned out to be, in the words of an experienced welfare official, "a scandal much worse than the hotels had ever been. . . ." Department of Welfare personnel had been careful to ensure that the new shelter would meet the most rigorous standards of safety and cleanliness for its inhabitants. They did such a good job of making it livable that no one wanted to leave. Henry Rosner, presently Deputy Administrator of Human Resources for the City and a long-time welfare official, comments:

> The trouble was that it was so deluxe the women didn't want to move back into apartments. No one wanted to leave the shelter. We got to the point where there were no more rooms there, so we had to go back to using hotels. We had provided all kinds of services: clean linens, nice curtains, a day-care center to watch the children while mothers went to look for apartments.

It also turned out that the shelter cost more per family than the hotels had.

In the next administration the department went back to housing families in hotels. As Rosner explains:

> The shelter was filled; the only alternative was to build another family shelter, but that was absurd. It cost too much money and we didn't receive any federal or state aid for shelters during the early days. The City Budget

Director came to me one day and asked how we could cut the City tax-levy funds for welfare. We received no reimbursement on public institutions, but hotels were paid for under the Public Assistance program, so we could be reimbursed [by the State and Federal governments] for using them. Therefore, I told him to drop the shelter. We did.

Virtually all of the newspaper pieces that documented the 1947 welfare hotels crisis focused on the errors of the Welfare Department in paying vast sums for hotel accommodations. They paid little attention to the housing shortage for poor people. Commissioner Rhatigan, speaking that spring before an association of social service groups serving the City, pointed out that "The Department of Welfare is caught in the housing crisis" and noted that "We are averaging three evictions a day of relief clients. Yesterday alone there were nineteen evictions of families who were not on relief, but who had exhausted their resources and could find no place to live." The Commissioner clearly recognized the likelihood that the actions of welfare officials, rather than conditions of the housing market, would continue to be the public target. In concluding his speech he asserted, "If this community fails to mobilize on the question of providing housing, obviously there will be a constant and unremitting series of difficulties and public criticism and press criticism, because the Welfare Department may not and will not allow anyone [eligible for assistance] who makes application to it . . . to sleep in the park."

It seems clear that more dominant in the public mind than the housing problems of the poor was the resentment that a few dozen families were receiving free benefits regarded as vacation luxuries by even comfortable, middle-class people. The amounts spent by the department for food and lodging were not excessive, given the necessity for using hotels at all. Costs were high because the families placed in hotels were usually large, and hotels charged by the person. Commissioner Rhatigan pointed out the comparative costs for one family with nine small children:

To live in a hotel and eat at a restaurant at minimum prices for eleven people required a grant of $630 a month. It sounds like a lot in a headline, but divide that sum by 330 person days and the result is less than $2 a day. I submit that this was a cheap price to pay for keeping this family together. We could have taken the children away and placed them in foster care at a cost of $60 a month per child, or $540 a month for the nine children. For an additional $90 a month, the difference between $540 and $630, we kept this family together. Once a family is broken up, it is difficult to reunite them, and this cost might have gone on for years.

Neither the general public nor its leaders cared about these justifications. On October 25, after the issuance of a report on Welfare Department operations by the Mayor's Committee on Administration, Commissioner Rhatigan resigned. In the view of more than one official, the welfare crisis led to his ouster. Former Deputy Commissioner of Welfare Philip Sokol says that state and City Hall pressure combined to make Rhatigan the "scapegoat" in a situation where the fundamental issue—the lack of decent housing for welfare clients—was never addressed.

II

In the twenty-three years between 1947 and 1970, housing opportunities for New York City's welfare clients did not improve. What had appeared in 1947 to be a temporary problem caused primarily by the shift to a peacetime economy became a permanent, and worsening, dilemma. Rehabilitation of older buildings lagged, constrained by rent control, rising construction costs, and zoning regulations. Private construction of new low-income housing could simply not keep pace with the demand for it. Public programs could not ease the shortage much, either. So it was inevitable that welfare hotels could once again become a dramatic public issue. In November 1970 a long, investigative article on page one of *The New York Times* proclaimed, "Welfare Cases in Hotels Called a Modern Horror." It concluded that the practice of placing welfare families in squalid hotels "has created a way of life that experts in the field describe as potentially explosive and benefiting almost no one except the hotel operators, who are making substantial profits." That story was followed by others in the City's papers, and Mayor Lindsay rushed to deplore the situation and to promise action on it.

When it comes to the daily degradations of the poor, the memories of both the politicians and the public are often very short. To everyone but a few durable bureaucrats in the Department of Social Services (formerly the Department of Welfare), the welfare hotels problem appeared to be new and unique. Though its symptoms were more acute, however, both its nature and its causes were familiar to anyone who knew the 1947 story.

This time more people were involved, staying in a greater number of hotels for longer periods. Instead of 37 families, the figure was over 1,100—about .5 percent of the total 1970 welfare caseload of one million, rather than .1 percent of the 223,000 people on welfare in 1947. Instead of staying a week or two in hotels, the average family remained four and one-half months. About forty hotels were in the welfare business, with seven of them containing more than half of the families.

Most of the welfare hotels were filthy, overcrowded, and unsafe. Murray Schumach, who first wrote about the situation in *The New York Times*, described what he saw:

> Children are jammed five and six in a room, sleeping on mattresses dropped on the floor, on broken sofas, crowded beds. Dingy rooms and dark hotel corridors are their playgrounds, shared with roaches and mice. Ceilings are peeling, and walls have holes as large as two feet high and four feet wide.

A *Village Voice* reporter told of her visit to a hotel which at one time held over 400 welfare clients:

When you visit the Kimberly, it's wise to hug the building to avoid the debris periodically descending from above. "Last summer," a resident explains, "someone threw a broken bottle out of a window and killed a man right in the middle of the street." Crushed glass littering the sidewalk offers ample testimony to that possibility.

When the Department of Health found the Hamilton Hotel "unfit for human habitation" in December and ordered the welfare families out, the conditions they cited included human excrement in the hallways and holes in the lead-painted walls of rooms where small children lived. Mayor Lindsay called the hotels "notorious sore spots," and Congressman Koch labeled them "hellholes."

The squalor of the hotels brought death and disease to children who lived in them. Dr. Eli Pascarelli, chief of Roosevelt Hospital's community medicine division, reported on the findings of a team of doctors and nurses who went around to welfare hotels to treat the residents:

> Dysentery is almost epidemic. There is a much higher incidence of respiratory and strep infections among these children than among other poor children. We are finding mastoid infections for which there is really no excuse any more.
>
> And lead poisoning. Here the city is spending $6 million a year to prevent lead poisoning among poor children. And then it spends even more millions to spread lead poisoning.
>
> How can you calculate the developmental damage to children raised under these conditions? Imagine the frustration of mothers in this environment.

And chronic health problems were not the worst of it. Serious accidents were frequent, caused by open elevator shafts, fires set in rubbish-strewn corridors, and violence among the addicts, pimps, and prostitutes who also lived in the hotels. Within a period of a few months, eight children died from causes directly attributable to the special hazards of living in these hotels: seven-year-old Juanita Sheppard was killed when the freight elevator of the Hotel Earle crashed down on her head; an eight-year-old boy fell to his death down the elevator shaft of the Kimberly; two children died in a fire in the Sanford Motor Hotel in Queens; a four-year-old boy fell through a broken railing down the stairwell of the Broadway Central. And there were others.

Costs to the City of keeping welfare families in hotels were difficult to determine, because separate figures including food costs had not been broken down in the expenditure report of the Department of Social Services (DDS). Robert Carroll, then Director of Public Relations, estimated that $7.5 million would be spent for hotel families in fiscal 1970–71; Howard Blum of *The Village Voice* figured the amount to be $14 million for 1,000 families. And Assemblyman Andrew Stein alleged at a hearing held by Congressman Koch that $2.5 million was going to house 700 families in hotels. A Special Assistant to the Commissioner says candidly, "There is no way of knowing the costs. The figure in the paper has no bearing on reality." In any case, the amount was a far larger proportion of the total welfare budget than the proportion that hotel families comprised of the entire client population. As of the summer of 1971, the average hotel room cost per person per day was $5.05, an amount which, if multiplied out as a month's lodging for a family of four, would be about four times the normal rent allowance for a welfare family in an apartment.

The owners of the hotels were in a perfect situation. Since most reputable hotels would not accept welfare clients, the welfare hotels had no competition. They charged welfare clients by the head instead of by the room. They increased their profit margins by stuffing welfare families into small rooms and giving them no services. Robert Jorgen, Director of the DSS Hotel Task Force created when the issue became public, describes the process:

The hotel people are making a fortune. Let's say you have a non-welfare family of two that is paying $50 a week for a single room with a double bed. They move out; DSS calls the hotel and asks if they have a room for four. The hotel owner takes two cots, places them next to the double-bed, puts in a hot plate and small fridge, and now he can get four people into a two person room and charge us $20 a day, so that now he'll be making $140 a week instead of $50. Landlords will throw many of their regular tenants out so that they can put in more welfare families. Once a welfare family moves in, services drop: he throws some cheap paint on the walls, stops changing linens, doesn't repair peeling hallway walls, doesn't provide facilities for kids. Naturally living in a place like that with nothing to do, the kids often break things. The guy [the landlord] doesn't replace any wreckage. If a chair is broken, he throws it out and there's one less chair in the hotel. He takes his bread and runs.

One reporter noted that the hotels were often scheduled for rehabilitation or demolition and that taking welfare families was a way of filling a hotel during a period when it would normally be vacant and unprofitable.

Both laymen and experts often see urban problems as "crises." This is a dangerous tendency, because it often leads to a superficial interpretation of the causes of the problem. The welfare hotel situation is an example. It appeared to some to be short-term, an aberration of an otherwise adequate system, an instance of simple and possibly cynical mismanagement on the part of welfare workers and their supervisors. But its historical precedent should have indicated that the problem did not stem just from the ineptitude of the Department of Social Services. The recurrence of a hotel scandal must force us to ask: What is the nature of the forces that produced the modern crisis? Are those forces likely to produce yet another crisis? How deeply rooted is the problem? What underlying social problems and bureaucratic failures forced DSS workers to use hotels as the quickest expedient for homeless welfare families?

The general housing shortage of the late 1940s has not really eased at all, though there have been brief periods when the production of luxury housing has met the demand of affluent New Yorkers. Rent control—both the sign of a tight housing market and its partial cause—extended into the 1970s on a reduced basis. In 1969 new legislation "stabilized" rents in the hitherto-uncontrolled market of newer middle- and upper-income housing. Newcomers searching for apartments in the city are inevitably stunned at how much one pays and how little one gets. The overall vacancy rate in the later 1960s was usually below 1 percent.

For the poor, the problem is particularly acute. There is no financial incentive for private landlords to build or maintain low-income units. Basic returns are simply too low, and the instability of poverty-stricken tenants makes the risks too great. As the President's Committee on Urban Housing reported in 1968:

> The root of the problem in housing America's poor is the gap between the price that private enterprise must receive and the price the poor can afford. In short, the basic source of the problem is not poor housing or a faulty production system. It is poverty itself.[4]

Not surprisingly, welfare families have even more trouble finding houses and apartments they can afford than other poor people.

In the private housing market the stigma against welfare families is extreme. Even where it appears clear that the Department of Social Services' rent grant will exceed what a nonwelfare family would pay, landlords discriminate against welfare families. They maintain that the presence of welfare clients is disruptive in the neighborhood, that people on welfare are more destructive, and that there is a higher rate of crime and addiction in welfare families than in others. Although state and federal laws prohibit a landlord from discriminating against potential tenants on the basis of race, religion, or ethnic background, nothing prevents him from refusing to rent to welfare clients. New York City Welfare Commissioners have repeatedly tried to get the state legislature to pass such a law, but to no avail.

Not all landlords spurn welfare tenants. Many exploit their limited range of choices by giving them small apartments—improperly maintained—for large rentals. A former official of the City's Human Resources Administration (the umbrella agency administratively responsible for DSS) reports that it is a common practice in slum neighborhoods for a landlord to divide large apartments into two, make a few superficial improvements, and on that basis receive approval from the rent control office to charge rents that are often higher for half of the old apartment than for the original whole. Having once found lodging, a welfare family will probably not be very likely to consider moving or withholding rent payments because the landlord does not repair peeling walls or provide regular extermination services.

The alternative to finding apartments for welfare families in the private sector is to place them in public housing. In 1970 there were about 150,000 low-income housing units administered by the New York Housing Authority (HA), roughly 20 percent of all public housing in the nation. Although New York City's program was by far the largest in the country, it did not reach as large a proportion of the truly poor as programs in some other cities. Only 23 percent of the families housed by HA were on welfare. Many of those were the elderly, the blind, and the disabled—people for whom the housing shortage was not so acute as it was for the often sizable families in the categories of Aid to Dependent Children and Home Relief. Even 23 percent was substantially more welfare clients than had been admitted previously; in 1966, when Mayor Lindsay took office, the new Commissioner of Welfare, Mitchell I. Ginsberg, had found that only 6 percent of the units were occupied by welfare families. It had taken a series of heated meetings among the top officials of HA and DSS (then the Department of Welfare) to reach agreement that HA

would henceforth adopt admission requirements that
would make more people on welfare eligible for public
housing.

From its inception, the public housing program in the
United States has generally evaded responsibility for the
poorest citizens. Conceived and enacted during the Depression, the basic federal legislation creating public housing
was aimed at "poor but honest workers—the members of
the submerged middle class, biding their time until the day
when they regained their rightful income level."⁵ After
World War II that day came. The families for whom the
program was originally intended moved out, and the "permanent poor" took their places. The federal government
had left virtually all responsibilities for building and regu-
lating public housing to the local housing authorities, be-
lieving that it would be unconstitutional and improper to
do otherwise. Anticipating the social problems that the
truly poor might bring to the projects, many cities instituted eligibility requirements that effectively excluded
those who most needed subsidized housing.

New York was no exception to this pattern. As early as
the 1940s, HA discovered that a few disruptive families in
a project would cause more stable ones to leave, so it
adopted guidelines for eligibility intended to protect the
latter group. (At one point, HA tried to put the "problem
families" together in one Brooklyn project, but neighborhood complaints caused the discontinuation of that policy.)
The 1961 "Desirability Standards for Admission of Tenants" stated as its objective "to create for . . . tenants an
environment conducive to healthful living, family stability,
sound family and community relations, and proper upbringing of children." The list of twenty-one "potential
problems" that could cause rejection of an application for
public housing included alcoholism, out-of-wedlock children, spouses under eighteen, irregular work histories, and
common-law marriage. Evidence of behavior that revealed
a "clear and present danger" to other tenants—such as a
record of criminal violence or narcotics addiction—was *ipso
facto* grounds for rejection. After Commissioner Ginsberg

and Walter Washington, then Chairman of the Housing
Authority, agreed upon a new set of eligibility criteria,
many of the "potential problems" were no longer grounds
for exclusion, but families with one addicted member or
someone "with a recent history of criminal behavior" were
still excluded. In addition, the "Standards for Admission of
Tenants" adopted in the late 1960's leave great room for
discretion and interpretation; a family is considered ineligi-
ble for public housing if it is found to be

(1) a detriment to the health, safety, or morals of its
neighbors or the community,

(2) an adverse influence upon sound family and community life,

(3) a source of danger or cause of damage to the premises or property of the Authority,

(4) a source of danger to the peaceful occupation of the
other tenants,

or
(5) a nuisance.

The arguments for controlling the percentage of "problem families" in public housing make sense if HA is to be
viewed essentially as a business. With a waiting list of 150,-
000, HA, as the purveyor of a scarce resource, can hardly
be blamed for choosing to admit only those tenants who
seem to be the best risks. As one DSS official commented,
drily:

HA is not a social agency; it's a landlord. If you have
a choice between Miss Jones, unmarried and with five
kids, or Mr. and Mrs. Smith and their stable family, it
makes good business sense to take the Smiths.

HA officials argue that they have a responsibility not only
to low-income applicants not on welfare but also to people
who already live in their projects. That responsibility con-

sists of maintaining practices that will keep the projects desirable places to live, as the present tenants define that standard. Such a view means that, in addition to being as crime-free as possible, the projects should not become entirely black or entirely filled with welfare families or entirely populated with the "permanent poor." Urban housing expert Roger Starr comments: "Now if Congress provided money for *all* poor people, then I would say HA should find housing for all; however, since there is a limited supply of money and housing, we have to exclude certain people." Inevitably those "certain people" are poor, black, and on welfare—people for whom often no housing at all can be found except decrepit hotels.

Sometimes welfare families cannot find housing, simply because they need large apartments. The families who were the focus of both hotel crises had as many as twelve members. HA units generally have one, two, or three bedrooms. As of January 1971, 400 families were categorized by HA as emergency cases waiting for larger apartments, and officials estimated that that number would rise in the future. Cost limitations imposed by the federal government on the public housing program and the lack of supplemental City funds make construction of four- and five-bedroom apartments virtually impossible. Even where large units are available, they are bleak places indeed. Roger Starr summarizes the problem of Congressional allocations for public housing and its results:

> Of course, $4,250 per room sounds like a lot of money to the Senators from Idaho and Nebraska. The $20,000 limit per apartment seems high enough in the Marlboro country, where land costs are low and the same figure would build a ranch home surrounded by a big spread of land. But substitute land at $10 a square foot (more, on occasion) for land at $200 an acre, labor at $5.50 an hour for labor at $2.50 an hour, and you find you can't build single-family homes in the city itself. You must build houses strong enough so that they can

rest on top of one another; sufficiently permanent so that the government will not have to renew them in less than fifty years. This leaves precious little money for clarity of architecture, experimentation in ornament, generosity in construction, the human touches that would make the public projects an accomplishment of great pride.[6]

The problems detailed in the preceding pages created the emergencies that led to housing families in hotels. They were defects in the structure of the housing market which had other important implications besides the hotels situation. But many of these emergencies could have been prevented. The actual placement and maintenance of the families came about as the direct result of a number of operational dilemmas within the City's welfare bureaucracy. It is impossible to detail all these dilemmas, but perhaps the example documented in the following pages will convey a sense of the institutional impediments to handling the housing shortage effectively.

In his first *New York Times* article, Murray Schumach reported that the hotel population had grown to problem proportions partly "because the rents in [the welfare clients'] former apartments—while cheaper than the hotels—became too high for welfare regulations." And the Mayor, speaking to *Times* reporters on the following day, blamed the hotels situation on "obsolete state and federal regulations [which make] it completely impossible for the City to use the millions of dollars spent each year on housing public assistance clients in any kind of creative way." The supposition was that because hotels were considered "emergency" lodgings within the meaning of the statutes and regulations, payments to them would be reimbursed by the state and federal governments, whereas apartment rent payments that exceeded the local ceilings would not be. This was not true. In most instances caseworkers and top welfare officials alike were unaware that in exceptional situations support for permanent housing was available at rent levels above the limits set forth in the DSS regulations. This misunderstanding was not the only cause of the hotel problem. But its roots and dimensions reveal much about the bureaucratic problems that led to the crisis.

The federal Social Security Act defines categories of public assistance and provides for federal support for needy persons falling within those categories. It leaves to the states considerable discretion for setting grant levels and administering social services and determining eligibility. Each state must have its public assistance plan approved by the Department of Health, Education and Welfare (HEW), but the specifications for approval are often general and ambiguous. (For instance, the Secretary of HEW must be assured that state administration of a plan will be "proper and efficient," a vague standard that allows the federal government to ride herd on some states and leave others to work out their own programs.) Individual states may enact more extensive programs than are provided for in the Social Security Act as long as they do not conflict with federal law.

Similarly, localities may regulate where the state has not spoken. Bernard Shapiro, New York State Deputy Commissioner of Social Services for New York City Affairs, describes the process:

> The state legislature promulgates the laws; the Social Service Board translates these laws into Board rules; the Department then translates them into procedurals and guidelines; New York City can then translate these regulations into their own language, as long as they don't contradict state laws. The Department (state) supervises administration of these laws and policies.

In New York, many areas of welfare administration are covered in detail by state law, but others allow considerable local freedom. For example, the amounts of many kinds of welfare grants are prescribed, but not shelter payments.

Instead, the Social Welfare Law mandates that each locality shall establish its own rent schedules, and the state describes its standards in terms of general public health rather than the amount of the grant. With respect to families, section 350.1 (a) requires that "allowances shall be adequate to enable the father, mother, or other relative to bring up the child or minor properly, having regard for the physical, mental, and moral well-being of such child or minor. . . ." Emergency assistance may exceed the schedules set by localities, and courts have held that the latitude allowed to Commissioners of the state's social welfare districts precludes them from using their rent ceilings to refuse reasonable allowances in emergency situations. A report prepared in the wake of the 1970 welfare hotels crisis by Martin A. Hotvet of the Columbia University Center on Social Welfare Policy and Law concludes that:

> What the State Department of Social Services has done, then, is to delegate to local welfare departments the responsibility for setting rent maximums. But these shelter allowances are required to meet certain standards. Family stability and the child's welfare are to be paramount goals. Rental allowances must allow the rental of housing which will foster these goals. Emergency assistance is authorized to give the district every power to assure accomplishment of the goals. Shelter allowances must be such as to allow needy, aged, blind, and disabled persons, as well as those on home relief, to stay in their homes. In short, the regulations track and to a certain extent supplement the standards for rental allowances required to be maintained by the State statutes.

And New York State Commissioner for Social Services George K. Wyman has said:

> All rents would be reimbursable by the federal and state governments. If a center was to exceed the limit,

as long as they had the proper authority to do so, they would receive the regular reimbursement rate, 75¢ for every dollar they spent.

If local rent allowances could be stretched to meet the emergency needs of welfare families, why was it not done? DSS Commissioners were men of goodwill who would not knowingly have denied adequate housing to relief clients. They could surely perceive that costs to the City of placing people in hotels would be greater than costs of increasing rent allowances for a few hundred families each year. Furthermore, there were career officials around them who could have interpreted the state regulations to allow for rent payments that would have kept families out of hotels. But solving this problem before it reached crisis proportions would have required a smooth flow of information within DSS. An examination of the bureaucratic divisions of DSS reveals how unlikely that was.

At the bottom of the DSS hierarchy were the caseworkers, about 12,000 of them working in forty-two Social Service Centers around the city. (The system is described as of 1970; a recent reorganization has made some fundamental changes in the nature and functions of many workers' jobs.) At this level, morale was low and turnover high. Caseloads were too heavy to give personalized service to clients. The paperwork necessary to process simple modifications in a client's status was so overwhelming that the worker often either refused help or became too harassed to attend to the client's other, more intangible needs. One former DSS caseworker says:

> The system was designed to complicate everything. . . .
> If you needed to get a special grant everything was tied
> up, sometimes for days, while the welfare client waited
> in the outer office . . . I quit when I couldn't apologize
> for the system one more time.

The swelling of the welfare rolls in the late sixties caused administrative shortcuts that have had the greatest impact on the caseworker. The three-week training course for new caseworkers was shortened, and first-line supervisors no longer need have three years of casework experience. A DDS study of the period between June 1968 and February 1970 found that 43.7 percent of caseworkers sampled left their jobs at DDS within a year; 63.7 percent were gone by the end of their second year. Furthermore, 70.2 percent of those who scored between 80 and 100 percent on the civil service exam left within a year, with 60 percent of them citing "dissatisfaction with job" as the reason. The study concluded:

> If the entrance score can be considered an indicator of ability, then we can say that our most capable people, or those in the 80–100 group, left within one year of employment.

Overworked and undertrained, the caseworkers could not be expected to know all of the "procedurals" intended to guide their decisions about client problems. Besides, the regulations were often neither clear nor comprehensive. They did not indicate, for example, the leeway allowed by the state to the City in determining rent allowances. Caseworkers received a schedule of maximum rents for families of different sizes. Approval for rent above those maximums was to be sought from different kinds of supervisors according to how substantially the rent exceeded the maximum. For example, approval of monthly rent below $100 for a family of three could come from the caseworker's immediate superior (the Unit Supervisor); between $100.01 and $120, it had to come from the Case Supervisor or Assistant Office Manager; between $120.01 and $130 from the Senior Case Supervisor; and between $130.01 and $140 from the Center Director. There were no specific provisions as to rents above $140. A particularly careful caseworker might have looked to section 352.2(8) (c) of the state Social Welfare Law and found that: "Supplemental allowances and grants may not be made other than as authorized under the regulations nor in excess of established schedules." Unaware of the emergency provisions, the uninitiated worker would assume he had no further recourse, and would look to hotels, where no ceiling existed. In many cases, first-line supervisors did not know any better.

Often the problem was one of resistance, not ignorance. Older workers—both white and black—who had made a career in the old Department of Welfare often felt resentment toward the clients and refused to approve large rent allowances. Growing up in the shadow of the Depression, these veterans had worked long, dull years trying to insure a bit of security for themselves. Now they saw people whom they regarded as idle and lazy receiving these benefits. Even when the Commissioner ordered flexibility in rent allotments, the workers did not comply. James Dumpson, New York City Commissioner from 1959 to 1965, recalls one such incident:

> I remember once going down to a center in Brooklyn where there had been a large number of evictions, especially since I had sent out a directive stating that there were no legal rent restrictions and that if a family's well-being depended on it, high rents should be approved in order to prevent eviction. When I got there, they told me: "Sure, Commissioner, we got your memorandum about rent restrictions, but our workers are refusing to obey it. They say they can't afford to live in $200–300 apartments, and they are certainly not going to give one to a welfare family!"

Even if workers sympathized with their clients and knew that allowances above the rent maximums were possible, they sometimes failed to appeal to the central DSS office. As the caseload rose dramatically in the late 1960s, it became increasingly difficult to get extra benefits of many kinds out of the already beleaguered system. Welfare officials emphasized that funds were tight, and—perhaps partly for that reason—the time and energy required to get approval from the top was almost overwhelming. State

Commissioner Wyman notes, ". . . the centralized approval process slows everything down. Workers often don't bother to call the Commissioner's office for approval." By the end of the decade, approvals for amounts above the rent maximums were requested very rarely.

The ignorance of the regulations at both the bottom and top of the welfare hierarchy points up another of the system's problems. The welfare caseworkers cannot always look to the Commissioner for guidance and understanding. He and some of his assistants are political appointees—rarely people who have worked their way up through the system, and sometimes not even social workers. As a result, it is hardly surprising that they often cannot find their way through the maze of local and state regulations any better than workers at the bottom. Workers all the way down through the bureaucracy know this, and it has various consequences. Sometimes it means that more informed middle-management personnel who disagree with the Commissioner's general positions can withhold important information from him, or that caseworkers feel too alienated from the Commissioner to bring him their problems. Lindsay's first Welfare Commissioner describes the difficulties of being the top man and having to depend on others in a system where one's immediate access to information depends more on experience than on authority:

> We had a cabinet we used to meet with. I tried to give them a chance to discuss things. Remember, I was a neophyte; I didn't know the regulations. I would try to do something and Rosner [longtime head of fiscal administration] would give me a procedure with seven numbers, saying it was illegal to do that. I would tell him to go find me a regulation that says I could do it. In half an hour he would come back with a regulation saying we could do it.

A social welfare agency hovers between the traditional models of the professional and nonprofessional organiza-

tions. In the latter, the manager dominates, with his entrepreneurial objectives paramount. In the "semi-professional
organizations," as one analyst calls them, the principal authority is exerted through application of the regulations,
and the workers are evaluated according to their observation of those rules.[7] Tensions come about as the result of
identification by the primary workers with professional
groups. That identification often conflicts with the organizational regimentation that would not prevail in a truly
professional organization. New York City's DSS follows
this pattern, but its tensions are perhaps exacerbated by the
fact that top management is not usually perceived as sympathetic to the workers. Commissioners do not understand
the workers' operational problems, the argument goes, but
it doesn't matter much, because the top administrators
don't last long anyhow. As former Commissioner James
Dumpson has commented:

> I will always remember two things that were told to
> me by staff—"Commissioners come and Commission-
> ers go, but we stay on forever." The other thing I
> heard was, "Be sure to be nice to the elevator operator,
> he may become Commissioner some day." I've known
> staff who have laughed when I told them to do some-
> thing. The attitude was why should we listen? He'll be
> around next week, next month, maybe next year, but
> not longer than that!

With this mixture of ignorance at the bottom and the top
and hostility rife throughout the system, it is not surprising
that situations posing exceptional problems were handled
badly.

III

Murray Schumach's *New York Times* stories were not
enough to force the city to take prompt and decisive steps.
The Mayor stated immediately that his housing and wel-

fare officials had already reported to him on the situation, but several who were interviewed do not recall any document submitted to Lindsay. There is general agreement that whatever informal reporting was done did not generate any call to action. Public awareness of the problem resulted in letters to the editors and in Congressman Koch's public hearings, but bureaucratic and political responses were slower.

During December the Department of Health, prodded by public expressions of outrage and by Koch's statements, began to inspect the hotels that housed welfare clients. The first to be declared uninhabitable was the Hamilton, where eighty families lived. The Human Resources Administration had been informed several days earlier that a vacate order would be issued, and Administrator Sugarman had enlisted the help of the Department of Relocation in finding other accommodations for twenty-three of the families. But when the others were told that they would have to leave within ten days, they announced that clearly the hotel was unsafe now, and they refused to stay. Seventy women and children, led by day-care activist Dorothy Pitman Hughes, sat in Sugarman's office, around the clock for several days, demanding placement in decent housing.

The Hamilton Hotel incident galvanized DSS and the Department of Relocation into action. Human Resources Administrator Sugarman explained at the Koch hearings:

> . . . the order to vacate the Hamilton Hotel produced a crisis which was almost beyond the capacity of the City to handle; and in fact, in realistic terms, I would say we were not really able to handle that crisis. Why was that? Well, it was essentially because many of the families in the Hamilton Hotel were large families of six, seven, eight, nine, ten, eleven, and twelve people who required large-sized apartments in order to live decently, and despite a really enormous effort we have thus far been unsuccessful in finding the large apartments that are necessary for many of these families.
> What did we do? Well, we had, first of all, the most

intensive publicity on the situation that I think we
ever had. Every TV station, every radio station, every
newspaper carried the plea from Administrator Walsh
[of the City Housing and Development Administra-
tion], and from myself, for housing. Each of the City's
departments put more people onto the job of locating
housing, and we really went through a real crunch in
trying to find additonal sources of housing.

Sugarman then went on to say:

The arrival and stay in our offices of the recipients
certainly did dramatize the issue. It certainly led the
City to focus more intensively on the problem, and I
think it produced some action.

DSS was not the only agency to feel the effects of the
Hamilton incident. Carl Weisbrod of the Department of
Relocation angrily remarked: "The whole thing was a dis-
grace. . . . Everyone vowed there would never be another
Hamilton. What followed was a period of great paranoia
between Relocation and DSS. We were afraid that another
Hamilton would explode in our faces." The two depart-
ments divided up the families. DSS opened the Fahnstock
Nursing Home as a temporary residence for some, and
Relocation put others in the somewhat better hotels they
used for families who had been displaced by fires or urban
renewal projects.

The success of the press in rousing the public and its
officials became complete in late January. Three welfare
workers with a family to house bypassed the list of dingy,
DSS-approved hotels and put Mrs. Cleola Hainsworth and
her four children in the Waldorf-Astoria on Park Avenue.
The local papers were quick to proclaim the outrage—their
stay was costing the City $76.32 a night—and the incident
provoked Mayor Lindsay into a far stronger statement than
he had made in November. From Washington, where he
was attending meetings, he accused the workers of "mali-

cious intent" and suspended them from their jobs. The invasion of the poor into the resting places of the rich clearly had greater political impact than evidence of danger and death in the usual squalid hotels. It was only at this point that the City departments involved began to work seriously to change the practices that had led to the welfare hotels scandal.

In his initial *Times* article, Murray Schumach had summed up the process that put poor families into dilapidated hotels at high costs as "a way of life," and it was to that picture that people responded. The New York Urban Coalition reprinted press photographs of children sitting listlessly on their hotel cots, subdued and defeated by their environment. People saw in these families a special case of poverty, dependence, and neglect. Yet one wonders if the life of those people was really qualitatively different from the general degradation of the poorest families in the City. Social workers and reporters estimate that between 20 and 50 percent of the children living in hotels did not attend school. It is also true, however, that many poor children living in apartments attend school irregularly and that the truancy rate approaches 50 percent by the early years of high school. Special Assistant to the DSS Commissioner Herbert Rosenbloom has noted that some of the families who move into hotels have come from fairly stable neighborhoods and that their exposure to the hotel conditions causes "a breakdown in the family structure." But the same phenomenon occurs when a black family from the South travels north and finds instead of a promised land of freedom and opportunity the urban slum with its menial jobs —or no jobs at all—and its decaying tenements. Although the hotels are crowded and filthy with inadequate cooking and bathroom facilities, many of New York's poor also live in apartments with only a double hot plate to cook on and a bathtub in the kitchen.

The similarity in the conditions of welfare families in hotels and those of poor people all over New York City raises questions about why the welfare hotels situation is seen by the press, the public, and the City administration as a "crisis." An observer unacquainted with the persistent problems of inadequate housing, joblessness among minority groups, and an inefficient, arbitrary income maintenance system might think that the welfare hotels problem created a stir because of its reflection of the systemic weaknesses of urban American society at large. No such perceptions appeared in any of the reactions to the crisis. Welfare hotels became a scandal because they could not be rationalized within the accepted cluster of policies and practices that serves to make the poor of the city appear as a relatively undifferentiated mass. The procedures of the public welfare system generally permit most middle-class New Yorkers to ignore the individual dilemmas of those who live in poverty. Suddenly, more affluent citizens were forced to know of the daily encounters the poor have with violence, disease, and disorganization. In that confrontation—brought about by the sudden visibility of what had been generally invisible, and focused on symptoms rather than causes—those citizens were not likely to press for fundamental change. Instead, their reactions might speed up cosmetic repair of the immediate situation but actually gloss over and intensify the real problem.

Also contributing to the public furor over the hotels was the fact that they were being supported—to the tune of $40,000 a month to the Hamilton Hotel, and over $18,000 a week to the Manhattan Towers—with "the taxpayers' money." This news produced two kinds of reaction. Many were horrified that such vast sums should be spent on such "hellholes"; they tended to be sympathetic to the hotel families and critical of the City bureaucracies that had placed and kept them there. Others, in a reaction that was predominant in the 1947 situation, focused their ire on the people for whom the money was being spent. They saw the families in hotels as lazy and undeserving, living off the hard-earned dollars of the middle class. Both of these reactions undoubtedly had some influence on public policy. The concern of those who were irate that public money was being spent on such terrible housing surely stimulated at least a partial resolution of the immediate crisis. But perhaps the reaction of those who saw poverty inevitably linked with depravity and waste has had, and will have, an equally significant impact. The accumulation of information about the "crisis" of welfare hotels, and other similar "crises," may serve to reinforce their suspicions of the poor so that the angry group constitutes a powerful political force for opposing any fundamental change in the welfare system or the urban housing market.

Lindsay's ire over the Hainsworth incident served to focus and intensify the bureaucratic efforts at change that had already begun. The Mayor announced publicly that welfare families would no longer be assigned to hotels except in extreme emergencies such as fires or evacuations. He brought together officials from DSS, HA, and the Department of Relocation in an evening meeting at Gracie Mansion and ordered them to come up with a plan to remove families from hotels immediately. For the first time, the three agencies were forced to cooperate in formulating and applying a solution for the welfare hotels dilemma.

Although there were points of friction, the agencies worked quite effectively together. They had three key tasks: the prevention of further placement of families in hotels, the removal of families presently in hotels, and the establishment of alternatives to hotel housing for the future.

DSS began by reissuing, in stronger language, an earlier directive ordering caseworkers in local centers not to refuse rent allowances that exceeded the maximums listed in the schedules. New regulations provided for referral of high rent allowances to a central DSS office, where they were often approved. Furthermore, DSS agreed in emergencies to reissue rent checks that welfare clients had spent on other things. (The agency recouped its loss by deducting the amount, in increments, from the next few months' checks.) Those two changes prevented many of the evictions that had previously led to hotel placement. Human Resources Administrator Sugarman also centralized the hotel approval process; for a time, only the Commissioner's office could finally determine placement of a family in a hotel. The general effect of the adverse publicity given to hotel placements, and the procedural changes, led to an abrupt decrease in new hotel admissions. Where some officials estimate that as many as 300 families a month were entering hotels during the fall of 1970, DSS records show that only 214 new families went into hotels between March 1971 and the end of the year.

Cooperation between DSS, HA, and the Department of Relocation (DOR) was crucial in rehousing the families then in hotels. The social services of DSS, the apartments of HA, and the placement expertise of DOR all had to be closely coordinated to get 1,100 families moved quickly. For a time, the traditional bureaucratic antagonisms receded, so that the agencies together could meet the challenge of the political attack from outside. But the substantive causes of the agencies' complaints about one another had not really been removed. HA still refused to admit large numbers of welfare clients, and DSS still had no effective way of forcing private landlords to rent to its clients.

DSS was fortunate in having DOR to work on placing families in permanent housing. Responsible for the relocation of families displaced by urban renewal, public improvement projects (schools, highways, and the like), or such emergencies as fires, DOR has a better record of finding housing for its clients than DSS. When it cannot find apartments promptly, it too places people in hotels, but conditions are generally better than in the DSS hotels. Conscious policy keeps the Relocation population of any hotel below 25 percent, the hotels are chosen with more care, the room prices can be higher, and DOR staff are placed at the hotels to handle any problems that may arise.

DOR's greater success with hotel families was not due entirely to its greater competence and experience. Many of its families knew long in advance of their need for DOR services; the agency could even sometimes delay demolition or construction on an urban renewal project while it found apartments for the people living on the old sites. Furthermore, DOR had some state-supported resources— such as large finder's fees to give out—which DSS lacked. And it handled far fewer people, with a smaller caseload for each worker. Even with those advantages, DOR had many of the same problems. With welfare families, placement opportunities withered: middle-income Mitchell-Lama projects would not accept them, the state did not allow them in its projects supported by capital grants to tenants, and Relocation was not much more likely than DSS to persuade HA to loosen its restriction for keeping out "problem families." At the time of the welfare hotels crisis, DOR had about six hundred families in cheap hotels, and the average length of stay was three months, only six weeks less than the DSS average.

As a result of the conferences brought about by the crisis, DOR was given major responsibility for finding permanent housing for welfare hotel families, whether they had been placed in the hotels by DSS or by DOR itself. The Board of Estimate, trying to ease this burden, authorized a grant to DOR of $1.8 million to be spent for renting 1,000 apartments which DSS could then use for hotel families. This utilized DOR's expertise at finding housing and provided unusual guarantees to landlords. The City would pay the rent directly, and DOR and DSS agreed to assume responsibility for any tenant-inflicted damage in those apartments. That leasing program has been very effective, with 459 hotel families placed in leased apartments in its first 7 months of existence.

The Housing Authority also took on new responsibilities. On March 9, its Chairman, Simeon Golar, announced that HA would supply one hundred units each month until all the hotel families were housed. He planned to set up a special unit in the Tenant Selection Division that would give top priority to hotel families when HA apartments were vacated. It would expedite the processing of public housing applications, interviewing families and actually helping them to move in once arrangements were made. In addition, HA would offer as many jobs as possible to heads of households among the hotel families—jobs like those of housing caretaker and motor vehicle operator, which can pay as much as $7,300 a year. And finally Golar promised to begin searching for a building to use as transitional housing for families who would, in the past, have been sent to hotels.

The Housing Authority delivered on its promise. Within a month of the beginning of its program, its special welfare hotel staff had interviewed 415 families, made 170 apartments available, signed 107 new leases, and actually moved 97 families. For many months HA exceeded its promised quota of families, and by the end of 1971 all but 5 of the original group of hotel families had been moved into permanent housing, about 90 percent of them into HA units. Where the usual requirements of family stability and respectability could not be bent enough to accommodate a "problem" family, HA helped find other housing.

HA's performance has been generally praised, and most City officials feel that Golar has done, as one put it, "more than he had to." But there is some cynicism. One DSS administrator, calling Golar's expression of concern and intent "a fake," asks why HA could not have placed all the families immediately, since it has a turnover of almost nine hundred families each month. He suggests that the one-hundred-families-a-month plan was adopted for its publicity value, and that Golar volunteered his help only under great pressure from the Mayor. Relocation officials have complained that HA took the least troublesome families first, leaving the "disruptive" ones for DOR to work with. These complaints are probably unfair. Traditional division of function among the agencies would dictate that HA took the families easiest to place. Apparently the goals of the new program were not pervasive enough to displace established bureaucratic routines.

While HA did most of the actual rehousing, DSS was

responsible for monitoring the progress made in removing families from hotels. Its new hotels task force, headed by Robert Jorgen, sent workers into hotels to refer the families to social services they needed. They also helped people fill out applications for public housing, escorted them to HA interviews, located movers, and saw to it that they had checks to pay rent and purchase furniture. The Mayor's Project Management staff set up a reporting system, which was then taken over by the task force staff. For the first time, there was a way of knowing when each family went into a hotel, how long it stayed, what efforts were made to find permanent housing, and what the outcome of those efforts were. The income maintenance division of DSS provided a daily report to Jorgen of all new hotel placements —a practice that allowed him to question actions that seemed unnecessary.

Although the DSS task force was intended to be a temporary expedient, it has continued to operate now that hotel placements have fallen as low as eighteen per month (as of July 1972). Fifteen staff members do field checks in the welfare centers in order to keep the reporting system accurate and take on special assignments related to the welfare hotels problem. One group needing special attention is men getting out of jail on Riker's Island who go on welfare and search for housing. Community resistance to ex-convicts and/or addicts previously forced these men into filthy, decaying rooming houses. But now many of those rooming houses are being emptied and renovated as middle-class housing, and hotels are often the only possibility. The task force, working to develop alternatives, is trying to calculate the size of what DSS officials call "the hidden hotel population"—people who don't say they live in hotels or who are not reported by caseworkers as hotel occupants.

The hotels task force occupies a special position in the bureaucracy. Formed to respond to a crisis, it operates with greater freedom and flexibility than most DSS offices are able to do. Jorgen reports directly to a Deputy Administrator of the Human Resources Administration, and he confers regularly with top officials about the problems he is working on. He has been able to choose his workers from several branches of DSS, and the independence of his office enables it to shift activities and expand functions with a minimum of bureaucratic congestion.

But task force activity, no matter how competently undertaken, is by definition temporary. The shortage of low-income housing is not. Cheap hotels will continue to be an emergency solution to the homelessness of some welfare families. Already there are indications that the agencies involved have lessened their vigilance in keeping families out of hotels. The special HA unit has been disbanded, and hotel families no longer receive priority over others on the waiting list for public housing. In early 1971 approval for a hotel placement could come only from the Deputy Commissioner. That requirement has given way to approval several hierarchical levels lower—from the director of the local welfare center where the family first reported its plight. As that authority becomes more routine, the balance will surely shift to the point where it becomes much easier for a beleaguered caseworker to place a family in a hotel than to search out relatives or friends with whom the family can stay briefly or who can help find housing for them.

Efforts at permanent solutions have been made. One operates in the form of a negative incentive, imposed by the state legislature. DSS now loses state reimbursement for the expense of housing a family if it remains in a hotel more than six months. Another measure is seeking to provide a local alternative to hotels. HA worked for over a year to develop a temporary residence, run by the famous Henry Street Settlement, for homeless welfare families. A public housing project—Lavanburg Houses—has been turned into furnished apartments, some of them large enough to house families of ten or eleven. DSS loaned HA $25,000 to renovate and pay staff, and it pays rent for welfare clients who need emergency housing. The Urban Life Center, as it is called, has begun to house families for up to six months while City agencies try to locate permanent apartments. HA gives priority to those families who qualify. For those who do not, DSS and Relocation search for housing, and the center's special staff works to remove the causes of disqualification.

The Lavanburg family residence has a dual purpose. Intended primarily to provide temporary housing for evicted or burned-out welfare families, it is also seen by its administrators as a place where "disruptive" people can be socialized into behavior acceptable to the institutions and individuals that control the housing market they must face. One DSS official calls it a "halfway house," and Val Coleman, the Public Information Director of HA, says it will "provide training for living in public housing." This function points the way to a concern privately voiced by most of those who have worked to develop the center. Although Coleman estimates that more than 90 percent of the families can qualify for public housing, with the help of skilled social services, many doubts remain. What will happen to the families who do not want to make the effort to qualify and the core of families who cannot qualify because they have a member with a recent history of drug addiction or violence? Neither DSS nor DOR has the resources to guarantee housing, and negative public attitudes toward welfare clients as neighbors and tenants do not change because people are in desperate need. (Despite repeated radio broadcasts by HA and HDA officials at the time of the welfare hotels crisis, not one landlord offered to rent to a welfare family.) Families who enter the Lavanburg center are told that they may stay there only six months, but what if adequate housing cannot be found in that period? HA officials say they would be evicted, but that would surely raise public relations problems, and perhaps legal ones. Some DSS personnel are privately worried that the residence will fill up and stay filled with what one calls "a murderous group of families." It has also been suggested the center's function as a temporary residence for homeless families might be thwarted by welfare clients who get themselves evicted so that they can be put in the center and thereby get priority on the long waiting list for public housing.

For the most part, there is little awareness in the Lindsay administration that a temporary shelter for homeless welfare families was tried, unsuccessfully, once before. Middle-level DSS employees, when asked, say that hotel placements began in the late 1950s or early 1960s and do not know of the 1947 crisis. The men and women who remember the earlier problem appear not to have concerned themselves about its applicability to the present situation. Perhaps this is because they were not consulted. (Plans for the center seem to have been effected through arrangements between HA and the Henry Street Settlement, on the one hand, and HA and Commissioner Sugarman's office, on the other.) Perhaps their indifference is testament to the general tendency of employees of any large organization not to venture beyond the programs and routines to which they are assigned. In any event, no analysis of the failure of the earlier shelter has informed the planning of the present one. Henry Rosner, now Deputy Administrator of the Human Resources Administration, was skeptical of the effectiveness of a residence when it was first conceived, but he now thinks it has a good chance of success. By limiting reimbursement for emergency housing to a six-month period, the state has increased the incentive for workers to get families into apartments, and Rosner feels that the opportunities for welfare families in public housing and middle-income subsidized projects have opened up somewhat. At the same time, he thinks that society in general has very little interest in actively trying to absorb welfare recipients into it as tenants and neighbors as, say, Israel has done with its poor oriental Jews. "The Kerner Commission was right; this is a racist society," he says. "At best we have a housing shortage . . . the crisis is created by discrimination against 'problem families' in both the private and public housing markets." To counteract this discrimination, the City needs three thousand apartments each year set aside for the families no one else will take. Rosner also suggests that a national system of rent supplements for all low-income families would do a good deal to solve the problem of integrating poor people into middle-income housing.

Even if the new residence is efficiently run and permanent housing is found for most families, there will be other factors that mitigate against a permanent solution to the hotels problem. The build-up of hotel families in 1970 came about partly as an external effect of a 1969 state law prohibiting local welfare departments from issuing duplications of rent checks. Previously, if a family had spent its rent check on something else and was in danger of eviction for failure to pay rent, a center could reissue the check. Discontinuing that practice may have deterred some families from mismanaging their budgets, but it put others on the streets and into hotels. Now there is debate about giving families a "flat grant" for rent and other housing-related expenses —a standardized payment varying according to family size, rather than the present practice of a check made out in the amount charged for a given apartment. Many DSS officials are strongly opposed to this proposal, saying it will cause evictions, which will create a need for putting more people in hotels. The relocation process will also become more difficult, many think, if landlords cannot be paid what they ask.

Bureaucratic behavior will also help determine whether the accomplishments of getting and keeping people out of hotels can be maintained. During the crisis period, the City's housing and social service agencies cooperated in an unprecedented way—"one of Mayor Lindsay's major achievements," Henry Rosner notes. But, as another official remarked, "The crises push each other out," and there are always plenty of crises brewing in the welfare area. As the most publicly visible symptoms of the welfare clients' housing dilemma recede, the incentives for effective agency cooperation will also diminish. Already there is grumbling at DSS about the way planning for the Henry Street Urban Life Center was handled, and officials there question whether HA really wants the residence to work. Finally, no one agency or unit is willing to claim the hotels problem as its responsibility. The special HA Welfare Hotels Relocation Unit has been disbanded, and HA has not embraced any new policy giving general priority to the housing needs of welfare clients. (The percentage of welfare families in public housing units stands at 26 percent, with only 17 percent in the problem-ridden category of Aid to Dependent Children.) DSS works hard to keep the problem under control, but its housing unit disavows responsibility for anything except referrals, and the hotels task force is a temporary office with "borrowed" budget lines and little special expertise in relocation. The Department of Relocation does not owe its first duty to welfare clients, and beyond its new leasing program, it has no housing resources of its own to ease the housing shortage for the neediest families.

One consequence of acting in response to crisis is that only a piece of a problem may receive attention. This was the case with the hotel situation. In 1970 both the press and the government officials emphasized the bad effects of sleazy hotels on families. They paid little attention to the problem of single people in the hotels. Yet the City's single-room occupancy population has been growing rapidly in recent years. With many of the families gone, those hotels that remained in business took in more single tenants, many of whom were drug addicts and prostitutes. Criminal enterprises flourished in the hotels; welfare recipients were sometimes participants, sometimes victims. An early 1972 Bureau of the Budget study of the new hotel problem found that:

> Typically, they [residents] are dischargees from state hospitals and prisons, alcoholics, drug addicts, the blind, the sick, and the aged. Usually they are uneducated, unskilled, and, because of a long history of downward mobility, unmotivated.

The in-house study was not enough, however, to get the City moving on that aspect of the hotel problem. It took another series of *New York Times* articles before the government came in to close down some of the hotels and try to find other places to house single welfare clients.

Perhaps it is too much to ask that the City's agencies maintain a constant vigilance over the hotels problem. It is, after all, only one side effect of a massive social and economic dilemma beyond the control of any one group of bureaucratic actors. As a nation we have not yet decided that every citizen deserves adequate housing, no matter what his income or race. Until that time, perhaps the best we can expect from urban governments' efforts to maintain the cosmetic changes they achieve is competent lassitude.

8

Conclusion

The six previous chapters are largely stories of failure. We have not prevented lead poisoning, though we know how to do so. We have not found either a "cure" for heroin addiction or a way to keep its effects from harming nonaddicted members of society. Christodora House stands empty, while the neighborhood goes without a community center. Water supply planning is not notably more sophisticated than it was a decade ago. The City's prisons feel almost as oppressive to both inmates and correction workers as they did before the 1970 riots. It is as difficult as ever for the average welfare family to find decent housing it can afford.

Of course, we could view some of these outcomes in another, more favorable light. The City is now reaching most young children who live in ghettos to test them for lead poisoning. Those addicts who want to be treated can usually find a place in a publicly funded methadone or therapeutic program. Correction officers are learning to appreciate the problems of inmates, and some inmates are receiving both services and sympathy that they did not know two years ago. Welfare families who are burned out or evicted now have a place to go that is safer, pleasanter, and cheaper than sleazy hotels.

But I am not satisfied that the kind of progress the City has made in these areas, if extended to other programs, is sufficient to make our cities truly livable. Basically, the changes suggested above have not solved the problems posed at the outset. In each case, the accomplishments do not permanently improve and extend a basic City service. They do not alter the goals or functions of the organization providing the service, and they do not necessarily stimulate further change in related areas.

Our evaluations of change depend on the times. If we accept that urban America is now in a state of crisis, we may regard as mere concessions developments that, in normal times, might represent significant progress. In another era we might have felt that we merely needed more of the same—more policemen, better teachers, more frequent garbage pickups. Then we would have regarded a new medical lead-poisoning program as a quantum leap in the provision of social services, a sufficient innovation in City policy. We would have been able to define in detail the expected outcome of a proposed change. But these days we work from the premise that whole institutions must be overhauled or overturned; since we do not know very well how to do that, we cannot specify exact criteria for the changes that must take place.

Let me provide some examples. If we assume some normal base—a world far removed from the urban crisis of the 1960s and 1970s—we would not find the Lindsay years lacking accomplishment. We might be appalled by individual problems—for example, the extent to which municipal workers have gobbled up large chunks of the City budget in wage increases and pension benefits, or the dramatic rise in the City's welfare rolls. But if these problems did not combine with a dozen others to instill some ominous sense of a civilization imminently in danger of collapse, we would look with approval on the improved communications systems of the Fire and Police Departments, the Sanitation Department's ability to pick up half again as much trash and garbage as it did in the years before Lindsay took office, and the new comprehensive child health care program.

But our sense of progress depends as much on our expectations as on the extent of progress itself. We are no longer satisfied with incremental improvements in traditional City services. Now we want to use local government to redress societal grievances, to forge new relationships between formerly powerless citizens and their local political leaders, to create opportunities for those who do not find them in the private sector. Our standards for change are tailored to fit those ultimate objectives.

The consumers of local government—even these days—do not always make such grandiose demands. When a problem arises that requires immediate solution, people often propose the treatment of its symptoms rather than demanding eradication of its causes. The lead-poisoning activists stimulated community groups to press for a medical program first, leaving the housing problems in the background. The Health Services Administration concerned itself with meeting the public demand for drug treatment, not with pure research or experiments that might lead to the adoption of chemical drug antagonists or other drug-free preventive measures.

For purposes of discussion, we might call this most immediate and achievable level of change the *programmatic* level. Programmatic change addresses the solutions of problems of individuals as they define them when the problems become acute. It sets up new activities likely to continue providing a service not offered previously. It goes beyond the mere improvement of a service to the kinds of changes the six stories recount. Welfare families are now

safely housed in a temporary residence, and the hotel crisis
has brought improved coordination among the City's agencies dealing with welfare clients. Prison inmates are now
more humanely treated by both correction officers and the
new paraprofessional employees; in addition, the reforms
have helped speed the development of a new civil service
category of prison worker who is much closer to the inmate
in background and values.

A second, deeper level of change may be called *structural*.
It focuses on root problems rather than symptoms. It can
usually come about only through the destruction or complete overhaul of a system of services that has outlived its
function. Slowly, even the most optimistic among us are
coming to believe that only this kind of change will improve the quality of life for Americans of all stations. Observers of American society have noted that it is no longer
tenable to call oneself a liberal; there seems to be room only
for supporters of the status quo (conservatives) and advocates of structural change (radicals). Reform as a concept
has changed drastically since the days of Lincoln Steffens.
It has moved from a call to rout the rascals, to a sober plea
for better management, to earnest attempts to meet the
rising demands of minority people, to the current concern
about breaking down institutions. Political scientist James
MacGregor Burns indicated the end of the path when he
wrote of Edward M. Kennedy in the spring of 1972, "He
shares the dilemma of any Presidential candidate who
'means it': the more he urges thoroughgoing economic and
social reform, the more he must be prepared to overcome
the 'tyranny of institutions' that has been obstructing major reform in this country for over forty years."[1]

Obstacles to overcoming the "tyranny of institutions"
are extraordinary. The institutions carry with them values
—or sentimentalities—that we regard as immutably
American. Millions of us teach and patrol and diagnose
within these institutions, our interests securely vested in
their perpetuation. It is a central human tendency to fear
the unknown; fearing the collapse of the known simply
reinforces this tendency.

This book has, in one sense, focused on certain critical obstacles to overcoming the "tyranny of institutions." Over and over, the preceding chapters reveal the variety and intensity of those obstacles. Throughout, the stories reflect a continuing confusion and imbalance between the kinds of changes people want and the kinds of changes that seem necessary to solve the specific problems they raise. The stories contain many threads of this dialectic between the demands and necessities for programmatic and structural change.

Sometimes the conflicts between wants and needs have operated at the most general level. Even when we know what problem we wish to solve, we do not demand the level of change necessary to solve it. We often choose to ask for programmatic change when structural change is necessary. (It is rarely the other way around.) The lead-poisoning case illustrates this pattern quite clearly; although everyone recognized the need for structural change, no one could commit himself to settling for nothing less. In a similar way, workers in government frequently know what level of change is needed but find that they cannot afford to provide it. Many correction officers understand the need for far-reaching penal reform better than the concerned public, but the structure of the prison hierarchy means that they cannot risk their jobs—let alone their lives—pressing for it. And sometimes these imbalances flow more directly from the basic divisions of power within the institutions than the personal perspectives of the workers. Even when government workers recognize the need for structural change and *can* afford to press for it, their ambitions are often frustrated because their individual agencies cannot pursue structural change. Henry Rosner in the Department of Social Services is fully aware that he cannot ultimately solve the welfare hotels problem without a national housing policy that guarantees the welfare client equal status as a tenant with others. Because of Rosner's seniority in the civil service, he could afford to make those demands. But the dominion of Rosner's agency precludes that sort of solution. He must accept the inevitablity of purely programmatic devices—in this case, the simple monitoring of local solutions for a limited number of families.

Sometimes—again at the most general level—incidental forces intervene to prevent a match of demands and needs. Take the case of Christodora House. The Tompkins Square residents were initially satisfied with a demand for programmatic change—the allocation of some Parks Department resources to provide them with a pool and a gym. In order to solve that "problem," simple programmatic changes were sufficient. But bureaucratic accidents intervened, preventing officials from meeting those demands. In response, the community people moved toward much more structural goals, involving the redistribution of some City power. Despite the interest of individual officials, the bureaucracies they presided over could not fulfill that demand.

Just as often, these conflicts between needs and wants have operated at much more specific levels, involving more subtle problems of change in City government. Several examples seem most important.

The first example involves the career horizons of government workers. The reformers of the Lindsay administration were always better able than the civil servants—not necessarily because they were brighter or more competent —to push for structural change. In both the tunnel dispute and the lead-poisoning negotiations, officials in the operating agencies returned again and again to standards of "professionalism," "past experience," and "responsibility" (meaning "turf") to support their positions. These were dependable notions, the observance of which had led to rewards in the past and would make recognition easier in the future. But standards of success for the reformer are constantly shifting; he has nothing as fixed, as reliable, as "professionalism" to define his achievements. The very ferment he creates becomes a measurement of his success. He is more likely to pin his hopes on process than on substance, more likely to think he will be judged by his ability to develop new ideas than by his competence at keeping something going. Not surprisingly, the reformer's tendency is to push for structural change, and the civil servant's is to accommodate as best he can to programmatic change. These conflicts often dominate substantive arguments about which kind of change is more appropriate in a given situation.

Often the success of a change of either kind depends on the public constituency that supports it. Sometimes a constituency is right there, sometimes it has to be developed—by publicity, by the organizing efforts of a small group of zealots, by community agreement. Much depends on the kind of constituency that emerges. The primary constituency—the direct beneficiaries of the change—may not be powerful enough to stimulate action. Jack Newfield's key contribution to the lead-poisoning cause was to develop a secondary constituency for the new program through his muckraking journalism. The poor families whose children were being poisoned did not have either the information about the disease or the clout with City officials that middle-class liberals who read *The Village Voice* would have. And one of the causes of defeat of the Christodora House plan was surely that the community residents did not ever get powerful individuals or institutions behind them as a secondary constituency for the changes they wanted to force upon the City government. Unfortunately, nothing guarantees that the constituency, once developed, will ask for what is needed to solve the problem. Or that members of the constituency will know what to do to press the governmental actors to go beyond what is easiest for them to do.

Several more examples involve the bureaucratic process itself. Max Weber believed that the rationalization of culture was the dominant force in modern society. He saw in it both beneficial consequences—the development of democracy—and crippling ones—the abandonment of personal, traditional, communal influences which support man's freedom of spirit. Since Weber's time, we have lived in an era of technological progress. Technological change

has always seemed compatible with the rationalizing processes—the specialized functions and elaborate rules—
within large organizations. So we have not been very aware
of the dangers of that rationalizing tendency. Now we are
beginning to find that bureaucratic rationalization works
against the kinds of change that we need to effect in urban
America. It particularly tends to inhibit agency personnel
from the creative risk-taking necessary to stimulate and
sustain structural change.

The impediments to change rooted in rationalizing
bureaucracies can be illustrated with several observable
tendencies of the agencies of New York City government.
The first tendency might be called the "barn door phenomenon." Over and over in City government, the barn
door is closed after the horse has fled; closing the door
simply prevents anyone from getting inside. Take the
problem of capital planning in the City. Maurice Feldman,
former Commissioner of Water Supply, told me in an interview, "The Marcus scandal slowed down many projects by
10 to 20 percent because they instituted a new set of procedures to prevent a repetition of that scandal." Similar problems abound with regard to welfare regulations: protec-
tions against obscure instances of fraud sometimes
necessitate elaborate arrangements before genuinely needy
families can get on the rolls. Reformers are often faced with
thickets of these "barn door" rules. Sometimes they resort
to extralegal procedures to bring about change, often en-
dangering their careers and providing fuel for public accusations of governmental corruption. Sometimes they
reduce their ambitions, seeking nothing beyond the incremental improvements that the system can tolerate within
its sets of rules.

Another problem results from the interconnections between rules and programs; it involves the rationalization
of function that I would call the "Pandora's box mental-
ity." Those who must implement change—either programmatic or structural—long ago discovered that they were
more likely to be criticized for doing something badly than

for doing nothing at all. (I have noted, however, that once public criticism of doing nothing gets started, it becomes more virulent.) And they know—often much better than the demanding public—that the problems clamoring for attention are related to other, as-yet-undiscovered problems. So they try as hard as possible to turn their backs on change, saying, in effect, that to do what is asked would open "a Pandora's box." (Dr. Conwell is said to have actually used that term in an early interview with the lead-poisoning activists, as he admitted that Health Department figures probably greatly underestimated the number of poisoned children in the city.)

The proliferation of formal rules is supposed to regularize the processes of government so that it can operate more effectively. But in a time when the political leaders know change is necessary, the regularized units of City government are often bypassed; everyone knows that they cannot adapt quickly to new goals or functions. At this point, rationalizing the activities of government with ever more rules confounds its original purpose. Great effort flows into evasion of the rules—through hiring "provisional" employees who will never conform to civil service regulations, or creating mini-agencies as branches of the Mayor's office which then do all the adventurous things the line agencies ought to be doing. It would surely be more "efficient," in view of these evasions, if we simply relaxed the rules within the line agencies to permit them to adapt positively to new problems.

Another example of rationalizing tendencies that inhibit change involves uncertainty. Many of the stories in this book convince me that our governments must be prepared, in times when structural change seems necessary, to live with great uncertainty. We should not rush—as Lindsay did with the drug problem—to embrace the quickest, boldest "solution" to problems whose outlines remain unclear. But uncertainty poses inherent conflicts with normal organizational aims and practices. To preserve a tolerance for uncertainty, an agency must at least leave its research department—if it has one—free of the usual restrictions on hiring. Agencies must be willing to admit how often they operate, in controversial and complex areas, by trial and error. (The agencies do, in fact, operate that way on occasion; they simply insist on a public and political certainty whose promises they can never fulfill.) Government ought not always to accept the conventional wisdom about the sources or nature of problems until careful investigation has established those premises. But these lessons themselves conflict with other important constraints on government action. Our political processes tend to ensure that governments will support and reflect the dominant public views. If bureaucratic exigency demands a tolerance for uncertainty, political constraints demand an equal obeisance to escalating political promises. If leaders do not want to appear too paternalistic, if they do not want to defy the public, they must often submit to the public's demands for quick results. This particular dimension of conflict may be impossible to resolve.

A final example further clarifies the obstacles to structural change rooted in the rationalizing processes of government bureaucracies. Agency policy-makers tend to choose the narrowest ground available for a decision, considering the issue to be resolved in terms of its most specific problems. The courts do this, too. They justify it with the argument that otherwise, as Felix Frankfurter put it, an "atmosphere of abstraction and ambiguity" would prevail.[2] Without this focus on specific issues the courts would not be granting Congress the careful consideration it must have applied in its own legislative deliberations. In the agencies, the tendency does not spring from philosophical principle at all. Instead, it stems from caution about upsetting essential bureaucratic routines in the agency directly affected—and perhaps in those with related functions. A natural outgrowth of bureaucratic rationalization, decision in the narrowest terms possible always creates a bias toward programmatic change. It also tends to convey to the public a sense of indifference about its demands; many clients of the bureaucracies interpret this narrow perspective as a sign that the workers in the bureaucracies delight in holding back progress. Few recognize the tendency as a persistent bureaucratic phenomenon.

Do all these impediments to structural change mean that it is impossible to achieve? Are there no examples of structural change that our cities have themselves promoted and controlled?

In 1971, New York's child welfare system began to undergo a thorough overhaul. Although the transformation is still incomplete, the process of change helps clarify the forces that promote and permit structural change. While the system has encountered many of the same kinds of bureaucratic obstacles that have plagued other efforts at change, the reform seems likely to have permanent structural effects. In essence, child welfare in New York has been moving from a custodial system to a service system.

Fifty years ago there were already many unwanted children who became public charges in New York City—16,000 in 1919, as compared with 27,000 in 1972. They were cared for through private social service agencies, usually with a religious focus. By and large the needy children were white —in 1919, 70 percent were Catholic—and did not remain homeless for long periods. Adoptive homes were easily found for babies and young children.

In fact, for many years it seemed that most kids who became public charges were wanted by some loving adult, and the principal task of the child welfare system was simply to match children without parents and families without children. Because there were many more parents than children, elaborate restrictions grew up, designed to produce the perfect match—with respect to religion, eye color, background—of parent and child. Although the child's interests were, of course, considered, a dominant aim of child welfare was to meet the needs of childless, middle-class couples.

Gradually, the problems of both the children and the

potential adoptive parents changed. On the parents' side, medical advances made infertility rarer, and childlessness lost much of its stigma. The pool of available children also changed drastically. Increasing acceptance of illegitimacy meant that many fewer unwed mothers put healthy babies up for adoption. More widespread birth control information reduced the incidence of unwanted babies among many classes of parents. Problems of urban poverty and alienation caused more older children to be neglected or abandoned. Statistics from the City's public child care agency, the Bureau of Child Welfare (BCW), show that the number of black children who were public charges almost doubled between 1960 and 1970, while the number of white children declined by more than 10 percent. Now there were two increasingly distinct groups of children for whom help was needed: healthy babies, both white and black; and older black or racially mixed children, usually with mental, physical, or emotional handicaps. Adoptive and foster homes were easy to find for the former group, often impossible for the latter group.

The shift in the population needing child welfare services began several years ago to shape both the services themselves and the attitudes of those providing them. Many of the social service agencies (usually called "voluntaries") initially balked at accepting black children, particularly those with handicaps of some kind. They argued that these children needed special care, and that adoptive homes for them were almost impossible to find. Foster care became an increasingly important activity, and even though payments to foster families were generous, the voluntaries often maintained that they couldn't find homes for the children who needed them. In 1949 BCW opened a foster care unit in response to the voluntaries' unwillingness to accept black children.

Public responsibility for New York's child welfare system is divided between the City and the state. The state passes the laws regarding public charges, provides financial support for certain types of care, and monitors the agencies that directly serve the children. The City purchases service (with city, state, and federal funds) from the voluntary agencies, coordinates various child welfare activities, initiates court actions with respect to public charges, and provides some child care of its own. Within the past few years, it has become increasingly evident that the state's funding structure has been perpetuating some of the inadequacies of the New York City child welfare system. Although the state pays $11 a day for each child in foster care, it does not subsidize agencies' expenses in finding adoptive homes. This forces many agencies to opt for "temporary" foster care rather than permanent adoptive homes. The state also does not pay for many of the social services needed to prevent children from becoming public charges at all. And there is no reimbursement for the expense of court actions which are often required to free a child for adoption.

By the late 1960s the child welfare system was simply not responding adequately to the needs of the City's homeless children. Although legislators, City officials, and voluntary agency heads all emphasized the goal of permanent homes for public charges, more than two-thirds of the children were in foster care, with half of that group remaining there to the age of eighteen. The City was not searching aggressively for homes for "hard-to-place" children. Agencies rarely took the legal steps necessary to free children for adoption, although it was clear that children had been abandoned.

The problems extended beyond the issues of adoption and foster care. The City was clearly full of children that needed help desperately but who still lived at home. Workers in the child welfare field had become concerned about the dramatic increase of reported child abuse. There seemed to social workers to be an increase in the numbers of children, especially in the ghettos, whose mothers left them alone all day, locked in empty apartments or roaming the streets. Many retarded or otherwise damaged children got little or no public attention. The massive social problems of the city seemed to be afflicting many of its children with particularly cruel force.

Both the City and state made efforts to improve matters.

In 1964 a special unit had been set up in BCW to investigate reports of child abuse; that office established a telephone number that any citizen who had witnessed a beating could call. The state passed a law requiring the responsible agency to review the status of a child who was still in foster care after twenty-four months, and also instituted a program whereby low-income foster families could be subsidized to adopt a child in their care. But these changes had only limited effectiveness. They did not confront the causes of child abuse or indifference of many communities to the children in them who need permanent, loving homes.

In early 1970 the *Daily News* ran a series of articles criticizing the City's children's shelters, where children are placed if an emergency situation keeps them from living at home or if no foster home can be found for them. In the aftermath of those articles, Mayor Lindsay met with a number of advisors to discuss the City's responsibilities in the child welfare field. He asked Mrs. Barbara Blum, then Deputy Commissioner of the Community Mental Health Board, to conduct a survey of the City's activities and make recommendations for improving them. In October the study was ready, and it has provided the basis for major changes in child welfare services. It is far from clear that the changes will all come to pass, or that they will all have the desired results. But they are aimed at bringing the child welfare system into the 1970s, at meeting the needs of neglected children and their families, *as they exist today.*

The most important single emphasis of the changes is the concern with keeping child welfare out in the communities where neglected children have lived. Mrs. Blum (who is now an Assistant Administrator of the Human Resources Administration and Commissioner of the newly created Special Services for Children) reasons that many children would never need placement—or would not need it for such lengthy periods—if services were provided to them and their families before the home situations became unbearably tense. To this end she is developing "preventive service programs," which include such services as home-making help, day care for small children, and psychiatric counseling. An "unmarried parents program" supplies prenatal care of many different sorts, referrals to maternity shelters if needed, training in child care and job counseling for mothers who plan to work. All of these services are provided as near the family home as possible.

For children who, for one reason or another, must be put in institutions rather than in foster or adoptive homes, Mrs. Blum favors care as close as possible to normal community life. She is pressing to close the City's largest detention center. (Special Services for Children [SSC] has taken over juvenile detention from the Department of Probation.) It seems likely that in the next few years SSC's efforts will produce a number of small group homes for children who do not adjust well to being part of a nuclear family but need more personal contact than can be provided in a traditional institution.

The reforms under way in the child welfare field have met with many of the same obstacles as those described in the preceding chapters. The habitual tension between the voluntary agencies and the City has not vanished. Some of the older BCW workers feel many of the same anxieties about reform noted here among correction officers and Health Department personnel. There is not nearly enough money to do things as well as the reformers would like, and the problems of coordinating such a variety of services are immense.

But Mrs. Blum is unusually skillful at avoiding pitfalls. She has built up a new staff of program planners, superimposed on the old BCW structure, but the new employees are able to mix with people who "know the ropes" from the days before reform. At this early stage, one can only speculate that this commingling of personnel is effective in providing incentives for reform within the agency. That speculation, however, seems borne out by the fact that many old-line BCW employees are enthusiastic about Mrs. Blum and the work she has done. They note that she visits the children's institutions regularly; that she goes to the voluntaries for meetings, instead of always having their staffs come to her; and that she badgers state legislators to pass laws and create programs that will make her employees' jobs easier.

Perhaps Mrs. Blum should not be compared with administrators in other agencies. After all, she is working within a much smaller system than many of those that this book has looked at in other chapters. Her clients are helpless children, a group likely to attract more sympathy than drug addicts, criminal defendants, or welfare families. Although child welfare problems had been in the news, the initial reform objectives for the system were not formulated in an atmosphere of public pressure or under the probing eyes of a group of persistent public-interest advocates. And finally, most importantly, external societal conditions had altered; not only was the system no longer able to provide the service its clients needed, but it could not much longer have sustained itself. Voluntary agencies that had long ago prepared themselves to deal with babies and relatively problem-free young children had empty beds in the late 1960s; they had no programs that would address the needs of the new pool of needy children; and they could not find clientele for the services that they had performed so well in a simpler era.

But Mrs. Blum must be given a good deal of credit. Leadership does matter; it is what keeps the organization thinking ahead to a time when even its most adventurous reform objectives will not meet the needs. As I interviewed hundreds of thoughtful City workers for this book, it was only at BCW that I met people who were trying to project who their client group would be ten or twenty years from now and what that group would need. They may not know what to do when the City's needy children are *all* disturbed adolescents who would—on the surface, at least—rather roam the streets than live in any sort of enclosed environment, but they are trying to figure it out.

The experience of altering the child welfare system suggests that in order for local government to effect structural change, certain external conditions must prevail. Some sort of structural change must already have altered the world of the clients and constituencies of government. Perhaps, indeed, structural change brought about by government can only reflect the fits and starts of larger societal developments. In the case of child welfare, two social forces created the potential for success. First, the structure of problems concerning neglected children had fundamentally changed, forcing government agencies to fish or cut bait. Second, the public at large was forced to recognize the need for these changes because Americans cannot easily ignore the plight of abandoned children. Both these changes—in structural social conditions and in the level of public sympathy—were necessary to overcome "the tyranny of institutions."

In most of the situations described in this book, either one or both of these pressures was missing. With correction reform, for instance, structural changes in the patterns of crime had begun to require fundamental changes in the operations of our courts and prisons. But the public was not yet prepared to consider the human needs of either prisoners or correction officers as matters which might justly require their own personal sacrifices. Until the public and government acknowledge both the need for structural change and the changes of personal motivation necessary to sustain reform, we are not likely to progress beyond the worthy, but superficial, changes described here.

Notes

Introduction

1. Frances Fox Piven, "The Urban Crisis: Who Got What, and Why," in Robert Paul Wolff, ed., *1984 Revisited* (New York: Random House, 1972), *passim*.

2. Philip Slater, *The Pursuit of Loneliness* (Boston: Beacon Press, 1970), pp. 12–13.

3. Murray Edelman, *The Symbolic Uses of Politics* (Urbana, Ill.: University of Illinois Press, 1964), p. 82.

4. Norton E. Long, "Political Science and the City," *Urban Research and Policy Planning*, eds. Leo F. Schore and Henry Fagin (Beverly Hills, Calif.: Sage Publications, 1967), p. 247. See also Long's discussion of metropolitanism in Chapter 2 of his book *The Unwalled City* (New York: Basic Books, 1972).

5. Edelman, *op. cit.*, p. 74.

2 / Getting the Lead Out

1. J. Julian Chisholm, Jr., M.D., "Prevention, Diagnosis, and Treatment of Lead Poisoning in Childhood," *Pediatrics,* August 1969, pp. 291–298.

3 / The Junkie Dealers

1. Claude Brown, *Manchild in the Promised Land* (New York: The Macmillan Company, 1965), p. 100.

2. Joseph H. Brenner, Robert Coles, and Dermot Meagher, *Drugs and Youth* (New York: Liveright, 1970), p. 77.

3. Kenneth Clark, *Dark Ghetto* (New York: Harper and Row, 1965), p. 90.

4. From an interview in Jeremy Larner and Ralph Tefferteller, *Addict in the Street* (New York: Grove Press, 1964), p. 161.

5. Brenner, Coles, and Meagher, *op. cit.,* p. 15.

6. For a good description of the effects of heroin and methadone written by a layman for laymen, see James V. DeLong, "The Drugs and Their Effects," in *Dealing with Drug Abuse: A Report to the Ford Foundation* (New York: Praeger, 1972), pp. 62ff.

4 / The Sixteen-Story Misunderstanding

1. Quoted in Daniel E. Button, *Lindsay: A Man for Tomorrow* (New York: Random House, 1965), p. 199.

2. Nat Hentoff, *A Political Life: The Education of John V. Lindsay* (New York: Alfred A. Knopf, 1969), p. 84.

3. From the Library of Congress (Manuscript Division) collection of Jefferson's letters to John Adams, as quoted in John Dos Passos, *The Shackles of Power* (Garden City, New York: Doubleday and Co., Inc., 1966), pp. 225–226.

4. Alexis de Tocqueville, *Democracy in America*, J. P. Mayer and Max Lerner, eds. Trans., George Lawrence (New York: Harper and Row, 1966), p. 218.

5. Richard Hofstadter, *The Age of Reform* (New York: Random House Vintage Books, 1955), p. 167.

6. *Ibid.*, p. 183.

7. John V. Lindsay, *The City* (New York: W.W. Norton, 1969), p. 92.

8. Hentoff, *op. cit.*, p. 127.

9. *Developing New York City's Human Resources* (New York: Institute of Public Administration, 1966), p. 8.

10. Peter Marris and Martin Rein, *Dilemmas of Social Reform: Poverty and Community Action in the United States* (New York: Atherton Press, 1969), p. 171.

11. Lindsay, *op. cit.*, p. 100.

12. *Ibid.*, p. 101.

6 / Locked In

1. Ricardo de Leon, "Rebellion in the Tombs: An Inmate's Chronicle," *The Village Voice*, November 5, 1970.

2. For a brilliant description of the process of inmate accommodation to a prison or asylum, see Erving Goffman, *Asylums* (Garden City, N.Y.: Anchor-Doubleday, 1961), pp. 12–74.

3. Goffman, *op. cit.*, pp. 83ff.

7 / A Hotel Is Not a Home

1. *The New York Times*, January 2, 1947, p. 20.

2. *The New York Times*, May 20, 1947, p. 1.

3. *Ibid.*

4. The President's Committee on Urban Housing, *A Decent Home*, 1968, p. 47.

5. Lawrence M. Friedman, "Public Housing and the Poor: An Overview," *California Law Review*, 54, p. 34.

6. Roger Starr, *Urban Choices*, p. 180.

7. See Amitai Etzioni, *Modern Organizations* (Englewood Cliffs, N.J.: Prentice Hall, Inc., 1964), pp. 87–89.

8 / Conclusion

1. *The New York Times*, April 19, 1972.

2. See *Adler* v. *Board of Education*, 342 U.S. 485 (1952).

Abbreviations

Listed below are abbreviations used frequently in this book:

Chapter 2

ALA—delta-amino-levulinic acid
CELP—Citizens to End Lead Poisoning
ERP—Emergency Repair Program (of the Housing and Development Administration)
HSA—Health Services Administration
SCPI—New York Scientists' Committee for Public Information

Chapter 3

ARTC—Addiction Research and Treatment Corporation
ASA—Addiction Services Agency
COC—community orientation center
HSA—Health Services Administration
NIMH—National Institute of Mental Health
OCAP—Office of the Coordinator of Addiction Programs

Chapter 4

NENA—North East Neighborhood Association
TSCC—Tompkins Square Community Center

Chapter 5

BOB—Bureau of the Budget
CPC—City Planning Commission
EPA—Environmental Protection Administration
PPC—Policy Planning Council

Chapter 6

CJCC—Criminal Justice Coordinating Council
CO—Correction Officer (in the New York City Department of Correction)

Chapter 7

DOR—Department of Relocation
DSS—Department of Social Services
HA—New York City Housing Authority
HEW—United States Department of Health, Education and Welfare

Chapter 8

BCW—Bureau of Child Welfare
SSC—Special Services for Children

Index

About the Author

Since shortly after graduating from Harvard Law School in 1964, Diana R. Gordon has specialized in policy problems of urban government. In 1965–66 she was a program analyst for the federal Office of Economic Opportunity. Between 1966 and 1970 she worked in New York City government, first as an assistant to the Deputy Administrator of Human Resources and then as a legislative assistant to the Director of the Budget. In 1970–71 she was a Fellow of the Institute of Politics of the Kennedy School of Government at Harvard University. She is currently a consultant on urban problems for the New York State Charter Revision Commission for New York City and for the Fund for the City of New York. Raised in Williamstown, Massachusetts, and Pasadena, California, she now lives in New York City, where she plans to remain—despite the findings of this book.